ECONOMICS OF INFORMATION AND LAW

ECONOMICS OF
INFORMATION AND LAW

Ejan Mackaay

Kluwer · Nijhoff Publishing

Boston The Hague London

DISTRIBUTORS FOR NORTH AMERICA:
Kluwer Boston, Inc.
190 Old Derby Street
Hingham, Massachusetts 02043, U.S.A.

DISTRIBUTORS OUTSIDE NORTH AMERICA:
Kluwer Academic Publishers Group
Distribution Centre
P.O. Box 322
3300AH Dordrecht, The Netherlands

Library of Congress Cataloging in Publication Data

Mackaay, Ejan.
  Economics of information and law.

  Reprint. Originally published: Montréal : Groupe
de recherche en consommation, 1980.
  Originally presented as the author's thesis
(Amsterdam)
  Includes indexes.
  1. Commercial law. 2. Trade regulation.
3. Liability (Law) 4. Records. 5. Economics.
I. Title.
K487.E3M3 1982   346'.07   82–72
ISBN 0–89838–100–2   342'.67   AACR2

CONTENTS

Acknowledgments

In bringing this book to its present form I have incurred many debts of gratitude. I should like to mention the most important ones: to H. Crombag and H. Franken at the University of Leyden; to A. Heertje, at the University of Amsterdam, who will find here the effect of his teachings of almost twenty years ago; to Y. Kotowitz, R. Prichard and M. Trebilcock at the University of Toronto, where a large part of this text was written during a sabbatical year; to M. Boyer, F. Lebeau and A-M. Morel at the University of Montreal; to my students in the law and economics course, whose most pressing demand, that I put all these ideas into French, I am only beginning to fulfill.

I am very grateful to the editors for removing many infelicities from the text and drawing my attention to others. They have also undertaken the ungrateful task of bringing the text in conformity with American usage. All remaining barbarisms are, of course, my responsibility.

PART I

The Promise and Premises of Economic Analysis of Law

CHAPTER 1

The Promise

"Old" and "New" Economic Analysis of Law

Among the interdisciplines that have sprung up around the law in this century, the economic approach, although of recent origin, occupies a prominent place. Its aims are ambitious. In the words of one of its ardent champions, R. A. Posner, the new discipline addresses itself to the

> central institutions of the legal system, including the
> common law doctrines of negligence, contract, and property;
> the theory and practice of punishment; civil, criminal and
> administrative procedure; the theory of legislation and of
> rulemaking; and the law enforcement and judicial
> administration.[1]

The economic approach to law appears to be very fertile. Since the classic papers of Coase and Calabresi[2] in the early 1960s, hundreds of articles, several "readers,"[3] and a few monographs[4] on the subject have appeared. Many scholars in North America would no doubt agree with Posner's optimistic assessment that these publications "in number weighted by quality, already overshadow the non-economic quantitive work."[5]

Economic methods were used well before the 1960s in the analysis of legal problems. But the earlier applications, which Posner designates as the "old" economic analysis of law, were limited to areas of law that affected the workings of the economy directly. Competition and tax law, as well as the regulation of stock markets, public utilities, and common carriers, reflect this "older" link between law and economies.[6]

It was not until the 1960s that Coase and Calabresi[7] drew attention to the possibility of a much broader connection between the two disciplines. The flurry of articles, theoretical as well as empirical, that followed analyzed the effect of alternative legal arrangements on the allocation of scarce resources, the central concern of the economists. These explorations have covered virtually all areas of the law, from company law to fields that, at first blush, would seem forbidding to the application of economic thinking — for example, family law, legal procedure, and human rights. This broad link between law and economics, which recognizes no limit in principle to the applicability of economic logic to legal questions, is known as the "new" economic analysis of law.

The economic approach to law starts from the premise that one cannot understand the nature of legal institutions by limiting oneself to legal argument alone. It is essential to consider as well *what effect those institutions have on society and what reactions they will evoke from citizens as a result.* Economic analysis of law is thus part of a larger family of "functional" approaches to law, in which one also finds, within the past twenty years, empirical studies of the "impact" of legal rules by sociologists of law[8] as well as analyses of judicial behavior and attitudes by political scientists,[9] to name but a few examples.

Interesting though these studies may be, they have not led to what one could qualify as even moderately comprehensive theories of legal phenomena from which verifiable propositions can be derived and that empirical studies tend to support.[10] The promise of the economic approach is that it will provide such a theory. It proposes a very general conception of human behavior, covering significant portions of what people have been observed to do in a variety of circumstances. It has developed powerful methods to derive precise predictions from the theory, and it has accumulated a great deal of experience on the ways in which the forecasts can be tested against observation.[11]

The promise of economics is aptly expressed by the economist G. S. Becker, in the introductory chapter to his *Economic Approach to Human Behavior*:

> Indeed, I have come to the position that the economic approach is a comprehensive one that is applicable to all human behavior, be it behavior involving money prices or imputed shadow prices, repeated or infrequent decisions, large or minor decisions, emotional or mechanical ends, rich or poor persons, patients or therapists, businessmen or politicians, teachers or students.[12]

Economics, in Becker's view,[13] is better described by its approach than by its subject matter. The economic approach assumes, as he sees it, "perhaps more explicitly and extensively than other approaches,"[14] that people tend to maximize something of interest to them, be it utility or wealth (the postulates of rationality and of self-interest). The economic approach assumes further "the existence of markets that with various degrees of efficiency coordinate the actions of different participants. . . ."[15] And finally, it does not make statements about how preferences are formed, but simply assumes them not to change substantially over time, nor to be very different between wealthy and poor persons (in Becker's terminology, the postulate of stable preferences).[16]

Taken together, these assumptions form, in Becker's view, the core of the economic approach, which he believes to be applicable to the study of all human behavior. A very general implication of these postulates is what hereafter we shall refer to as *Becker's precept*:

> When an apparently profitable opportunity to a firm, worker or household is not exploited, the economic approach does not take refuge in assertions of irrationality, contentment with wealth already acquired, or convenient ad hoc shifts in values (i.e. preferences). Rather it postulates the existence of costs, monetary or psychic, of taking advantage of these opportunities that eliminate their profitability — costs that

may not be easily "seen" by outside observers. Of course,
postulating the existence of costs closes or "completes" the
economic approach in the same, almost tautological, way
that postulating the existence of (sometimes unobserved) uses
of energy "completes" the energy system. . . . The critical
question is whether a system is completed in a useful way.[17]

Moreover,

the economic approach does not assume that decision units
are necessarily concious of their efforts to maximize or can
verbalize or otherwise describe in an informative way reasons
for the systematic patterns in their behavior.[18]

Whether the promise of economic analysis as formulated by
Becker can in fact be sustained must ultimately be decided by the
"forum" of scientific users and fellow researchers.[19] The decision
will no doubt be based on the empirical evidence amassed in support
of the approach as well as on the generality and coherence of the
underlying theory. But long before this lasting acceptance, a new
theory must be provisionally accepted to justify the effort involved
in studying it, determining its implications, and undertaking empirical studies to seek out its support. After all, if Becker is correct,
scholars make rational choices among the ventures, in their case
the theories, in which they could invest their time, energy, and
funds.

Before the main argument of this study is set out, we should
like to provide the reader with the grounds on which such provi-
sional acceptance of the economic analysis of law could be justified.
To an extent, the very generality of Becker's statement and the
liveliness of the "law and economics" literature might convince
him. Even so, it would seem appropriate to give a few simple and
straightforward examples of how the economic approach is applied
to legal questions. To these we now turn.

Three Straightforward Examples

The examples to be discussed as illustrations of what economic
analysis can do for lawyers are drawn from consumer protection
law. They concern credit rate ceilings, limitations of creditors' remedies, and rent controls. In each of these cases, the intervention in

the normal freedom of contract is based on the premise that the consumer has become, as one study puts it, "a contracting party who can be exploited at will" and that "the principle of equality of the parties to a contract has turned into a mockery."[20] The *intention* of the legislator in issuing the forementioned rules is clear: to "give the consumer a break." The relevant questions here are what their *effect* is and whether it can be said to constitute a *success* in the light of the legislative intention.

At the outset a general observation should be made. The practices that consumer protection legislation seeks to eradicate are prevalent in low-income areas. Several studies have found that indeed "the poor pay more."[21] Yet at the same time there is no evidence that the merchants who serve these groups make excessive profits. In fact, a study by the Federal Trade Commission found that "low-income retailers earn *substantially less* on invested capital than general market retailers."[22] One must conclude that the higher prices paid by these consumers do not reflect monopoly profits or another exploitative phenomenon. Instead, they appear to represent the normal cost of doing business with these groups, a conclusion to which we will refer several times in what follows.

Credit Rate Ceilings

Credit can be granted by money-lending institutions or by vendors as an incidence to the sale of goods. These modes, usually referred to as *lender credit* and *vendor credit,* will be dealt with separately.

Lender Credit. Rate ceilings are usually thought of as a reaction against "usury" interest rates on loans. The term *usury* suggests that undue profits are made, a practice that it is only proper to prohibit. In what follows, economic principles will be used to argue that the level of the interest rate, even where it is well above that of the commercial banks, is not necessarily indicative of excessive profits.

To see why this is so, one must consider what it means for a money lender to make a reasonable or competitive return on his business. It would be misleading to think that all of the interest payments are a net return to the lender; they must also cover the expenses of the money-lending business. Moreover, if indeed all interest payments were a net return to the lenders, one would expect a massive inflow of capital into this sector, where returns well in excess of what is possible elsewhere can be made. Such a movement would lead in due course to a lowering of the interest rates at which loans are offered and taken, according to the usual laws of supply and demand operating in open markets.

Be that as it may, the explanation of why rates provide only a reasonable return lies in the nature of "expenses." Apart from the cost of administration, these expenses must cover the recovery of the capital (collection costs) and the possibility that it cannot be recovered (insurance). The former include the cost of exercising creditors' remedies, legal fees, and the like.

In a number of instances, the lender will be unable to recover part, or even the whole, of the sum he lent; the debtor may go bankrupt, disappear, or otherwise frustrate recovery. To secure a reasonable overall return on capital, such a loss must be covered, and this is done through a form of insurance. The lender acts as his own insurer, and the insurance premium for the default on some debts is paid by all his debtors in the form of higher interest rates. The good risks pay for the bad.

Of course, such a pooling is not much to the liking of the better risks, and they will attempt to convince the lender that they contribute less than the average to the insured risk and hence should pay lower rates. If some lenders agree, competitive pressure will lead all others to follow suit in due course.[23] The favorable rates granted to the better risks force the lenders to charge more than average to the bad risks. This process of differentiation will go on until it costs the lenders more to investigate prospective borrowers within a single risk class in order to subdivide that class than the better risks would save through reduced rates.

The cost and the effectiveness of such investigations may vary among lenders; as a result, one would expect that they would specialize in the groups they choose to serve or in the type of risk they will accept.[24] Financing companies usually take on cases of higher risk than would banks and credit unions, and this difference is reflected in the rates charged by these institutions. One also expects to find little variation in the rates charged by one institution to different segments of its clientele.[25]

If the foregoing analysis of the lending market is accurate, one would expect "usury" rates to be charged to debtors who are "poor risks." Moreover, such loans would be granted by specialized agencies (including loan sharks) who can, better than commercial banks, assess the actual risk involved and put pressure on the debtor for the repayment.

What will be the effect of the imposition of a rate ceiling? Lenders whose usual rate is above the ceiling will withdraw from the market, since their business is no longer viable. (Recall that no "monopoly returns" are made in these markets, as several empirical studies have found.) This means that their customers will no longer have legitimate access to capital. Some of them may forego the purchases they could previously make with that money. Others, whose demand for the money is, in the economist's terms, very inelastic,[26] will be prepared to acquire it at even higher prices, and a black market is likely to arise to serve this group.

The rates in the black market are particularly high because they must cover not only the costs already mentioned, but also those associated with the risk of detection and punishment for the lenders. Furthermore, as the risk of default in this group of borrowers is rather high, various repulsive collection procedures (harassment or physical violence) may well be "cost effective" for the lenders.

Evidence from American studies suggests that stringent rate ceilings, the "6 percent usury" laws in force in many of the states at the beginning of the century, led in fact to substantial development of loan-sharking operations.[27] The Uniform Small Loans Law, drafted by the Russell Sage Foundation, was meant to meet this problem. It proposed to allow licensed lenders to charge interest rates commensurate with risk. Its introduction in numerous states appears to have had the effect of limiting the room for loan sharks. This became dramatically obvious in 1946 when the Missouri Supreme Court turned the clock back by declaring the uniform small loans legislation unconstitutional and de facto reinstating the older, "usury" law. Legitimate lenders were seen to disappear in favor of loan sharks until new legislation in 1951 put an end to it.

Vendor Credit. Restrictions on the rates that can be charged by money lenders would be ineffective if they did not also cover credit granted by vendors on goods purchased. For many high-risk debtors this may well be the most important source of credit. The problem with setting ceilings for this group is that the vendors would react by recovering some of the cost of credit in higher prices for the commodities, possibly combined with discounts for cash payment. Various studies have shown that this is indeed the strategy the vendors follow. While interest charges for vendor credit in low-income areas are only slightly higher than those prevailing among retailers in general, the markup on goods among the former was found to be three times that of the latter group.[28]

It might be thought that price controls would provide a further means to be considered here. Leaving aside the difficulty and the cost of their enforcement, such a policy could be expected to lead to the withdrawal of some vendors and to the development of a black market in other instances.

Restrictions on Creditors' Remedies

The exercise of creditors' remedies is, as Cayne and Trebilcock put it, one of "the most visible and distressing symptoms of overcommitment."[29] They include the repossession of sold goods, seizure of salary or property, credit blacklisting, as well as direct harassment. It is "natural enough, as a first instinct, to respond to these symptoms by advocating their removal."[30]

Yet the effect of such removal, the economic approach would lead us to predict, is to make credit costlier for the groups concerned or to make lenders turn to costlier or less effective and more repulsive methods of collection. This has in fact been the pattern in Pennsylvania, according to Cayne and Trebilcock.[31] When wage garnishments were forbidden there, the attachment — and in some cases the sale — of the debtor's home became commonplace.

Rent Controls and Accommodation Rehabilitation Requirements

Rent controls are thought to protect tenants against "abusive" increases in rent. Such increases are thought to be a major contributor to inflation. In low-income areas, rent controls as well as accommodation rehabilitation requirements are thought to be justified by an apparent disproportion between the rent and the quality of the accommodation provided.[32]

The imposition of rent controls appears to be beneficial to tenants in the short run. The tenants occupy premises for which, without rent controls, they would presumably have to pay more. They need no longer fear that at the time of lease renewal they will be forced to agree to substantial increases by the threat of the costlier alternative of moving to different premises.

How will the controls affect landlords? If without controls they would make excessive profits, the controls would help to shear these away. But are excessive profits being made in the market for rental accommodation? Such a situation would be possible where the market had monopolistic aspects — a small number of landlords or difficulties for new ones in entering the market — or other imperfections.[33] But such elements should not be lightly assumed. In the Montreal market, for instance, there is substantial dispersion of ownership and, until recently, new buildings were regularly put on the market. Hence one must assume that, in such a market, rents, in the absence of controls, would cover only the expenses of running the buildings and a normal — competitive — return on invested capital.

Under these circumstances restrictions on rent increases in times of mounting costs simply reduce the landlords' return and induce them to cut their costs or to withdraw from the market and invest their money elsewhere. Let us examine the hypothesis of cutting costs. Initially, landlords might attempt to save on decoration and "frills," then on services to tenants and on such items as repainting apartments and hallways, and finally on the basic upkeep of the building. For the tenant this drop in quality amounts to a rent increase, although, of course, on the surface his out-of-pocket expenses have not increased. Be that as it may, some tenants may find the degradation intolerable and will move to a "better neighborhood." As rents are higher in such a neighborhood, the system accomplishes indirectly for this group what the rent controls are meant to prevent directly.

But this is not the end of the story. While the landlord may maintain reasonable returns on capital by cutting running costs, what he does amounts in fact to "eating up his capital." This comes to the surface when he sells the building; buyers can be expected to offer no more for the building than the sum on which the excess of the controlled rents over normal running costs would constitute a reasonable return. What are normal running costs will depend on the expectations and requirements of the tenants and perhaps on the courts' interpretation of the term. As a result of the sale, the old landlord will take a capital loss, and the new one can make a reasonable return on the building at its *depreciated* value.

In the chain of events, one would further expect that, as land lords are seen to take capital losses on the sale of their buildings, the attractiveness to builders or developers of investing in construction will change and very likely diminish. Cheaper buildings may be put up, and there may be a decrease in new building projects. It is this last effect that will lead in due course to a shortage of housing. This, in turn, will tend to put upward pressure on the rents according to the laws of supply and demand, and, since rents are controlled, this pressure will take the form of requiring "key money" from prospective tenants or other symptoms of a black market. Such practices have in fact been observed in many jurisdictions subject to stringent rent controls. Of course, the very shortage of housing combined with these easily publicized black-market phenomena may be expected to lead to cries for further, more stringent, controls, which, according to the above analysis, would in fact aggravate the problem.

Of course, one might leave newly constructed buildings out of the controls. In such a regime the rents in these buildings would be substantially higher than those in the older, controlled buildings, and one would expect different rates of vacancy for the two sectors: a very low rate in the controlled sector and a higher rate in the "open" market. Of course the high rate of vacancy in the open market will affect the profitability of buildings in this sector, and this in turn will reduce the attractiveness of new construction. Differential vacancy rates between controlled and open markets have been observed recently in Montreal and previously in many other cities in which such markets coexisted.[34]

These general considerations allow one to analyze slum-area housing problems and to predict the effect of measures designed to provide relief for the tenants in such areas. The basic problem here is the poverty of the inhabitants. It leads to overcrowding in the apartments[35] and hence to a greater need for repairs and basic upkeep. And yet the poverty and frequent unemployment also increase the likelihood of default on rental payments, a direct cost increase for the landlord, as one may conclude from the discussion of credit. One can therefore predict that rent controls will lead to neglect of upkeep, which in turn will give rise to calls for more stringent controls. These new controls may require landlords to make basic improvements to substandard housing in order to be entitled to the rent, or they may declare minimal habitability standards.

Since landlords in these areas make minimal returns on their capital at best, their reaction to such requirements would be to withdraw from the market. And even this may be difficult, given the very uncertain and unfavorable outlook for the potential buyers, as has in fact been observed in the city of New York.[36] Landlords then abandon their buildings, and, if one attempts to come after them in spite of that, they may have the buildings set afire and collect whatever the insurance company will pay. Of course, all these moves will effectively diminish the quantity of housing — whatever the quality — available for the poorest. In this light it is not surprising to find judges in New York refusing to enforce legislation forcing landlords to make improvements; such a judgment would only hasten the abandonment.[37]

Conclusion

In each of the three examples discussed above, one could derive from economic theory predictions with regard to the way in which people will be affected by legislative measures and will react to them. These predictions turn out to be substantially confirmed by evidence on the observed effect of such measures. This correspondence between theory and reality is all the more relevant because on most accounts the legislation would be judged at best only partly successful in the light of the evidence,[38] and *this outcome could have been predicted* — in much more detail — *in the manner outlined in the previous section.* This result confers, in our view, a good deal of initial plausibility on the economic approach to law.

The next chapter deals with the scope of the economic approach — that is, the type of question it can answer, given its assumptions, and the type of answer it will give. This discussion is a prerequisite for the critical examination of what appears to be the most ambitious application of economic reasoning to law — namely, the analysis of the core common law doctrines — that will be undertaken in the third and fourth chapters.

CHAPTER 2

Economic Premises

The field of economics on which the new economic analysis of law draws heavily is *welfare theory*. This branch of economics studies what affects the welfare of society as a whole. An area within this large field of particular relevance here is the study of how prices are formed in markets, traditionally known as *price theory*. One might see economic analysis of law as applied welfare theory, and one author uses the significant title "Price Theory as Jurisprudence."[1] To understand the potential and the limits of economic analysis of law, one must be aware of the more fundamental limitations of the theory on which it is based.

The currently accepted focus of discussion within welfare theory is a formally elaborated set of theorems known as the *neoclassical model*.[2] By means of this model, it can be shown that under some, admittedly restrictive, assumptions, reliance on competitive markets will lead to optimal welfare for society as a whole, defined in a technical sense to be discussed below. The political relevance of this proposition is obvious; some would like to read it as an argument for "free markets" and absence of "state intervention," barring special circumstances. Discussions in welfare theory concern, among other things, the question of whether this political conclusion may be drawn. Against such a move it is argued that actual markets systematically fail to conform to the "competitive markets" assumed in the model, and, more fundamentally, that the interpretation given to the idea of collective welfare in the neoclassical model excludes significant aspects of an intuitive understanding of that notion.

The present chapter summarizes this discussion. The first section gives the essence of the model. The second section deals with "market failure" and "imperfect competition." The third section covers the limitations of the welfare concept used in the neoclassical model. The final section discusses propositions for a broader welfare concept and draws parallels between this and Becker's precept. The distinction between the neoclassical and the broad welfare concept appears to be what separates two major thinkers in the law and economics field, R. A. Posner and G. Calabresi.

The Neoclassical Model

The fundamental problem studied by economics is scarcity: the limits on the means at our disposal to influence our welfare. The economist answers such questions as whether a different allocation of scarce resources would increase the satisfaction people derive from their use or to what extent the pursuit of one form of satisfaction requires abandonment of another form in the face of scarce resources.

The neoclassical model postulates what economists call *methodological individualism*.[3] By this is meant that the individual is considered the atom of the analysis. Society's welfare is no more than the welfare of each of its members. Decision making by groups is nothing other than the decisions of the individuals who compose them, combined according to procedural rules and other constraints particular to the group. In this approach one would analyze decision making by "the government" by referring to the constraints applicable to the individuals who make up the political bodies and the bureaucracy.[4]

Methodological individualism should be contrasted with approaches in which group phenomena are thought to have an autonomous existence and to influence or even "determine" individuals. Such approaches can, for instance, be found in sociology. Boudon describes them as "descriptions which depict *homo sociologicus* as a being moved by social forces which are external to him. . . . [They represent] the model current in contemporary sociology, of a *homo sociologicus* whose *actions* would have the status of responses determined by social 'structures.' "[5] He himself rejects such approaches, preferring instead explanations that always attempt to "retrace individual actions behind the regularities observed at the macrosociological level."[6]

The neoclassical model makes two further important assumptions about people's welfare. It postulates that individuals are always able to judge their own welfare and that their judgment does not depend on the welfare of their fellow citizens. These postulates rule out, among other things, systems in which some members decide what is best for others (paternalism and dictatorship) as well as those in which people's sense of welfare depends on that of their neighbors and peers (jealousy).

How does one translate the welfare of all individuals into a single welfare function for society as a whole? Arrow has shown that, if majority rule were adopted, where there are more than three individuals and more than three issues, one cannot be certain that a consistent ranking will result.[7] Of course, one might weight certain votes less than others, or not at all, but that would be dictatorial and contrary to the assumptions.

The usual way out of this problem is to adopt a less demanding criterion for social welfare, but one that does not lead to a ranking of all objectives under all circumstances. The criterion adopted is named after the Italian sociologist and economist, V. Pareto. It states that a movement from one situation to another constitutes an improvement of society's welfare if no individual's welfare is reduced and at least one individual is made better off. The new situation is said to be *Pareto superior* to the old one.

Strictly speaking, the criterion does not allow one to judge a change in which one individual gains and another loses. If, however, there were a way in which the "winner" could *compensate* the "loser," changes might still be said to constitute Pareto improvements if the gains were sufficient to cover the compensation and still left a net benefit.

There are two problems with this expanded version of the Pareto criterion: that of the holdout and that of the feasibility of compensation. Let us illustrate the first problem by an example. Consider a plan to establish in a depressed region a factory that will procure jobs and manufacture products at highly competitive prices but that creates some river pollution. The plan would lead to a Pareto improvement if the gainers could compensate the losers, in this case those who stand to suffer from the pollution. Suppose that some of the pollutees have agreed to a settlement offered by the developers. If the plan could go ahead only if it brought a Pareto improvement, the remaining pollutees could decide that any sum of money was not worth the degradation they would suffer or, at the very least, they could insist on very substantial sums, well in excess of what other pollutees had been paid.[8] In the first case, they would halt a project that a very large group of individuals would have preferred to go ahead. In practice, mechanisms are found to override the preferences of such "holdouts," and, to the extent that this is true, the modified Pareto criterion is not an adequate representation of how collective priorities are set in reality.[9]

The second problem with the compensation idea is that it may not be realistic to assume compensation after each project. As many moves go on at once and most individuals stand to gain by some and to lose by others, it may be preferable to think of compensation over numerous projects. Under these circumstances one would judge a project to be a Pareto improvement if the winners could, ultimately, compensate the losers: the *potential compensation criterion*.[10]

The concept of a Pareto improvement can be used to define a *Pareto optimum:* a situation in which no Pareto improvement is possible. *The central point of the neoclassical model is that under certain assumptions an economy consisting of competitive markets, i.e., having many sellers and many buyers, for all goods and services as well as productive factors would bring about a Pareto optimum and be in equilibrium at that point. The theorem implies that, even though no one deliberately pursues the common good, but instead each individual looks after his self-interest, the result of these efforts will be best for all.*[11]

The demonstration of the theorem and the precise assumptions underlying it will not be restated here.[12] Generally they describe a system in which productive factors and end commodities can be freely exchanged between suppliers and purchasers. The exchanges take place in what are called *markets.* These are characterized by the presence of many persons both on the supply and on the demand side. Exchanges are facilitated by the use of money rather than barter. Under these circumstances, it can be demonstrated that all commodities and productive factors "gravitate towards their highest valued use."[13] Exchange will cease when no further gains will result from it. The collection of goods has then reached the highest achievable value at the prevailing prices. Of course, if initial resources or wealth were differently distributed among individuals, demand for various goods might well be different. Hence the prices in the market, determined as they are by both supply and demand, would be different, and a different collection of goods would be optimal.

In summary, the neoclassical model shows that universal, perfectly competitive markets bring the economy to a state that is Pareto optimal, *given the initial distribution of wealth*. A different distribution of wealth would lead to a different optimum. It is therefore meaningless to speak of *the* Pareto optimum without specifying the distribution of wealth, a point to which we will come back in the third section.

A further important proposition derived from the theory is that when the economy is at its optimum, prices are equal to *marginal cost* — that is, the cost of producing the last unit of the commodity or service involved. The importance of the "marginal cost pricing principle" as a normative guideline had been recognized independently in various segments of the economic literature, as Graaff notes in his well-known book on welfare economics.[14] Of course, a particularly gratifying aspect of a theory is that it allows one to "find back" themes developed in earlier literature.

An interesting feature of the prices in a Pareto optimal state is that they accurately reflect the relative scarcity of the commodities or productive factors to which they are attached. This finding is particularly interesting to those who like to analyze the economy as a cybernetic system reacting to scarcity;[15] the price system in this structure is a most effective distributor of (feedback) information about scarcity.

Deviations from Neoclassical Assumptions: Market Failure and Imperfect Competition

The economy described by the neoclassical model will, if left to its own devices, move to a Pareto optimum. Much research has gone into the question of the realism of the assumptions and of the direction in which the economy would autonomously move if they are not met. Of special concern are the assumptions regarding the exchange process. If they are not fulfilled, there is said to be a *market imperfection or failure*. The prices of the commodities in the imperfect markets do not reflect marginal cost — i.e., scarcity — and this failure would tend to misdirect the use of resources: too much, relative to other commodities or factors, given their scarcity, would be used of the underpriced items, too little of the overpriced ones. In what follows we discuss some of these market imperfections.

Market Imperfections

Nonuniversality. The first assumption is that market are all-encompassing, that everything affecting consumers' well-being can be exchanged.[16] Trade barriers and inalienable rights violate this assumption.

Public or Collective Goods. The model further assumes that all resources are owned, in the sense that some person to the exclusion of all others can decide on the uses to which each will be put. This is not the case for so-called public or collective goods, alternatively defined as those from whose use nobody can be excluded or those whose use by one person does not diminish their utility to any other person.[17] The usual example of such a good is national defence. Information, as we shall argue in Part II, assumes public-good characteristics in certain circumstances, as does the protection of the environment. The problem with such goods is that if they are available free of charge, everyone will be tempted to make excessive use of them; whereas if one is asked to contribute to their creation, one will have an interest to understate one's desire for them, in the hope that one will pay less than one's share while retaining the full benefit. This last strategy is usually called free-riding.[18]

Costly Transactions. A further assumption is that exchange is instantaneous and costless. This assumption, usually referred to as that of zero transaction costs (ZTC), is particularly relevant in the legal area, in the context of the so-called Coase theorem, to be discussed in Chapter 3. In practice, the assumption is violated in a multitude of ways. One cannot, for instance, "buy" one's safety from every possible car driver who might involve one in an accident;

the costs of locating the contract partners and agreeing with them on the terms of the contract are clearly prohibitive. Again, many people may suffer from dog owners who let their pets defecate indiscriminately. They might even be willing to pay the dog owners to stop the practice or scoop up. Yet the effort and cost required to bring the sufferers together for such an exchange is so great that none will in fact come about. As a third example, consider the cost of negotiating complex agreements involving substantial sums of money. The cost and effort that go into foreseeing a variety of contingencies and formulating clauses covering them that are satisfactory to the negotiating parties are obviously quite substantial. Indeed, it is conceivable that mutually advantageous exchanges will not be undertaken because of the costs of negotiating them.[19]

Uncertainty.   Related to the preceding assumption is the one stipulating the absence of uncertainty or risk. Such uncertainty might involve imperfect knowledge of what techniques will be available in the future or risk stemming from anticipations of future wealth as they affect one's present well-being. It is, as Graaff argues, very unlikely that people will agree "on the proper [risk] premium to add to (or subtract from) marginal cost."[20]

External Effects.   If prices are to reflect scarcity, they must cover the cost of *all* scarce resources used to produce a commodity. Thus, if the production process entails pollution of the environment and yet the price for the product reflects only the direct production costs and not those associated with "using up" the environment, there might be overconsumption of the product in question. The production process is said to generate unfavorable external effects or spillovers on the environment;[21] the *private* cost of the product — that is, the factors considered by the manufacturer in setting its price — is not equal to its *social* cost.

Usually the unfavorable spillover is to the detriment of identifiable persons — as opposed to future generations, in the case of the environment in general — and one might say that the value of their property right has effectively been reduced, a partial expropriation in disguise. One of the surprising conclusions of Coase's article,[22] which we cited earlier as a classic in the law and economics literature, is that if parties can negotiate without costs, the existence of external effects will *not* prevent the economy from attaining a Pareto optimum, although it will affect the distribution of wealth between parties to the spillover. This means that, *in the absence of transaction costs, the precise division of property rights between owners whose use of them will conflict is of no consequence for the optimal allocation of resources in the economy as a whole.* In Chapter 3 this proposition will be discussed further. In the present context, we note, following Schultze,[23] that the problem of external effects can be restated as one due to high transaction costs and free riders.

Imperfect Competition.   The last assumption of the neoclassical model to be discussed here is that all markets are perfectly competitive. This assumption is necessary to ensure that no producer or owner can sell his wares above marginal cost and make excessive profits or "rents." This condition is violated by the existence of monopolies or oligopolies, on which an extensive literature exists. Usually these phenomena are referred to as market imperfections, as opposed to the market failures analyzed in the preceding subsections.

Conclusion.   The preceding discussion has allowed us to identify four general phenomena that are incompatible with the assumptions of the neoclassical model:

1. Collective goods (free rider problem),
2. Significant transaction costs,
3. Substantial uncertainty,
4. Imperfect competition.[24]

We must now discuss the consequences of this finding for the usefulness of the neoclassical model.

The Correction of Market Imperfections and the Problem of Second Best

The observation that there are significant discrepancies between reality and the assumptions of the neoclassical model might lead one to reject that model as a description of reality, and even more as a basis for policy statements. Yet this conclusion is understandably not usually drawn, considering the absence of an alternative to the neoclassical model that is equally well formally developed and general. Instead, it is thought that such imperfections can be remedied by government intervention and that, to the extent that this result is achieved, the economy as a whole moves closer to a Pareto optimum. Thus, public goods are supplied by the government and paid for out of taxes; transaction costs are reduced — among other things — by a legal system that supplies standard solutions for a number of potential conflicts.

Intuitively plausible though this attitude may be, it cannot be taken for granted that by moving the economy closer to the required conditions through piecemeal moves — to which policymakers are limited in practice — its performance will come closer to a Pareto optimum. In a fundamental article written more than twenty years ago,[25] Lipsey and Lancaster demonstrated that if the economy deviates from some of the assumptions required for it to reach a Pareto optimum, it is not necessarily helpful — indeed, it may be positively harmful — to try to make it conform to other assumptions. This conclusion is known as the *principle of second best*. It seems to imply that unless all assumptions can be satisfied at once, it is futile to pursue any at all. Such a conclusion would, of course, be devastating for much practical policy making.

Davis and Whinston argue for a more refined use of the theory of second best.[26] The theory should, in their view, be used to determine under what conditions piecemeal policy is justified and under what conditions it is not. Generally, policies in a restricted area are justified if changes in that sector have only negligible effects on the prices of goods and resources in the remaining sectors of the economy.[27] Thus, the theory of second best may serve to develop "principles for the designation of 'natural units' for the concern of policy."[28] Within such units the various Pareto assumptions must be satisfied all at once, and different policies must be coordinated to this end, but the effects of the policies on other sectors may be neglected. Whether these guidelines are viable in practice is, as Mishan points out,[29] open to question.

We would draw the following conclusions from the foregoing discussion. A Pareto optimum of the economy may be achieved through competitive markets as well as other institutions or government interventions. If a Pareto optimum for the given distribution is society's goal and if it wishes to achieve it through decentralized markets, the question of how market imperfections must be handled arises. The theorem of second best suggests that piecemeal correction of these imperfections may be counterproductive. This paralyzing result can be avoided if corrective action takes place within what the literature on second best calls "naturals units" of the economy. But a fundamental question remains: Can it be taken for granted that the pursuit of a Pareto optimum is society's objective or even one of its objectives?

Limitations of the Pareto Optimum as a Description of Society's Welfare

The historical relevance of the notion of "Pareto optimum" lies in its relation to perfect competition. From Adam Smith on, "there has never been absent from the main body of economic literature the feeling that in some sense perfect competition represented an optimal situation."[30] The nature of this "optimal situation" is that of a Pareto optimum. Discussions of the desirability of perfect competition and, by extension, of the free market system may therefore be reformulated as the question of whether the Pareto optimum covers one's intuitive notion of what is socially best. This section deals with that question.

In a Pareto optimum, "the pie of final goods and services would be as large as possible given available resources *and* the ingredients of the pie would best suit the tastes of consumers who could exercise effective demand for slices of it."[31] Such a situation is said to attain *allocative efficiency* in that no reallocation of goods could improve anyone's situation without at the same time depreciating someone else's. There is no "waste" of resources, and in this sense such a state of economy is "efficient."

The concept of a Pareto optimum is very general. It covers *all* goods and services that can be made available through production and exchange. It avoids, as Hennipman has convincingly shown,[32] many of the restrictions on the package of goods and services that are implicit in earlier concepts of optima, such as maximal real income, productivity, or social product.

In spite of the generality of the concept of a Pareto optimum, various authors have raised doubts about the appropriateness of choosing the attainment of a Pareto optimum as the sole objective of economic policy.[33] It has been asked in particular whether the objective of economic policy can exclude the question of the distribution of wealth.

It will be recalled that a Pareto optimal state of the economy is defined for a given distribution of wealth.[34] What that distribution is, or should be, lies outside the discussion of what the optimum is and how it can be attained. The proper distribution is, in the view of many orthodox neoclassicists, an issue best left "to the preacher and the politician."[35]

Yet in practice, as Mishan points out, "some of those who are made better off [as a result of a Pareto improvement of the economy] could be among the very rich."[36] This would tend to widen the distance between rich and poor and offend many people's sense of social justice. This observation holds in particular for Pareto optima that might be pursued by reliance on decentralized competitive markets.

It might be thought that this need not unduly worry us since "each consumer can *expect* to come out ahead *in the long run* if the efficiency criterion is used. . . ."[37] But such an expectation does not imply that each individual will *in fact* gain, and even casual observation of North American society suffices to convince one that there are in reality distinct groups of losers (nonwinners).

All in all, it would seem that a proper concept of social optimum should contain some reference to an acceptable distribution of wealth as well as to efficiency in the allocation of scarce resources. Unfortunately, these two objectives are not independent, as the neoclassical model might suggest. One cannot in practice decide on a distribution of wealth, institute it and subsequently pursue efficiency unhampered. Redistribution goes on continually and may "entail adverse effects on economic incentives of the rich and the poor, and the administrative costs of tax-collection and transfer programs."[38] These adverse effects and administrative costs mean that the production of some goods and services may have to be foregone to achieve the desired distribution. But it is quite conceivable that the desired distribution of wealth can be realized *only* at such a sacrifice.

Various institutions used in Western economies to redistribute wealth limit freedom of exchange in the market. An interesting example of this phenomenon are the inalienable rights attributed to all citizens, which prevent them, for instance, from selling themselves or their family into slavery.[39] Okun, who mentions this example, argues that minimum-wage laws and work-safety legislation belong in the same category of prohibitions on exchange born of desperation.[40] In each of these, and in many other cases that could be cited, the pursuit of efficiency without consideration for equality or vice versa would be a move away from the social optimum as many would understand the term.

The Broad Concept of Welfare

Definition

The foregoing discussion leads inevitably to the conclusion that a Pareto optimum cannot be the sole guide to economic policy in any existing society. What could take its place? Surely not more limited concepts, such as "maximization of real income" or of the "social product." Instead, the solution proposed is *to abandon the idea that economic activity is necessarily aimed at particular goals that can be specified by postulate.* To use Robbins's phrase, *"there are no economic ends."*[41] *Any objective that contributes to society's welfare in the sense that it satisfies the wants or desires of some citizens — or more generally, of those whose preferences count — and that requires decisions on the allocation of scarce resources is a proper goal for economic policy and should be studied as such by economists.* This statement defines the *broad concept of welfare.*[42]

In this view of welfare economics, "the job of the economist is not to try to reach welfare conclusions for others, but rather to make available the positive knowledge — the information and the understanding — on the basis of which laymen (and economists themselves, out of office hours) can pass judgment. . . . One of the tasks of theoretical economics is then simply to *predict* what particular index numbers (of output or consumption) will be in the future (or explain why they were what they were in the past), and not to say what they ought to be if welfare is to be maximized."[43]

To be sure, if there were extensive agreement on various ethical matters — the objectives that citizens thought it worthwhile to pursue and their relative priority — it might be possible, though complex, to formulate normative statements. But, as Graaff notes, "it does not seem to be realized how *detailed* the agreement on ends must be if a consistent theory of welfare economics is to be erected."[44] In the absence of such agreement on fundamentals, "the elegance and simplicity of *laissez-faire* welfare theory, which is largely concerned with demonstrating the optimal properties of free competition and the unfettered price system,"[45] is an illusion.

For those who accept the broad concept of welfare, it is meaningless to distinguish between "economic" and "noneconomic" goals if both kinds require the use of scarce resources. Freedom, trust, cultural development, public health, justice, international peace, or the avoidance of social and political strife can all very well be objectives of economic policy. It may be true that such objectives are less readily quantified than those that are found in traditional economic discussions. Yet, once scarce resources are used, they fall within the purview of economics, whether satisfaction is attained through the production and the acquisition of income within organizations traditionally considered part of the economic system, or outside of it.[46] Moreover, some of these objectives might be considered "irrational" by traditional standards. To this objection, Heertje's reply is particularly fitting: "for economics, too, it is rational to take the irrational into account."[47]

What meaning can be given to the notion of "efficiency" under the broad concept of welfare? Hennipman, who has given prominence to the broad concept of welfare, writes that "efficiency" loses most of the technical sense that it assumes in the neoclassical model.[48] Efficiency in this general sense would be achieved if choices regarding the allocation of scarce resources were based on correct insight in economic phenomena and their relations. "A policy would be 'uneconomical' in this sense, not if it deviates from certain objectives or rules of conduct, but if it is based on incorrect or incomplete knowledge of economic facts."[49] It is the task of economics to provide this knowledge of economic facts, of links between means and ends. How far economics has in fact progressed, of how much help it can be in practical situations where several, conflicting ends are pursued, is a different matter.

The Broad Concept of Welfare and Becker's Precept

At first glance there is a great deal of affinity between the broad concept of welfare and Becker's precept. Both conceptions give a wider scope to economics by making it applicable to areas previously considered to be "non-economic." In both cases this extension is motivated by the desire to include in the notion of welfare, collective in the first instance, individual in the second, factors that were heretofore held to be too subjective to be dealt with.

The boundaries set for economics appear to differ in the two conceptions. In discussions of the broad welfare concept, economics is held to encompass any question involving choices of allocating scarce means among competing ends. Becker finds "this definition . . . so broad that it is often a source of embarrassment rather than pride to many economists, and [that it] usually is immediately qualified to exclude nonmarket behavior."[50] He proposes to characterize economics instead by its approach and refers for this purpose to the combined assumptions of maximizing behavior, market equilibrium and stable preferences. Yet, considering the analyses assembled in the book from whose introduction these remarks were taken, one can hardly avoid the conclusion that, much as he may feel embarrassed by it, Becker relies in fact on a broad concept of economics.

The difference between the approaches lies perhaps in the faith they place in the neoclassical model. The broad welfare concept expresses the idea that it is not for economics to indicate particular aims of economic policy, especially not the pursuit of a Pareto optimum. Strictly speaking, this position is neutral with regard to what are in fact society's objectives and therefore consistent with a possible finding that it is indeed the collectivity's desire to strive exclusively for a Pareto optimum. Yet implicit in many of the discussions of the broad welfare concept is the belief that allocative efficiency is *in fact not* a complete description of what society is after, and hence that there is reason for caution with respect to the practical uses to which the neoclassical machinery can be put.

It is this implicit idea that conflicts with Becker's position, which appears to favor the use of the neoclassical model as much as possible but focuses on the individual decisionmaker and allows for considerable refinement of the meaning given to the basic terms of the model. Whether the use of neoclassical machinery in this more restricted context is less objectionable than at the level of the collectivity as a whole is a debatable question. Whatever the answer, there is no denying that the problems associated, at the level of the collectivity, with the variety of people's values and objectives come back at the individual level as questions about what are to count as costs and benefits.[51] At both levels the notion of welfare from which we start must rest on observation, not on postulation.

Practical Consequences of Adopting the Broad Concept of Welfare

The adoption of the broad concept of welfare implies that it can no longer be maintained as a matter of economic insight that Pareto improvements are socially desirable. The relevance of the notion of a Pareto improvement and with it, of the neoclassical model, depends on the extent to which people actually desire efficient allocation of resources.[52] This question is not readily answered by a survey. As we saw earlier, the notion of a Pareto optimum is less straightforward than it might appear to be at first glance. And even if we agreed on a definition, the question of whether efficient allocation, rather than more redistribution or other objectives, is desired is not of a kind for which people have ready answers.

Must we then leave neoclassical theory on ice until we have better ways of ascertaining what people actually desire? That position would be devastating to the discipline, since, as Arrow notes, "no really cohesive alternative which aspires to the same level of completeness [as the much-abused neoclassical theory] exists."[53] He adds that

> one cause for the persistence of neoclassical theory in the face of its long line of critics is precisely that for some reason of mathematical structure, the neoclassical theory is highly manipulable and flexible; when faced with a specific issue, it can yield meaningful implications relatively easily.[54]

In applying economic theory we are therefore faced with a dilemma. We can place our faith in the neoclassical model as a solid tool and attempt to widen its admittedly restricted applicability by giving broader interpretations to its basic terms. Or we can, from the outset, admit all conceivable objectives — a perhaps more faithful description of reality — but find ourselves hampered by the relative crudeness of the methods available to determine how these objectives can be pursued and to what extent the pursuit of one interferes with that of others. We must, in other words, weigh the predictive power of the tools against their descriptive relevance, and this requires a value judgment.

For our part, we would subscribe to the statement that "efficiency [is] surely an important, if not necessarily paramount, value in society."[55] It follows that we shall judge results derived from the neoclassical model not only as correct or incorrect but also as relevant. We shall therefore make liberal use of the neoclassical model in what follows, but, forewarned by the discussion of the broad welfare concept, we shall be aware that its results provide only some of the considerations on which the weighing of social choices is based. We shall try to extend the scope of the model by taking into account, contrary to its assumptions, that scarce resources must be devoted to the acquisition and processing of information used to reduce uncertainty and to effect transactions.[56]

CHAPTER 3

Economic Analysis of Major Common Law Doctrines:

The Mainstream View

Schools of Thought

The few examples of economic analysis of law given in the first chapter may have left the reader with the impression that this new discipline provides clear answers to the questions it raises and that there is little scope for controversy among its disciples. This idea must be dispelled. Within the "law and economics" literature there is no less disagreement than in the traditional legal literature.

To cite but a few examples, Posner believes that negligence rules can induce people to observe the efficient level of caution, whereas Calabresi maintains that, at least in the field of automobile accidents, they will not have that effect.[1] Again, with respect to the policy of adopting safety standards for various consumer products, Oi sees no market imperfection with respect to safety features and, hence, believes that these standards unnecessarily reduce choice for those prepared to take risks in order to pay less. By contrast, Goldberg argues — for reasons to be explored in Part II — that people are unable to form an informed preference with respect to safety and, hence, that standards, while imposing a uniform safety level on all consumers, bring most of them closer to the safety level they prefer than would be possible by other means, in particular the market.[2]

Disagreements are not limited to theoretical argument. Empirical work may be equally contested, as was Peltzman's study of the effect of automobile safety regulation.[3] These disagreements do not usually turn around technical flaws in the argument of one or the other of the disputants.[4] In most instances they concern fundametal issues, parallel to those discussed in economics generally, such as were reviewed in the preceding chapter. The controversial questions are, in other words, those of the faith to be placed in autonomous market forces as opposed to government intervention, the appropriateness of "efficiency" as a policy objective, and, accordingly, the uses to which the neoclassical model can be put. In what follows we review what appear to be the main lines of thought.

The Mainstream Position

The mainstream position in the "law and economics" literature generally accepts the neoclassical view of the world. It may admit that economics should not — and even, cannot — prescribe goals for economic policy. It may further admit that the community's objectives need not be restricted to "efficiency." But not much seems to turn on this, since most analyses by this group[5] are limited to results derivable in the neoclassical model or to empirical tests of such propositions.[6]

The primary function of the law, in this view, is to facilitate the functioning of markets. To this end the law should define very general property rights so that every object can be exchanged; it should set out general terms of contract, covering major contingencies, in order that exchanges are smooth, as parties succeed in avoiding disagreements that might have arisen out of misunderstanding or unforeseen circumstances. Where a transaction is not feasible, as between a person and all others who might inflict accidental injury on him, the law should institute dispute-resolution facilities that imitate the market, in that they adopt solutions that the parties would have chosen had they been able to negotiate before the actual injury. In this manner all citizens are made aware of the actual costs of their behavior and can make the appropriate choice with regard to care. Generally, the mainstream position is that the law can contribute to efficiency by reducing the transaction costs of market exchange, by correcting other market imperfections — discussed in Chapter 2 — and, where actual markets are not feasible, by adopting solutions that imitate market exchange results.

The Critics

Criticism from Within the Neoclassical Paradigm. The criticism of the mainstream position may take one of two forms. The first, staying within the neoclassical framework, points to forms of market imperfection that had not been recognized and that call for unusual remedies. The second kind attacks the mainstream position on more fundamental grounds, contending that to consider "efficiency" as the policy objective is irreparably unrealistic.

Criticism of the first kind is at the root of much legislation for the protection of the environment, where it is alleged that there are substantial, hitherto unrecognized, externalities.[7] It is also invoked to justify much consumer legislation, on the ground that consumers are thought to have insuperable problems in acquiring or processing the information necessary for them to make appropriate choices in the market.[8] In both instances the freedom of autonomous market forces is clearly curtailed.

A similar critical position underlies efforts to show that institutions replacing the market are justified because they are less costly than the — imperfect — market would be. Such a comparison of costs and benefits of market and nonmarket institutions can be found, for instance, in Goldberg's articles on regulation as an administered contract and on safety standards.[9]

Fundamental Criticism. The second group of critics argue that the view limiting society's objectives to "efficiency" concerns is so incomplete as to be misleading. Such a position is an implicit argument for a broader concept of welfare than is used by the mainstream. One of the principal factors that these critics wish to include in the analysis is the distribution of wealth, in forms as varied as subsidized housing (Ackerman)[10] and spreading of accident costs (Calabresi).[11] This position will be discussed further in Chapter 4.

Outline of Chapters 3 and 4

In the remainder of this chapter, we shall summarize the analysis of common law fields, such as property rights, contracts, torts and procedure, as they are presented in the perspective of the mainstream, mostly by Posner. This summary does not purport to do full justice to the wealth and detail of the analyses published by mainstream authors, but it should be sufficient to give the reader an idea of the essentials and to allow him to see the difference between the mainstream view and the critics.

Chapter 4 deals with the criticism of the mainstream view. Since the critics are rather heterogeneous in their views of what is wrong with the mainstream position, we have not attempted to synthesize their opinions. Rather, it seemed preferable to focus on a single critic, whose thinking we believe to be very rich and to encompass much of what the others have advanced. The critic we have in mind is Calabresi, and Chapter 4 deals with his writings and his exchanges with Posner.

The Goal of the Common Law

The general efficiency objective of law as viewed by the tenants of the mainstream position in law and economics can be particularized as follows:

> The common law method is to allocate responsibilities
> between people engaged in interacting activities in such a
> way as to maximize the joint value, or, what amounts to the
> same thing, minimize the joint cost of the activities.[12]

To the objection that this looks like a truncated view of the common law, Posner, from whom we took the statement, responds by showing that the observance of various moral precepts, such as honesty, trustworthiness and truthfulness, which the law is thought by some to encourage, should be analyzed as means to reduce transaction costs and to facilitate market exchange.[13] On a refined analysis, in other words, they turn out to be but instruments in the pursuit of efficiency.

Posner concedes that distributive justice cannot be reduced to efficiency in this manner. But, he contends, "it is rarely suggested that the common law is based on distributive justice, as distinct from corrective justice [i.e., disguised efficiency, as discussed above] or efficiency."[14]

This argument leads Posner to the conclusion that *the one and only goal of the common law is to promote the efficient allocation of resources, albeit in many, differently disguised forms.* In spite of its normative form, this statement must be understood as a *descriptive* hypothesis. Posner submits that this is in fact society's objective in shaping the institutions of the common law. If one accepts the hypothesis, one could make the very important inference that *"it may be possible to deduce the basic formal characteristics of law itself from economic theory."*[15]

Given this substantial promise, the methodological task is to determine whether observation, in particular of common law doctrines in recorded cases, *supports* Posner's hypothesis, rather than a rival one such as Calabresi's. But empirical support would not be the final word on the confidence one could have in this economic theory of law. One would also like to have a theory that *explains* how this remarkable result comes about. In what follows we shall be concerned with both these kinds of support for the thesis.

A last general remark is in order. If the descriptive hypothesis advanced by Posner were confirmed, it would *not* of itself justify the normative proposition that the efficiency objective *ought* to be pursued in the future development of the common law, or of any other area of law. Hence, to deplore the inefficiency that certain rules are thought to display, as Posner does on occasion when he contrasts judge-made rules with those issued by legislatures,[16] reflects an unwarranted value judgment.

Property Rights

Function

The function of property rights is best understood by imagining a world initially without them. Let us think of a common pasture open to all herdsmen in a village.[17] Each herdsman will try to keep as many cattle as possible on the commons. This arrangement may work satisfactorily as long as diseases, wars and other causes of attrition keep the number of men and cattle well within the carrying capacity of the land. But as advances in medicine, science and social development push back the effect of such causes, the day inevitably comes when the commons is saturated, when no more cattle could be added without reducing below the vital minimum what is available for the animals already there.

Once this point has been reached, the herdsmen are in a predicament. Each of them would be tempted to add one more animal to the herd for his own benefit; he can reap the benefits from this extra animal without very much suffering the detriment — overcrowding — resulting from it. And yet since all other herdsmen will follow this reasoning, collectively they face disaster. Hardin puts in poignantly as follows:

> Each man is locked into a system that compels him to
> increase his herd without limit — in a world that is limited.
> Ruin is the destination toward which all men rush, each
> pursuing his own best interest in a society that believes in
> the freedom of the commons. Freedom in a commons brings
> ruin to all.[18]

Such predicaments are not only found in land use. In modern times, polluting industries may treat the air and the rivers that surround them as a commons for waste disposal. The fish stock of rivers and oceans may be treated as a commons by the fishermen of different nations, and overfishing as well as the extinction of certain animals has been seen to occur as a result of excessive and indiscriminate hunting.[19]

In all these situations the participants are likely to find it profitable to come to an agreement with each other that will limit their collective demand on the common but scarce resource. The allocation might be organized in several ways. People might be assigned quotas, with or without compensation. Or some might be excluded from the commons, by lottery or other means. The arrangements would, of course, have to be "policed," since the incentive for an individual to cheat when others observe the agreement is particularly great. The "policing costs" may well be a factor that influences the nature of the arrangement chosen.

While arrangements of this kind will avoid disaster, they are cumbersome in that the consent of the entire group is necessary to modify them when circumstances demand such a change. Of course, one could leave this task to a council or other representative or administrative body, but that solution has its own problems[20] and would probably not be as responsive to individual needs and preferences as the institution of property rights, which we shall now discuss.

Property law consists in assigning to individuals (or groups) rights to *use* a designated piece of the commons and to *exclude* others from it. Moreover, since people may come to differ in their ability to make productive use of the land — due to unexpected illness, or, on the contrary, because one has a knack for it or a large family — property law makes these rights *transferable* among people.

A rearrangement of the use to which the land (or other resource) is put now involves no more than agreement among the *two* parties involved, rather than the entire community or its representative body. The ease in transferring rights will help people, as the economists would put it, to specialize in activities in which they have a comparative advantage over others and to be collectively better off as a result. Conversely, one would predict that as a community expects benefits from new forms of specialization and trade, a demand would arise for property rights in the objects concerned and facilities for their transfer. Thus, specialization in "risk bearing" might well explain property rights in "futures" and industrial stock; specialized research and development may be fostered — or so it is thought[21] — by industrial property rights; as medical science perfects techniques for transplanting organs, one would expect demands on the legal profession for rules to facilitate the transfer of organs.[22]

Property rights as a solution to a "tragedy of the commons" concern the relations among people at a given time: a static point of view. They have an equally important dynamic function. Who would invest his time and effort in preparing land and sowing if at harvest time anyone could come and take the crop? For any investment to be worthwhile, the investor must rest assured that he can exclude others from the fruits and trade only at terms acceptable to him.

Pejovich, in a very interesting theoretical article on the function of property rights, discusses examples such as those given above and concludes as follows:

> The logic of economics is then capable of explaining that (i) from the social point of view the creation of property rights assignments is a powerful and possibly necessary condition for more efficient allocation and use of resources, and (ii) from the individual's point of view the specification of property rights is associated with his search for more utility. I conjecture that this latter point relates the standard theory of production and exchange to the creation of property rights over scarce resources.[23]

Property rights exist where one can exclude others from the use of a resource. To the economist, all legitimate means of exclusion have the function of property rights, even though lawyers may give them different names. Economic theory predicts that property rights in this broad sense arise where the cost of excluding others from a resource is more than offset by the benefit one derives from the exclusive use of it.

The Efficiency of Existing Property Rights Systems

Does the common law on property rights conform to Posner's thesis about efficiency? Does it create as much as possible *universal* and *transferable* rights to use resources and *exclude* others from it? Most commodities for which exclusion is useful and feasible can in most systems be the object of property rights. Apart from property of movables and immovables, there are industrial and intellectual property rights and rights to control in corporations. The right to dispose of one's name and image is slowly being recognized. In general, one cannot use someone else's image or name — for instance, for advertising or in a television broadcast — without his prior consent. The recourses against such use are not limited to damages after the fact, but include injunctions before. The right to one's name and image thus clearly acquires the characteristics of excludability and transferability, which make it a property right in the sense in which economic analysis of law uses the term. It is interesting to remember, as Posner points out, that such a right is not fully recognized with respect to news photographs. The cost of negotiating with each person whose picture appears in a photograph of an accident, a demonstration, or a political rally is prohibitively high in comparison with everyone's interest in quick dissemination of news, at least in Posner's view.

There can also be little doubt that the variety of the property rights defined by existing legal systems generally facilitates exchange. Various limited forms of absolute right, such as easements (servitudes in the civil law) or mortgages (hypothecs), are defined as standard institutions to allow parties to negotiate a partial lifting of the owner's right to exlcude. Registration of such rights, while imposing an administrative burden, is likely to facilitate the transaction in that the uncertainty with regard to who holds what right on a given object is eliminated, or virtually so.

Pejovich, in the article from which we quoted earlier, offers examples from the development of property rights in European history in support of the thesis.[24] One of these is the development of property rights after the fall of the Roman Empire. Roman law had a fully developed concept of private property, the respect of which was guaranteed by state authority. After the fall of the empire, violence became the predominant method of resolving conflict among people, which is to say that the cost of exclusion from what one considered to be one's property rose dramatically. This normally would have led to a return to nomadic existence, relying on ample supply of land and breeding of cattle, whose use could more readily be supervised than that of land. However, given the density of population in the region, such a course was not really feasible, and, hence, one would expect arrangements to protect the use of land, thus making possible its intensive use in agriculture. The feudal system is, in Pejovich's view, precisely such an arrangement, providing for specialization in the functions of protecting and exploiting the land among a group of people.[25]

Demsetz cites the example of the development of property rights among Indian tribes. Before the advent of the whites, hunting was carried on primarily for the hunter's family's immediate needs. Once the fur trade became established, hunting was undertaken on a much larger scale, thus increasing the likelihood of conflicts among the hunters. There is evidence that this led the Indians

> to mark off the hunting ground selected by them by blazing the trees with their crests so that they may never encroach

on each other. . . . By the middle of the [eighteenth] century
these allocated territories were relatively established.[26]

While these observations tend to support Posner's thesis, there
are situations in which suitable property rights have not been defined. Examples can be found in the areas of water, air and noise
pollution. The economic model would lead to the prediction that,
in the absence of property rights,[27] there will be overconsumption
of such scarce facilities, and this seems to be amply borne out in
reality.[28] Consider also that we no longer recognize rights in the
use of public roads, and that in the cities, where this resource has
become scarce, one now sees substantial congestion.

All in all, the foregoing would seem generally to support Posner's thesis about the efficiency of property rights. The generality
of his thesis leads us to a further hypothesis, to wit, that the absence
of fully fledged property rights must be attributed to the fact that
the cost of instituting them — i.e., the cost of exclusivity — would
exceed the prospective gains and that the net loss would be larger
than that resulting from the absence of rights. This question is
examined in the next subsection.

The Efficiency of the Absence of, or of Restrictions on, Property Rights

At the outset, the following quotation from Hartle seems particularly relevant:

> If transactions costs were zero, property rights could exist in
> all scarce resources (e.g., pure water and air, privacy, and so
> on). Those who used them (made them even more scarce)
> could be required to pay for the benefits received because the
> information would exist about who was using what. Charges
> could be levied accordingly by those owning the rights. This
> would take care of the overproduction and/or
> overconsumption of goods and services with negative
> externalities. Similarly, if transactions costs were zero,
> perfect information would be available about how much
> everyone valued everything. Quality standards could be
> specified and enforced without controversy. Those who
> refused to pay for what they enjoyed could be readily
> excluded from the source of the benefit. Private suppliers
> could negotiate separate contracts with millions of people.

. . . It does not follow, of course, that where there are transactions costs, governments must necessarily step in and either subsidize or provide goods and services. Transactions costs are ubiquitous. They exist in all modes of economic organizations, private and public.[29]

Problems of Excluding and Transacting.   In Chapter 2 the problem of exclusivity was raised in the context of the clearest example of its absence, some of the collective goods, such as national defence. As a further example consider that legal systems generally do not recognize property rights in *ideas,* an issue that has come to the fore in attempts to patent computer programs. This policy would seem sensible, as it would scarcely be possible to police the ideas people use and, even if this could be done, for the owners to transact with all those who would wish to use them. Moreover, society may attach such a high value to the generation of new combinations of ideas that it would not wish to institute such restrictions, even where it is feasible. This might well be the reason why, in practice, copyright in scientific work is only partly enforced; one can liberally photostat it (indeed, libraries contribute to the practice by providing machines at subsidized rates) under protection of the "fair use" doctrine, although for reprinting it permission of the copyright holder must be sought.

Precisely how useful property rights can be and, hence, how much one would expect this solution to conflicting uses to be favored would depend on the actual cost (feasibility) of exclusivity. This is quite plain in the case of pollution. While most people would now agree that substantial damage is done if *pollution* is left unchecked, one does not always have inexpensive yet effective measures to determine exactly who pollutes how much (among many who dump waste in a river) and what the monetary value of the damage is (recall that optimally prices should be set equal to marginal cost in the neoclassical view). The policy of allowing owners of polluted river beaches to take out injunctions against the polluters does not appear to have led to satisfactory solutions in general. The courts are faced with terrible "measurement" problems for which they are ill equipped, and, if an injunction is granted, the transaction cost of contacting all pollutees and agreeing with them on some compensation would frequently be prohibitive for the polluter and lead him instead to adopt possibly costlier purification measures.

As a result the property rights solution has not generally been followed in coping with the problem of pollution. Davis and Kamien list a variety of other strategies, such as specific prohibitions, directives on use, voluntary cooperative action, regulation (issuance of standards, mandatory equipment, and so on), taxes and subsidies, none of which is without its problems.[30] Schultze has recently argued that many of these solutions do not take proper account of the incentive structure facing the people to whom they apply and lead to somewhat perverse results (recall the three examples discussed in Chapter 1). He submits that it would be desirable to rely more frequently on marketlike solutions, in which "pollution licences" are auctioned off at prices such that "the costs and gains [polluters] confront also reflect, as far as possible, true *social* costs and gains."[31] As our capacity to isolate polluting agents improves, such solutions should become viable.

The question of negative spillovers crops up in a different manner as well. As an example, Posner discusses *water rights* recognized in certain western states of the United States.[32] These entitle the holder to divert water from a natural stream and use it for irrigation or other purposes. Some of the water flows back into the river, and, hence, its content affects the water rights of holders further down the stream. As the rights are transferable, these holders have a great interest in ensuring that in any transfer "upstream" their rights are not harmed. Such harm would result if the new owner were to take more water or return improper water to the stream.

To avoid complex negotiations among all the owners when one of them wishes to sell his lot, the law requires the parties to a transfer to work out arrangements that avoid injury to the rights of other users of the stream. Posner points out that this solution is asymmetrical in that if the new owner *improves* the quality or quantity of the return flow, he cannot capture the benefits to downstream users. It is, of course, costly and perhaps difficult to collect payments from the downstream users. Be that as it may, the result is that property owners have a smaller incentive to make improvements than if they could collect payments. Notice that in similar situations of interdependent interest elsewhere, different legal structures have been adopted — for example, zoning bylaws with respect to the quality of city neighborhoods and owners associations in the case of condominia.

The last example to be discussed is that of *airlines' using the space over people's land.* Normally, property rights in land are thought to reach up to the sky. Yet airlines are not made to pay royalties to the owners for use of the land when flights go over it. Airlines may therefore "dispose of" their noise above people's land. The reason for this arrangement presumably lies in the transaction costs. The flight patterns of aircraft may change according to weather conditions, and one can well imagine the enormous number of people with whom agreements would have to be made on compensation if the owners could stop the overflights.

These transaction costs are arguably substantially in excess of the inconvenience suffered by owners, and, hence, property rights in the use of the sky over one's land are not upheld against airlines. Notice, however, that the matter is looked at differently around airports.[33]

All in all, the restrictions on property rights discussed in this section could be justified, or so it would seem, on the basis of the costs of excluding and of transacting. These few examples also suggest, we believe, that when these costs change, a different view is taken of the appropriateness of instituting property rights.

Other Restrictions.   In some cases people are given exclusive use over some resource but are forbidden to transfer it. One cannot *sell himself into slavery*, much as one can be gainfully employed. Calabresi, in an article with Melamed,[34] speaks of "inalienable entitlements" in such cases. These restrictions on transferability can best be seen, as Okun has forcefully argued, as "prohibitions on exchanges born of desperation."[35] One could perhaps argue that they are compatible with a concern for efficiency in that exchanges under those circumstances can hardly be beneficial to both parties and, hence, will not enhance total welfare. But this interpretation seems strenuous. It would be more plausible to see them as stemming from a minimal concern for equality among citizens.

In other cases restrictions are defined on the use, rather than the transfer, of commodities or resources. For instance, one may not treat one's animals cruelly, nor use one's house as a brothel. *Cruelty against animals* could be seen as a — not easily monetized — externality inflicted upon many people who are sensitive to the issue. It might then be argued that, in the absence of laws against cruelty, people offended by bad treatment of animals would band together and pay ("bribe," in the terminology proposed in the next section) the animal owner to refrain from his practices. Such an initiative would, of course, take a huge amount of personal time and money from those who take the initiative, and the enactment of the rules forbidding costs. The law, in other words, serves here simply to facilitate a transaction that would be much costlier — though no less desirable — without it.

But this argument is not entirely satisfactory, because the animal owner — assuming that he is not indifferent with respect to the cruelty — receives no compensation and is thus presumably worse off than he would be under a voluntary agreement. Nor are the animal lovers made to pay for the realization of their wish. All in all, it would seem that this kind of restriction on the exercise of property rights cannot be justified by a concern for efficiency through savings on transaction costs. Other values seem to be involved. While this may appear to detract from the strength of Posner's thesis, it should be recalled that restrictions such as these are usually defined in an act, rather than developed by the courts as part of the common law.

The *prohibition on keeping a bawdy house*, too, appears to rest on other than efficiency grounds. Perhaps such a prohibition, and more generally the restrictions on prostitution, are thought to contribute to the stability of marriage. Or they might reflect people's desire to restrain themselves from overindulgence in sexual activities, as they discourage themselves from excessive use of alcohol. Some would argue that such restrictions contribute in the long run to so fundamental an objective as survival of the species. Becker has made this kind of argument with regard to monogamy. In his view, "monogamous unions . . . predominate because it is the most efficient marital form."[36] Be that as it may, restrictions on prostitution obviously make some people worse off, namely, those who like to engage in it. Paternalism and values other than efficiency appear to play a role here, and, to the extent that public morality of this sort is part of the traditional common law, it constitutes an exception to Posner's descriptive thesis.

Conclusion

From the foregoing discussion, we conclude that there is ample support for Posner's thesis that property law generally contributes to efficiency by defining a variety of exclusive and transferable rights over virtually all scarce commodities and that in most instances where property rights are absent or incomplete, it could be shown that fully fledged rights would be more costly than the existing solution because of the costs of transacting or excluding others from use. We noted Pejovich's theory, which would account for the emergence of property rights by pointing to incentives for individuals to seek them as part of a larger quest for increased utility. However, we also encountered some cases in which restrictions on property rights could not in an obvious way be considered compatible with efficiency concerns.

Incompatible Uses and the Coase Theorem

One of the ideas the reader may have gained implicitly in the preceding section is that, if one pursues a Pareto optimum in the economy and to this end seeks to ensure that private costs (and benefits) equal social costs (and benefits), *external effects generated by a given activity should be charged to it, or "internalized."* The idea is no doubt congenial to lawyers since it appears to be the basis for compensation for nuisance, for expropriation, and for other well-known doctrines.

The Coase Theorem

Coase, in his celebrated 1960 article on social cost,[37] demonstrated that in a world such as the neoclassical model postulates — without transaction costs and perfectly competitive — this thesis is false. *"Internalization" is not required for an economy to reach a Pareto optimum.*[38]

The demonstration goes by way of an hypothetical example, where, in Coase's view, it would be unproblematical to most economists that the firm that causes damage must pay for it. The example concerns a cattle raiser whose animals stray into the fields of a neighboring farmer and trample part of the crop. Assume that farming as well as cattle raising are perfectly competitive industries and that, without the cattle raiser, the farmer would find his optimal crop size to be ten tons. Assume further that the relationship between the number of animals and the crop damage is as given by table 3.1

Table 3.1.   The Relationship between Herd Size and Loss Resulting from Animals Trampling the Crop.

Number in Herd (Animals)	Annual Crop Loss (Tons)	Crop Loss per Additional Animal (Tons)
1	1	1
2	3	2
3	6	3
4	10	4

The question that might come first to a lawyer's mind is how one could stop the cattle raiser from harming his neighbor's interests. Making him pay for the damage will not necessarily stop him from creating it, as we shall see in a moment. Nor would this necessarily be the efficient solution. One might just as well see the conflict between these two operations as the farmer's impeding on cattle raising. The choice is really between meat and wheat.

How is this choice made? If the cattle raiser makes on his first animal a net revenue higher than 1, it pays him to raise that animal and compensate the farmer for his losses. Similarly, he should expand his herd to two animals, if he nets more than 3 on them, and so on. Clearly, if consumers value meat sufficiently, liability by the cattle raiser for damage to the farmer will not stop the trampling of the crop.[39]

This might be true even if we granted the farmer an injunction against the cattle raiser; the cattle raiser would further delve into his net revenues to pay the farmer. The agreement is satisfactory to both parties, since the cattle raiser still has some net profit and the farmer is left with more than if he were farming without the interference. Of course, the possibility of an injunction allows the farmer to extract more from the cattle raiser than would simple liability for damage.

Suppose now that it is technically feasible to erect a fence that stops the cattle from straying onto the farmer's land altogether. Will either legal rule lead the cattle raiser to install the fence? Not necessarily. If the fence costs 9 per year (annual upkeep as well as amortized capital cost), the cattle raiser will *not* put it up if, in the absence of this possibility, his optimal herd size would have been less than four animals and his payments to the farmer less than 9. Only with a herd of four — with damage payments of 10 — or if the farmer, under the pressure of the injunction, could extract more than 9 from him, would it pay the cattle raiser to put up the fence.

Let us extend the example somewhat by assuming that the farmer makes $2 net revenue from sales of $12, which it costs him $10 to produce. If the herd on the neighbor's property is only one animal, he will have damages of $1, paid for by the neighbor, and sales of $11 with a profit of $1, so that his net revenue is still $2. If the herd increases to two heads, $3 worth of damages will be caused. The farmer now sells for $9 what it cost him $10 to produce, a loss of $1, but collects $3 from the neighbor. His total net revenue is still $2. But notice that under these circumstances a different arrangement would seem to be more advantageous to both parties. If the farmer stopped farming altogether, his net loss would be $2. But this is less than the $3 that the cattle breeder would have to pay him if he continued his farming. Hence, there is room for an agreement between the two in which the cattle breeder pays the farmer a sum between $2 and $3. It is again easily seen that under the assumptions of the example, no further rearrangement of the farming and cattle-breeding activities would improve their joint value.

All in all, in each of these cases, the parties, through negotiations or otherwise, would arrive at what for society is the least costly solution. The burden placed on the party that creates the damage in terms of the law will not necessarily prevent that party from carrying on his business. The precise balance between the two operations depends on their relative profitability.

The second part of the Coase theorem states that the *same* point of equilibrium between the two parties would be reached if the cattle raiser were *not* liable for damage done to the neighbor's crops. To see why this is so, let us first restate the argument developed until now. Suppose that the cattle raiser is contemplating an enlargement of his herd from two to three animals. This move is worthwhile if his revenues from three animals — net of the damages he has to pay — exceed those from two animals with the corresponding payments, or, formally if

$$R_3 - D_3 > R_2 - D_2$$

which can be restated as

$$R_3 - R_2 > D_3 - D_2 \qquad (3.1)$$

This simply says that the move is worthwhile if the increase in revenue exceeds the increase in damage payments.

Suppose now that the cattle raiser is not liable. In this case the farmer has a choice between assuming the loss inflicted by cattle roaming on his land and paying the cattle raiser to reduce his herd, installing a fence, or ceasing his operation altogether. Suppose the herd is now at three animals and the farmer must decide whether to pay his neighbor to reduce it to two. The comparison in this case is between the loss with three animals (D_3), on one hand, and the loss with two (D_2) plus compensation payment to the cattleman for profit foregone, on the other; or, formally, the farmer must accept to leave the herd at three animals if

$$D_3 < D_2 + (R_3 - R_2) \qquad (3.2)$$

But (3.2) is equivalent to (3.1). We may therefore conclude that *whether the cattle raiser pays for the damage he does to his neighbor or is paid by the latter to avoid that damage, the optimal size of the herd will be the same.* This result is completely general and could equally well be demonstrated in situations where, contrary to what was implied in the discussion above, the farming operation was the relatively more profitable of the two.

A very important implication of the Coase theorem is that once one abandons the idea of what is and what is not allowed as part of a property right in *existing* systems, it becomes obvious that the nuisance problem is symmetrical;[40] the cattle create a nuisance to the farmer, but the farming operation creates a nuisance for the cattle breeder. Hence, it is best to speak simply of *conflicting uses.*

We may now draw the general conclusion of the Coase theorem, which is that, under a set of assumptions to be discussed presently, *it is irrelevant for the optimal allocation of resources which of two conflicting uses of property rights legally prevails — that is, in which way the law defines the boundaries of property rights and consequently the liability rules for their transgression.* To put it differently, while it is important for the law *to delineate rights clearly,* the *actual* delineation is of no consequence for the attainment of a Pareto optimum. The initial assignment will be corrected, if need be, by market transactions which transfer and recombine these rights.

On further reflection, the Coase theorem is but the expression, in a particular context, of the general neoclassical thesis that a Pareto optimum will result from voluntary exchange. As such, it is subject to the reservations discussed in Chapter 2. We must now look at some of these more closely.

Limitations of the Coase Theorem

The Coase theorem has been the object of a host of comments, by economists as well as by lawyers.[41] Of the arguments made in this literature, three appear to us to be of particular interest. They concern the distributional consequences of the allocation of rights, the observation that what one is willing to pay to make someone else stop an activity may well be *less* that what one would accept as minimal compensation for tolerating that activity, and finally, that transaction costs are generally not negligible.

Distributional Consequences of the Allocation of Rights.   Whether, in the example discussed above, the farmer suffers the intrusion of the neighbor's cattle without compensation or can extract payment for doing so may not affect the composition of output in the economy, but it will certainly make a difference with respect to the wealth of both parties. Suppose that initially the cattle raiser is liable for damage done by his animals to the crop of his neighbor. In order for him to engage in cattle raising at all, the return of the operation, in which damage paid to the neighbor is a "production cost," must provide him with a living wage. But now let the rule be reversed and the cattle raiser no longer be liable. Coase has demonstrated that this will not affect the amount of cattle raising and farming, and Demsetz has extended the argument by showing that the change will not alter, even in the long run, the resources attracted into these activities.[42] But the new rule will have some effect, namely to give a *windfall gain* to the cattle raiser and a *windfall loss* to the farmer. These gains and losses will be reflected in the value of the land. Thus, if the rancher sells his land, he can expect to receive the initial value plus the capitalized worth of the increased returns resulting from the rule change. The new owner, buying the land at a higher price, should normally make no more than a living wage from the cattle-raising business even if he extracts some payments from the neighbor. Similarly, the loss to the farmer would be absorbed by the person who owns the land at the time of the rule change, while his successors buying land at a lower price would again make normal returns on it.

It is obvious, then, that the allocation of rights clearly affects the distribution of wealth. In this sense, the Coase theorem is subject to the same reservations as were expressed concerning the Pareto optimum.[43]

The Inequality of "Bribes" Offered and Compensation Accepted for a Given Activity. This argument is due to Mishan.[44] It says that the maximum someone will pay somebody else to stop some activity to which the latter is entitled — that is, the highest "bribe" he will offer — is limited by his resources, but that the minimum sum he would require to tolerate that same activity, if he was entitled to be free of it, is not dependent on them and, hence, likely to be higher. Let us illustrate this argument with Mishan's example of the aircraft noise. Individual A is exposed to it and could escape it only by relocating in some desert area hundreds of miles away. If the present law forced him to tolerate the noise of the aircraft, he would be willing to spend up to $5,000 per annum out of his $12,000 disposable income to be free of it. If, however, under existing laws, airlines could not fly over populated areas, he would require at least $15,000 to allow planes over his land.[45]

Let us assume that the interests of all individual landowners — 5,000 in all — can be costlessly determined and pooled and similarly for the airlines. Let us further assume that negotiations are costless. One can then determine whether negotiations will lead to a rearrangement of rights, as the Coase theorem asserts they will. These conditions for each of the alternative legal arrangements are as shown in table 3.2.

The first row indicates that airlines would require $55M to part with the right to schedule their air routes over the landowners' property, whereas the latter could offer only $25M to this end. There is a shortfall of $30M and, hence, no scope for an agreement. In other words, the existing law gives the optimal solution to the conflict. But observe now what happens if the law were changed

Table 3.2. The Asymmetry of Bribes Offered and Compensation Demanded
to Stop Conflicting Uses

	Airline Interests	Landowner Interests	Total
Law permitting overflights	−$55M	$25M	−$30M
Law forbidding overflights	$45M	−$75M	−$30M

Note: Assume 5,000 landowners. Positive amounts indicate "bribes" offered; negative amounts indicate minimal compensation demanded.

in favor of the landowners (second line). In this case the airlines would not be prepared to pay the minimum sum landowners require to give up their right to be free of the aircraft noise and, hence, one would have to conclude that in this situation, the existing law gives the best solution as well.

One must conlcude that *the optimal arrangement under each state of the law is not optimal under the opposite state.* Hence, it cannot be maintained that, whatever the content of the law, there is a unique optimal state of the economy that will be reached under perfect competition and in the absence of transaction costs. In other words, the actual state of the law matters *even* for the allocation of resources. How one should rank the states of the economy that would prevail under alternative legal regimes is a question we cannot address here. Mishan has shown that the above paradox is not confined to matters of all or nothing, but can be extended to external effects that are perfectly divisible, such as the *number* of aircraft permitted to fly over a residential area.[46]

The crucial element in the demonstration is, of course, how large the bribe-compensation difference for one party is in relation to the other party's stake. If, in the example above, the landowners required only $35M — instead of $75M — to allow the flights, the solution under either legal regime would be that flights would take place over residential areas. Conversely, if they were ready to pay $60M to stop flights — instead of $35M — there would be no flights whatever the legal arrangement.

It is generally thought that the difference between the minimal compensation and the maximal bribe that a party would accept and offer, respectively, becomes significant as the amount at stake grows *larger in proportion to his total resources.* This would lead one to the conclusion that the Coase theorem would still hold if the amounts at stake were not of major significance to the parties.

Nonnegligible Transaction Costs. A further complication with the Coase theorem is that agreements that would be Pareto improvements may not be feasible because of transaction costs. Let us continue the example of the aircraft noise. The existing law allows the airlines to schedule their flights over residential areas, but they would be willing to reroute them for a compensatory payment of $50M. The landowners collectively would be willing to offer $55M to this end, but it costs $7M to contact them all, convince holdouts, cover lawyers' fees and so forth. As a result, the agreement will *not* be concluded and, hence, a nonoptimal situation will be perpetuated.

This observation leads one to the prediction that if, as Posner submits, the common law is indeed organized so as to promote the optimal allocation of resources, *it would contain measures to reduce transaction costs and, where these costs would be high in spite of those measures, it would seek to institute directly rights and liabilities compatible with the optimal allocation of resources.* These ideas are discussed in separate subsections.

The Reduction of Transaction Costs

Mishan, in discussing the difficulties facing the victims of pollution in trying to come to terms with the polluter, lists the following items as elements of the transaction costs:

(a) Costs associated with taking the initiative,

(b) Costs of identifying all parties (victims) involved,

(c) Costs of communicating with them,

(d) Costs of persuading enough of them to make an offer,

(e) Costs of reaching an agreement on the total sum offered or to be accepted and each person's share in it,

(f) The cost of the negotiation itself.[47]

It is obvious that costs (b) to (e) increase rapidly with the *number* of persons and their *geographical dispersion*. Their reduction is much affected by technical factors. The law can clearly be seen to deal with the problem, for instance, in the case of a meeting of creditors for the purpose of considering a compromise offer by the debtor to avoid bankruptcy, or in the way in which, in a class action, its intended beneficiaries — usually consumers — are contacted (public notice, possibility of objection, or withdrawal): in both cases, a substantial simplification from what would be required for unstructured action. The law may further offer standard rules of procedure for the conduct of meetings, which would tend to reduce (e).

The costs of taking the initiative (a) are due mainly to the uncertainty associated with the ultimate outcome of the process. As we shall see in Part II, markets for uncertain events are not as easily and generally established as those for known commodities and services. A reduction in transaction costs might hence be expected from arrangements that facilitate the pooling of risks. This seems indeed to have been the thinking behind suggestions to let lawyers take the initiative in class actions and collect substantial fees from a damage award won or a settlement, but none where the action is rejected. The lawyer pools the risks over various actions and is probably the best person to do so, as he can best evaluate the chances of winning the action and has control over the precedural moves while it goes on.[48] In a different way, such a reduction of costs is achieved where the government provides public trustees to take care of personal bankruptcies; given the uncertainty of recovery of his fee in small cases, no trustee would take them and, as a result, there could be no effective liberation of debtors in this category.

Finally, the costs of negotiation themselves are substantially affected by the number of issues that must be covered, in particular, the number of questions in which, because of uncertainty, parties take special care in seeking arrangements that will protect them against unforeseen losses. The law is seen to reduce costs of this kind (f) by pointing to the contingencies that may befall parties and by providing standard solutions on which they can rely without explicit negotiation. Of course, to be effective in this function, such standard clauses must generally reflect arrangements that parties would have worked out themselves. But this means precisely that they must propose efficient solutions, which is what one would expect if, as was assumed at the outset, law is to promote allocative efficiency. Of course, even where parties wish to deviate from the arrangements suggested by law with regard to uncertain events (who bears the risk of impossibility of performance, and so on), the mere fact that the contingencies have been made explicit may facilitate the negotiation. This theme is further pursued in the next section.

The Choice of Entitlements

In spite of efforts to reduce transaction costs, there are many situations in which an agreement between holders of rights, as presumed by Coase, is not feasible at reasonable cost. One cannot in practice negotiate with all those who might cause one accidental harm (say, a car accident). Moreover, as Demsetz notes, "for most uses of property rights only some beneficial and harmful effects are easily known. Other effects can be discovered only with great cost."[49]

Under these circumstances the initial assignment of rights is likely to be final, and this may *well* affect the allocation of resources. Imagine that in the example used before negotiations between the farmer and the cattle breeder were prohibitively costly. In that case, the solutions in which the cattle breeder pays the farmer to stop farming altogether or to put a fence around his fields are excluded, and it is quite conceivable that the herd the former decides to keep under these conditions is smaller than what would have been considered optimal where negotiations are possible.

If Posner's thesis about the tendency in the common law toward efficient solutions is accurate, one would expect that the magnitude of transaction costs in a given area would substantially affect the way in which rights and liabilities or, to use Calabresi's term, entitlements are defined.[50] Specifically, one might make the following predictions:

1. That the role of the law is more important where transaction costs are high than where they are low,[51]

2. That in areas of high transaction costs, the law would exhibit a particular concern to find the optimal solution and, in particular,

3. That in these areas, the law would be readily adjusted by the courts where its rules appear to give nonoptimal solutions, whereas in areas of low transaction costs, such changes would

be much rarer. The latitude for the courts to adjust the rules might be reflected in the fact that the law in the area consisted in a few general rules and that the concepts would allow reinterpretation as need arose.[52] By contrast, the low-transaction-cost fields would have many detailed rules and the concepts would be clear.

Existing legal systems appear to bear out these predictions. For instance, torts, in the civil law, are defined in a few general sections of the Civil Code, whereas property rights and contracts (obligations) call for many more detailed rules.[53] The notion of "fault" in the civil law allows for considerable discretion by the courts.

It should be noted that while the courts have some discretion to reinterpret rules and de facto change them, this power must be exercised with caution if the law is to show a trend toward efficiency, as Posner presumes. If changes were too frequent, the rights or liabilities in question would appear to be ill defined to their users, and, at the limit, one would slide into a "tragedy of the commons." These costs of the uncertainty of the law must be weighed against the loss resulting from leaving in place a rule imposing an "inefficient" solution.[54]

Transaction costs are also thought to affect the choice between property rights and simple entitlements to compensation. Posner illustrates this through the example of the common law on pollution.[55] Where a factory creates a nuisance to neighboring homeowners through smoke pollution, one can well imagine a solution whereby the homeowners are given an absolute right, enforceable by injunction, to be free from it. Suppose now that the factory values its right to pollute more than the homeowners their right to be free of it, and that in good Coasian fashion, it would be willing to pay off the homeowners — that is, to buy the right to pollute. It is unlikely that such a solution could come about in practice, for the transaction costs are likely to be prohibitive. Apart from the sheer number of landowners to be dealt with, each of them has an incentive to hold out in the hope of extracting a higher price from the factory owner. The upshot of this argument is that legal relations in terms of absolute rights under these circumstances are likely to lead to welfare losses since they cannot be adjusted by the parties when the comparative value of the conflicting uses changes. This conclusion holds equally well in the opposite case where the factory has the absolute right to pollute and homeowners would have to band together to buy it off. The courts in these cases have recognized more limited rights only. Injunctions will not lie; damages will be awarded, but only in cases of unreasonable use. Posner summarizes the law as follows:

> Pollution was lawful if reasonable in the circumstances,
> which meant (but only approximately) if the benefit from
> continuing to pollute exceeded the cost to the victims of
> pollution of either tolerating or eliminating it, whichever was
> cheaper.[56]

The question may be looked at in a slightly different light. The holder of a property right is entitled to forbid use of his land. Any interfering use of it can take place only with his prior consent. But since the consent is given (presumably) for a price, one might say that compensation for the nuisance is established by the parties and prior to its taking place. In contrast, under a rule of liability, the amount of compensation is fixed by a third party and after the fact only.[57] Given the key role of voluntary exchange in the concept of efficiency, the first solution should be preferred unless exceptional circumstances make it costlier than the second. High transaction costs are such an exception. Posner asserts that the law generally conforms to this hypothesis.[58]

Conclusion

A superficial reading of the Coase theorem might suggest — and this is in fact the conclusion that several authors in the mainstream tradition such as Demsetz draw — that "little or no government intervention is usually the best rule."[59] We differ with these authors, not only because that statement implies a value judgment that is, in our view, unwarranted, but also because it bypasses the most interesting function the theorem fulfills with regard to situations in which its conditions are not satisfied. This is perhaps most eloquently expressed by Calabresi:

> Coase's analysis . . . gives us an admirable tool for
> suggesting what kind of empirical data would be useful in
> making resource allocation decisions, and for indicating what
> kinds of guesses are likely to be justifiably made in the
> absence of convincing data. . . . His analysis combined with

common intuitions or guesses as to the relative costs of transactions, taxation, structural rules and liability rules, can go far to explain various types of heretofore inadequately justified government actions."[60]

We would, of course, read this statement descriptively.

Contracts

Function

In the mainstream view the function of contract law is to maintain incentives toward, and to facilitate the conclusion of, exchanges that move resources from less to more valuable uses.[61] From this definition it follows that the law should not uphold agreements in which the consent is defective, such as cases of error, fraud or duress; in such instances, it cannot be presumed that the exchange would in fact be to the advantage of both parties and, thus, constitute a Pareto improvement. It is also easily seen why the law refuses to enforce preliminary agreements in which some of the elements of the full contract have been specified, but others, such as the price or the method of computing it, are yet to be determined. In such cases the common law detects absence of "consideration." The refusal to enforce such agreements is compatible with the objective stated before, in that parties are in a much better position than the courts to determine what is to their mutual advantage, and the policy encourages them to complete their negotiations.[62]

Breach of Contract

Contract law without the possibility of enforcement resembles a "commons" in fhe field of property law. Exchange would be considerably hampered. Given the advantages of specialization, for which effective exchange is essential, one would expect costly private measures by both parties to ensure that the other will live up to its contractual commitments: deposits or other security, credit bureaus to investigate the credit-worthiness of prospective contracting partners, contracting only on the basis of personal knowledge or through reference, performance, in contracts which call for performance in stages, only as payment has been made for the preceding stage, and so on. In a sense such protective measures are similar to the arrangements made to safeguard private property under the feudal system, discussed earlier. In both situations general protection of reliance interest by the state appears to be a less costly solution, or a more effective one, to ensure the functioning of markets.

While, in general, one would therefore expect that the efficiency objective in the common law — Posner's descriptive hypothesis — leads to the enforcement of contractual obligations, this does not mean that each contracting party should always receive that to which he was entitled under the contract — that is, *specific performance*. Posner gives the following example.[63] Suppose I sign a contract with A to deliver to him 100,000 items of some sort at $0.10 apiece. After the signature, B comes to me and explains that he needs 25,000 items in a hurry and is prepared to pay $0.15 apiece. Now if I accept B's offer and A, as a result of my delay in performing under the contract, suffers damages worth $1,000, the breach would still be "value maximizing" since I make an additional profit on the sale to B of $1,250 and, hence, can pay A's damages and still have a positive net revenue. Had I refused to deal with B, he could presumably have negotiated with A to have the 25,000 items, but this additional step would have resulted in higher transaction costs. All in all, the breach of contract in this case should, in Posner's view, be allowed — even encouraged — on the ground that it brings resources to higher-valued uses than was initially foreseen and thus would improve welfare for society as a whole.

The breach of contract in this example might be analyzed analogously to a conflict of uses in the previous section: A's rights under the contract conflict with my use of resources in the new contract with B. The solution — if one is to pursue efficiency — is to have the highest valued use prevail but to make sure that the decision on what is the highest valued use is made by the best placed person and with proper care. It is to this last end that the party breaching the contract is made to pay damages. If such decisions were lightly and inaccurately made, contracting parties would face substantial uncertainty with regard to their rights under contract — a minor tragedy of the commons — which would be costly and lead to a net social loss.

The common law's reluctance to enforce *penalty clauses* is perfectly explicable in this analysis; it would be inefficient to discourage breach of a contract if such action promised a net social gain. Penalties beyond the value of the damages suffered could constitute such a disincentive. Note, however, that parties may well wish to save the transaction costs of determining what the actual damages are by agreeing, in advance, on a reasonable amount. Unlike penalty clauses, such "liquidated damages" would facilitate proper decisions regarding breach of contract; hence, one would expect the law to uphold such provisions in contracts, as in fact it does.[64]

Latent Defects in Sale

In many instances problems arise in contracts of sale because the object sold lacks some good qualities the buyer expected to find or presents some unexpected defects. Should the buyer have a recourse against the vendor to annul the sale or to have part of the price reimbursed to him? Or should one follow the maxim "caveat emptor" and deny all recourses to the buyer?

Kronman has written a very enlightening article on the subject.[65] It is clear, he submits, that disputes of this kind would not arise if the parties were aware of the precise qualities of the object and could adjust their negotiations accordingly. The central question is, then, how this information should be generated, if at all.

With respect to apparent defects, defined here as those that the purchaser can detect himself by inspection, the law denies the purchaser recourse for defects. And this is reasonable since the means of knowledge regarding these qualities are equally available to both parties, and the purchaser is clearly the best person to determine whether observed qualities are those for which he is looking.

But assume now that the seller became aware that the buyer had overlooked an important, but apparent, feature. Should he draw the buyer's attention to it? In Kronman's view he should, and if he does not, he should be liable in damages. The reason is that in this case the vendor is the cheaper "mistake preventer," and, since his knowledge of the buyer's mistake is not the fruit of deliberate and costly searching, the vendor's obligation to warn the purchaser will not discourage him (or other vendors in the future) from acquiring that information.

In recent years the common law, in Kronman's analysis, has also increasingly shown a tendency to hold the vendor liable for latent defects that were not divulged to the buyer. In these situations as well, the vendor is generally the cheaper "mistake preventer." It is true that where the defect can be detected only by expert examination, the parties are at a par. But where it reveals itself through use or where previous owners knew about it, the vendor clearly has better access to the information. For this reason the law obliges him to divulge information known to him. It is unlikely that this obligation will curtail the production of useful information. For instance, homeowners have an independent interest to acquire it, namely, to protect their investment. And this might even be true for sellers of goods since, in Kronman's view, the expertise they acquire would make them more efficient in the purchase of materials and reduce the likelihood that they fail to identify any special advantage their goods enjoy and that would allow them to ask a better price.[66]

The problem of latent defects in manufactured goods has given rise to the field of product liability. Posner deals with this question in his chapter on torts, as it raises many of the issues of the choice between strict liability and negligence. It will be dealt with in the next section, in the discussion of strict liability.[67]

Unforeseen Contingencies

In some cases a party may fail to fulfill the promised performance due to circumstances not of his own volition, which make fulfilment impossible, impracticable, or exceedingly costly. The question is then whether the failure to perform should be treated as a breach of contract or, on the contrary, the performing party should be excused from performing. The common law has developed the doctrines of "impossibility," "impractibility," and "frustration" to determine in which cases nonperformance because of such fortuitous events should be excusable.

Posner and Rosenfield, who examine this question in a lengthy article,[68] submit that common law doctrines promote efficiency in that they tend to put the burden of the fortuitous event on the party they call the "superior risk bearer." A party may be best able to bear risks for two reasons. One is that one party may be better (or more cheaply) able than the other to prevent the risk from materializing. Cost would then be minimized by making the first party liable. Whether it is preferable to prevent rather than to let the risk materialize and assume its cost is then for this party to decide. The argument here follows the logic of negligence rules, which will be examined in the next section.

The second reason why one party may be better able to bear the risk than the other is that he has a comparative advantage in spreading the risk, in particular, that he can better insure for it. Insurance, as we shall see in more detail in Part II, is the exchange of a large, uncertain loss (the insured risk) against a much smaller, certain one (the premium). The existence of the flourishing insurance market shows that people are willing to pay for the avoidance of risks, i.e., that risk is a cost.

The cost of insurance in the market depends principally on two factors. The first is the costs associated with assessing the risk. The insurer must accurately estimate the probability of occurrence and the size of the loss if it occurs. The process of measuring itself, and the errors in assessment are costs to the insurer that must be covered in the premium. Moreover, where the insured can to some extent reduce the probability of loss, but at a cost to himself, he has an interest in being unusually careful while the assessment takes place and assuming his usual, more casual behavior after the insurance contract has been established. This would lead the insurer to ask a lower premium than is warranted by the actual risk he assumes, but, foreseeing the problem, he would charge all insured a certain sum for the "misrepresentation" that he cannot adequately control. This phenomenon is known as "moral hazard."

The second factor affecting the cost of insurance is the resources that must be devoted to reaching clients and setting up contracts (agents' and lawyers' costs). They are a form of what were called transaction costs above.

In many instances insurance takes the form of a contract with an organization specializing in that activity. Yet, where it is feasible, parties may prefer to "self-insure," thus saving transaction costs and avoiding moral hazard. Investors keep a diversified portfolio in the expectation that losses in one area will be offset by gains in another. A large transportation company may create an internal fund for liability; the size of their operations is such that they can pool these risks as well as an outside insurer would.

The discussion of these problems suggests the approach to risks one would generally expect to see in contract law if the pursuit of "efficiency" were the objective. One would consider for each party the optimal "mixture" of prevention of the risk (through avoidance measures or search of more information) and its assumption in the form of self-insurance or insurance through the market. The costs associated with these optimal solutions by either party would be compared and the cheapest one retained; the party in question would be made liable for the damages.

One can now readily follow the analysis Posner and Rosenfield present of a variety of common law cases. One class of these concern contracts for the delivery of agricultural products, where delivery has been made impossible by an unexpected event such as a flood or a severe drought. The courts in these cases have granted discharges to individual growers, but not to wholesalers or large dealers. The distinction is sound in the framework presented here since, between individual grower and purchaser, the latter can more readily assume the risk of bad weather conditions by spreading his purchases geographically. As between large dealers and purchasers, the former group has better facilities to spread the risk.

The authors present a similar analysis of the *Hein* v. *Fox* case.[69]Fox had agreed to drill a well on Hein's land. In the process of drilling he encountered layers of rock. Special equipment necessary to penetrate the rock was not available at the time, because of wartime regulations. Should Fox be discharged because of impossibility? The court decided that he should not be. In an economic analysis, one would argue that the driller was better able than his customer to estimate the likelihood of encountering rock below the surface and to choose different methods of drilling. Moreover, Fox could have spread the risk of such contingencies among all his customers.[70] Whether Hein could spread risk less easily is an empirical question.

It should be stressed that the common law on these questions provides only guidelines to the parties. They are free to stipulate that risks be allocated differently. Frequently the parties' intention with respect to particular risks is not clear on the face of the written contract. In this case the courts may well try to retrace their intention by looking at the price in the disputed contract in comparison with similar agreements elsewhere. The comparison might be cast in terms of "fair price" or "equity." Yet in an economic analysis the issue need not be regarded as one of equity. A higher price in the contentious contract might be interpreted as an indication that one party — say, the vendor — was meant to bear particular risks and that the higher price was to reflect the "insurance premium" for it.

Damages

In discussing breach of contract, we suggested reasons for making the breacher compensate his contract partner for exactly the damages suffered by the latter. This reflects a general principle that Posner attributes to Holmes, according to which:

> it is not the policy of the law to compel adherence to contracts but only to require each party to choose between performing in accordance with the contract and compensating the other party for any injury resulting from a failure to comply.[71]

Each party is, in other words, insured against nonperformance by the other, and the risk of "moral hazard" on either side requires that compensation is exactly equal to the damages suffered, neither more nor less.

It is easily seen that if total costs are to be minimized, the victim of the breach must be encouraged to keep his loss to a minimum. This would explain the doctrine of mitigation of damages know in common as well as civil law.

Damages are generally limited to the *foreseeable* consequences of the breach.[72] To see why this is in line with the pursuit of efficiency, consider Posner's example of a commercial photographer's buying a roll of film to take pictures of the Himalayas. The cost of development is included in the purchase price. After completing the assignment the photographer sends his pictures for development to the manufacturer. The film is lost by the manufacturer and never found.

The relevant question is whether the manufacturer should be liable for the entire cost of the Himalaya expedition. Case law is generally to the effect that he is not, and this is perfectly explicable on the assumption that the common law is formulated as though the pursuit of efficiency were its goal. As between manufacturer and user of the film, it is generally the latter who can more easily assess the value of the exposed film and take inexpensive precautions (several films, for instance) against the contingency. If he cannot recover damages beyond a new film or two from the manufacturer, he will have an incentive to take such precautions or, if the manufacturer can better bear the risk or take special precautions, to negotiate a special arrangement with him to that effect.

Full liability for the manufacturer, on the other hand, would simply lead to self-insurance by the latter, resulting in a price increase, or to costly negotiations in which the manufacturer would ascertain the use of the film or the value of the pictures on it in order to determine a proper price, including the cost of insurance. This solution entails, moreover, a risk of moral hazard on the part of the purchaser. Considering all this, it is quite likely that the vendor or manufacturer will limit his liability through a clause in the contract.

"Inequality of Bargaining Power" and Unconscionability

The current movement toward consumer protection legislation seems to be premised on the idea that the general rules of contract lead to undesirable results where they are applied to transactions between consumers and commercial suppliers of commodities and services. One author expresses it as follows:

> One observes in reality that the consumer is incapable of knowing the complexity or even the dangers of the products and services offered to him. He cannot, in the vast majority of cases, negotiate the price and the conditions of sale for these goods and services and he is all the more vulnerable as it frequently concerns essential products and services under the control of powerful firms, often monopolies. All these factors have made the consumer a contracting party who can be exploited at will. They have made a mockery of the principle of the equality of parties to a contract.[73]

Posner and others[74] are at great pains to argue that, whatever the source of the uneasiness, it should not lead one to doubt the soundness of ordinary contracting principles. As this question will be discussed more amply in what follows, we shall summarize Posner's arguments here.

Many contracts are offered in standard form, on a take-it-or-leave-it basis. The consumer can sign or not, but there is no negotiation over individual terms. From here it is but one step to argue that the consumer did not have a choice and should not be bound by the onerous terms of the contract. But this conclusion should, in Posner's view, not be drawn, as is obvious when one considers the reasons for adopting the standard contracts in the first place.

Posner advances two possible reasons, only one of them sinister. The first is that the standard contract economizes on the transaction cost of negotiating individual agreements and that the resulting saving, under pressure of competition, is passed on to the consumer.

It is true that the consumer's choice is limited; but he can still refuse to sign and go to a competitor. Competition will in due course lead to standard contracts that suit consumer preferences. Thus, while all firms in an industry (say, insurance, but also dry cleaners, bus companies and parking lots) will prefer standard contracts because of the economies of scale in this mode of transacting, the relevant question is whether competitive pressure will lead to terms acceptable to consumers.

Of course, standard contracts might also be used in industries where the consumer cannot effectively switch. The firm can then propose terms it could not maintain in a competitive market. But in these instances the problem is with the market imperfection (monopoly, oligopoly) and the proper remedies to look to are, in Posner's view, policies to restore competition.

It is further argued that standard contracts are objectionable because they are used to slip in fine print an onerous provision past the unwary customer. Posner's view on this seems to be that, unless this practice amounts to *fraud,* a doctrine of which he shows the economic rationale, there is no reason to interfere with freedom of contract.[75] Competitive pressure will presumably weed out clauses offered to consumers, even in fine print, that are fundamentally objectionable to them.

Finally, it is sometimes alleged that consumer contracts involve *duress,* in that the customer, especially the poor one, is forced to accept terms that are basically repulsive to him. Thus, he may have to give the vendor the right to repossess sold goods in case of default on a payment, even if most of the price has already been paid. Or he may find himself without effective redress against defects in the purchased commodity. Legal measures against the vendor are too costly, and stopping payments will lead to harassment — menacing letters, calls at work, threats of seizure or of bankruptcy — by the finance company to which the vendor has transferred his claims against his customers. Posner's reply to such remarks is that one should not attempt to remedy poverty by reforms of contract law — recall his earlier statement that no one suggests that redistribution is a goal of the common law — and that if one tries to stop these practices, the commodities or services in question will be available to the poor at even more draconian terms or not at all,[76] a prospect which appears to him to be a net social loss.

All in all, Posner doubts that the concept of "inequality of bargaining power" is useful in the discussion of consumer problems.

The same holds, in his view, for the very wide interpretation recently given to the general doctrice of "unconscionability" through which contracts were traditionally invalidated because of defects in their formation or in the capacity to contract of either party.[77] Following Becker's precept one might say that the rationality of these doctrines, which purport to protect consumers, or, what amounts to the same thing, their contribution to the efficient allocation of resources, cannot be shown within the limitations of Posner's economic analysis of law.

Conclusion

All in all, the traditional common law doctrines examined in this section appear to support Posner's descriptive hypothesis. But some recent case law in the area of consumer protection — and, of course, much legislation in that field — appears to be incompatible with that hypothesis.

Torts

Function

A lawyer, asked to state the purpose of the law of torts, might well reply that it is to *effect compensation* for losses sustained.[78] In terms of the concepts introduced in the previous section, one might say that the victim is insured against the effect of accidents that befall him. But in this formulation it becomes obvious that the idea of "compensation" is an incomplete description of the function of the law of torts. Some accidents do not give rise to full compensation for the victim (for instance, those in which he is contributorily negligent), and the use of such concepts as "negligence" or "fault" suggests that the law attaches particular significance to the conduct of the perpetrator of the damages.

If Posner's hypothesis about the pursuit of efficiency is accurate, one would expect the law of torts to be formulated so as *"to deter uneconomical accidents"*[79] — that is, those that could have been avoided at a cost lower than that of the accident. This idea is very clearly expressed in the negligence standard formulated by Judge Learned Hand:

the defendant is guilty of negligence if the loss caused by the accident, multiplied by the probability of the accident's occurring, exceeds the burden of the precautions that the defendant might have taken to avert it.[80]

This formula makes it obvious that the perpetrator of an accident is not liable under all circumstances — as a pure compensation rule would require — and that the aim of the law is not to discourage *all* accidents. Notice the similarity between this last principle and that attribtued to Holmes with regard to breach of contract. The infliction of losses is not to be discouraged if it promises a net social gain (contracts) or if its avoidance would be costlier (torts).

The purpose of tort law as expressed in the Hand formula is frequently formulated more generally as follows: that the law of torts would pursue efficiency by *minimizing the sum of accident and accident avoidance costs*. It is obvious that the Hand formula is a special case of this rule; it seeks accident avoidance by the perpetrator where that is cheaper than assuming the costs of accident, not in the opposite case. The general rule also covers the situation, strictly speaking not within the purview of the Hand formula, where precautions by the perpetrator could *reduce* accident costs (but not eliminate them) by more than their cost. More important, it also covers preventive efforts on the part of the victim, a subject to which we must now turn.

The Reciprocity of Incentives to Prevent Accidents

If, under the Hand rule, the perpetrator of an accident is liable, one would not have minimized the costs of accident and accident prevention if the victim could have prevented the accident at a cost even lower than that facing the perpetrator. The law appears to recognize the problem in its doctrine of *contributory negligence*. Under this rule the victim of an accident is barred from recovery if he could have prevented the accident for less than the discounted accident costs (i.e., loss multiplied by its probability). In other words the victim cannot recover if he was, himself, negligent.[81] But this rule suffers from the same lack of symmetry as the original Hand formula; it fails to take into account the possibility of prevention by the "other" party *as well*.

A further possibility is to adopt a *comparative negligence* standard, according to which the victim's recovery of damages is limited by the degree to which his own negligence contributed to the accident. But this solution, in Posner's view, may still not minimize the total cost.[82] Suppose that an accident of $1,000 (discounted) can be prevented by the victim for $50 and by the injurer for $100. Now if the parties expected that in case of an accident each would be attributed at least 25 percent negligence, each would have an incentive to engage in the full preventive effort — the injurer, because damage costs of at least $250 are higher than prevention costs; the victim, because foregone recovery of at least $250 is higher than his prevention cost. As a result, one might see *double* prevention.

Of course, knowing the possibility of double prevention, each party might gamble on the likelihood that the other would incur the cost of prevention and avoid the entire accident. And these strategic considerations may be reciprocal and lead actually to situations in which *neither party prevents*.[83] On the whole, then, if both parties can prevent accidents at low cost, it cannot be shown within Posner's framework that the rules of negligence discussed above will lead to the optimal allocation of resources, in the sense that it minimizes total costs.

Product Liability

Traditionally, the recourse open for damages suffered as a result of a defect of a manufactured good was governed by the law of contract. In practice, under the doctrine of *privity* of contract, the buyer had such a recourse only against his vendor — usually not the manufacturer, but a middleman — and similarly, the manufacturer's liability was only to his purchaser — usually the middleman — and not to the ultimate consumer. In the course of this century, this restriction has been gradually abolished; at present, according to Posner,[84] not only the victim but also members of his family and even bystanders have an action against the manufacturer.

This extension of the class of people from whom a consumer can seek redress would in itself be of only limited help if the consumer had to prove negligence on the part of the manufacturer. A second development — the principle of *implied warranties* — has loosened this restriction as well. This principle is now extended to cover generally freedom from hazardous defects.

It might be argued that these jurisprudential rules simply put the burden of precautions on the party who would have borne it as a result of voluntary negotiations, if high transaction costs did not effectively preclude these. In other words, these rules put the burden on the party best able to assume it and contribute to efficient allocation of resources by economizing the transaction costs otherwise required to bring about that solution.

Whatever the merit of the argument may be, it is not the main reason invoked for product liability. Rather, it is argued that this institution leads to safer products.[85] Posner goes to great lengths to refute this thesis, and, since it will concern us in the following chapters, it is useful to summarize his arguments.

Posner notes first that even without liability for his products, the manufacturer would have an incentive to take all cost-justified precautions. He will make safer products (and conduct research on safety features) if they are less costly than the accidents they avoid. If the manufacturer is strictly liable, this is the cheapest way of assuming the burden; yet, if he is liable for negligence, the Hand rule would give him the same incentives. Even in the absence of liability, Posner would argue, manufacturers who introduce these safety features should outsell their competitors, as consumers will realize their advantage.

Conversely, if the precautions are not "cost-justified," the manufacturer, under strict liability, will not introduce them, but will instead pay for the damages awarded in lawsuits against him. Under the negligence standard or in the absence of liability of the manufacturer, these costs fall on the consumers, and they would not demand — and hence the market would not supply — the costlier safety features in the product. Hence, whatever the legal regime, the safety features would not be installed if they were costlier than the accidents they prevented.

Although the institution of product liability instead of the common negligence rules will not, according to Posner's argument, lead to safer products, it is not without effect altogether. Where safety features are not cost justified, putting strict liability on the manufacturer amounts to instituting mandatory insurance for accidents by the manufacturer, paid for by consumers. This amounts to a loss for the so-called risk-preferring consumers, who would rather buy the product at a lower price, but without the "insurance," and assume the risk themselves and for those who feel that they can self-insure more cheaply than what it costs them to buy insurance from the manufacturer. The imposition of strict liability — as well as of safety features or norms, as could be easily shown[86] — appears to deprive these groups of the option they would have preferred if the matter were "left to the market," a loss of freedom that in Posner's view amounts to a net social loss.

Moreover, assume that product liability is considered on the ground that the manufacturer is a cheaper insurer than most consumers and that the transaction costs would be very high in relation to the insurance premium so that the market will not autonomously lead to insurance by the manufacturer. Even then there is no reason, in Posner's opinion, to extend the interference with free market forces to the point where one forbids clauses in which the manufacturer disclaims or limits his liability, thus shifting the insurance burden to those consumers who feel that they can bear it more cheaply.

One must conclude that, on the grounds discussed so far, it cannot be shown that the institution of product liability contributes more to efficiency in the Posnerian world view than a simple negligence standard would. Indeed, Posner argues that it might well contribute less, and he extends this argument to strict liability generally.[87] Admittedly, he mentions one further reason for strict liability, but he appears to find it unconvincing — that is, the difficulty for consumers in accurately assessing small risks. The issue will be taken up in the next chapter, since, as we shall see, Calabresi attaches a great deal of weight to it.

Damages

The principle here, as in the case of contractual damages, is to limit them to the foreseeable consequences of negligent behavior. This is explicable if the aim of the law is to induce potential injurers to make the appropriate choice with respect to accident prevention.

In some cases the courts award *exemplary* or *punitive* damages. This term is used sometimes where it is difficult to quantify the injury to the plaintiff, as in the case of defamation. More interesting are cases in which they are imposed on those who *intentionally* commit a tort.[88] Posner argues that punitive damages are to be accounted for here by a concern in the law to discourage people from substituting legal for market transactions.[89]

A last ground for punitive damages mentioned by Posner is present where the effects of the tort can be concealed. In this situation only a fraction of all tortfeasors are apprehended or, what amounts to the same thing, only a fraction of all the torts are discovered. The discounted accident costs of which these people are made aware by law suits are lower than the actual, social costs of those accidents; as a result, prevention will appear to them to be unduly disadvantageous by comparison. Socially, there would not be the optimal amount of prevention, or, where the torts "pay" — and more generally in criminal law — there would be insufficient motivation to stop them.

Conclusion

On the whole, we found in this section general support for Posner's thesis about the economic function of the common law. However, common negligence rules could, under quite plausible conditions, lead to a less than optimal solution, as Posner analyzes it. In a more general way, strict liability regimes could not be shown to be compatible with Posner's thesis.

Procedure

Function

Procedure is the law governing the functioning of the courts. The function of this branch of law is best understood as part of the overall role of the courts. Courts are generally thought to have two important functions — namely, to resolve disputes and, as an inevitable corrolary, to some extent to create legal rules. Let us restrict ourselves to the first function for the moment. Even in a rudimentary legal system, it would be worthwhile, from an economist's point of view, to have a relatively inexpensive mechanism through which disputes can be resolved. In this sense the courts are an alternative to be preferred to physical violence among disputants or to resolution by group decision, such as may have occurred in village or tribe councils in earlier times. In a more developed system, which recognizes property rights, contracts and torts, not only must disputes be resolved, but this must be done *according to the rules governing these institutions.* If, for instance, current legal rules stipulate that injurers are liable for a certain kind of accident and courts decide that they are not, there may well be more than the optimal amount of accident prevention; both potential injurers and potential victims would undertake some. Clearly, there is a social loss here. Similar remarks could be made with respect to the law of property and the law of contracts. All in all, we might say that an evolved legal system needs an inexpensive mechanism for enforcing the rights it allows to be created.

One would expect that procedural rules reflect a concern with allowing the courts to arrive at decisions concerning the enforcement of rights at minimal administrative cost. But this formulation hides most of the real problem — namely, that the rights to be enforced are not in all cases easily established. One must take into account the possibility of errors in the court's decision. They may result from gaps in the facts that can be proved or from lack of clarity in the law (a problem left aside here). Errors may consist in failing to enforce rights that exist or enforcing some that do not exist.

The effect of errors of this kind is to change the substantive rule. Suppose that we are interested in accidents caused by the product of manufacturer A under a negligence regime and that the courts make 20 percent errors in their findings, equally in favor of the manufacturer and the victims. Suppose further that of all actions against the manufacturer, one-half are in fact well founded, in the sense that they concern events that the manufacturer could have prevented at less than the cost of the accident (the Hand formula).

Consider first the cases in which prevention costs are higher than accident costs. According to the Hand rule, they should be left on the shoulders of the victim. If the victim sues the manufacturer, the judge should find the latter nonnegligent and dismiss the suit. In these cases an error consists in holding the manufacturer liable. How will judicial errors affect the manufacturer's behavior? Given the initial assumption about prevention costs, it is surely cheaper to assume these accident costs than to try to prevent them. Hence, the manufacturer "self-insures" against these judicial errors and tries to recover the cost of this "insurance" in the price of his product.

Consider now the opposite kind of case in which, according to the Hand test, the manufacturer ought to be liable because prevention costs are lower than those of the accidents in the absence of preventive measures. Contrary to the first kind of case, here judicial errors may well change the amount of prevention. If, for instance, accident costs are 100 and prevention costs 90, the manufacturer would normally prefer the latter option if the judicial system functioned flawlessly. If, however, in one case out of five the manufacturer, as a result of a judicial error, is not held liable, the actual burden of accident costs he faces is only 80. Obviously, in this situation, bearing the accident burden is cheaper than taking preventive measures. Judicial errors lead here to suboptimal prevention; to put it differently, because the manufacturer finds it preferable not to prevent accidents, the accident cost for society as a whole is 100, whereas the corresponding prevention cost would only be 90. There is a social loss of 10.[90]

The foregoing discussion should have convinced one that besides the administrative cost of the courts, one should also seek to minimize the error cost — that is, the likelihood of an error multiplied by the value of the social loss if it occurs. These two types of cost appear to be inversely related; a reduction in the cost of errors can usually be acquired only at the price of an increase in administratrive cost (fact finding, consultation of experts and so on). The central problem in procedure is therefore to find the optimal tradeoff between the two types of cost. The objective of procedural law in the mainstream view can now be formulated as the minimization of the sum of error and direct costs of the procedural system.[91]

The Cost of Enforcing Rights

In the example discussed above, it was argued that a 20 percent error rate in the courts' decision making would lead to a social loss and in effect to a change in the substantive rule facing the manufacturer. The conclusion that there will be a social loss must be qualified. After all, it is quite possible that a 20 percent error rate represents the optimal tradeoff between error and procedure costs, in the sense that a decrease in error costs would be more than offset by the increase in the cost of the procedures to attain it. In this case one could speak only of a social loss in comparison with some ideal world in which rights could be costlessly enforced. But that is a sterile argument, and one must accept that in the real world procedural constraints may change substantive outcomes without necessarily entailing a social loss in an economic perspective. To put it differently, the enforcement of rights uses resources as the production of goods and services does. In the example given above, these resources, or, alternatively, the cost of not enforcing one's rights (if that is cheaper), must count to those who suffer damages from the defective product as part of what it really costs them to acquire and use that product.

Consideration of the cost of enforcing rights allows one to explain several interesting phenomena. At one end of the scale, the stakes in a case may be so low that it is "not worth enforcing one's rights." This means that the minimal costs of enforcing one's rights through the courts are disproportionate to what one stands to gain. If this cost is reduced, as it is for small-claims courts, which have simplified procedures and, in some jurisdictions, bar lawyers, more substantive rights will be enforced; to some it might appear that the substantive law changes. This seems to have happened when landlords' obligations to maintain and repair could be enforced before rental boards and manufacturers' obligations of warranty before small-claims courts. It should be noted that the situation is not symmetrical, since landlords may find it worthwhile to enforce their rights even in the costlier court system, as the outcome in one case settles the issue in many others and, hence, the court costs can be spread over all these cases.

It might be thought that since litigants before small-claims courts are not charged the full social cost of their trial, there is an implicit redistribution from the taxpayers at large to those who proceed before such courts. But this conclusion is not necessarily justified. Suppose that each claim in small-claims court reflects a number of similar claims, which, because of the cost (or bother) of trial, will not be enforced. If a favorable judgment is issued in one case, all others will presumably benefit from it. Yet, since the claimant cannot collect contributions from the other claimants for "use" of his judgment, he has no interest in undertaking the law suit in the first place. A favorable judgment is a commodity created with scarce resources, yet one on which no property right can be effectively maintained. Hence, it assumes the character of a public good,[92] and one might justify subsidization of the courts (in particular the small-claims courts) on this ground.

It is now easy to see the justification of class actions. They are a means of aggregating all similar claims and spreading procedural costs implicitly over each of these claims. Admittedly, the mechanism raises other problems,[93] but in principle its purpose is clear.

It might be thought that the civilian rule, which obliges the losing party to pay the lawyer's cost of the winner, would overcome the hesitation to sue on the part of small claimants. And, indeed, this would be true in cases where the plaintiff could be perfectly certain of winning his case and was fully compensated for his expenses. Unfortunately, neither proposition holds entirely. Courts do make errors and one is not fully indemnified, if only for the time spent in court.

Where the stakes are very high, it is obvious that the cost of an error, if one occurs, is substantial and, hence, that very elaborate procedures are justified to reduce the likelihood of errors. This may explain why most jurisdictions have two or even more levels of courts of first instance for ordinary civil cases, with the highest level promising increased accuracy of decision because of the quality of its judges and its more detailed procedures. Appeal, in particular appeal to the highest court, is frequently restricted to cases with the highest stakes, and this, too, could be explained by the cost tradeoff. On the opposite end of the spectrum, it would justify the rule *De minimis non curat praetor.*

Study of Some Procedural Rules

In civil cases the judge decides according to the preponderance of evidence standard, while in criminal matters he will convict only if there is proof beyond a reasonable doubt of the guilt of the accused. The difference can perhaps be explained in the framework set out above, if one assumes that in civil matters the two kinds of error are considered equally serious, whereas the avoidance of one conviction of an innocent person is thought to be worth the acquittal of several guilty ones. If these premises are accepted, our analysis suggests that in civil matters one would aim at an equal likelihood of the two kinds of error and that in criminal matters one would optimally have a much lower likelihood of mistaken convictions than of erroneous acquittals.[94] The different evidence standards in civil and criminal matters seem to correspond to these prescriptions.

The question of admissible evidence under common law is dominated by the well-known rules requiring the "best evidence" and prohibiting "hearsay." These rules tend to increase the cost of producing evidence, but to reduce the likelihood of error. It is quite plausible that the latter gain is in general thought to outweigh the increased expense. This consideration would justify the rules in an economic analysis. A similar argument could explain the principle of the unity of time and place of a trial, which stipulates that all the evidence must be put before the court at the date of the trial.

Depositions of witnesses made outside the trial are generally not admissible; the witnesses themselves must be heard (again) in court.

Courts Versus Other Ways of Dispute Resolution

As means of resolving disputes, the courts compete with such substitutes as arbitration and agreements to settle disputes out of court.[95] It is interesting to consider what might motivate parties to choose any of these options.

Once a dispute has arisen, it is unlikely that parties will agree to arbitration rather than to a settlement of the dispute itself. If they violently disagree, neither way seems open; if not, direct settlement would seem preferable. Landes and Posner in a recent article state:

> One is not surprised to find that, in our society, private
> arbitration (or its equivalent) is largely limited to two types
> of case: (1) those where a preexisting contract between the
> parties requires submission to arbitration according to
> specified rules for selecting the arbitrator, and (2) those where
> the disputants belong to an association which provides both
> arbitration machinery for its members and a set of private
> sanctions for refusal to submit to arbitration in good faith or
> to abide by its results.[96]

Associations or groups of this kind may be securities or commodities exchanges, religious associations, universities, and so on. The sanctions include public ostracism and even exclusion from the group.

With respect to the first possibility, it should be noted that these agreements are effective only if the courts have a policy of sanctioning them. Of course, this reintroduces the courts into the dispute, but the question here — validity of the arbitration clause — is presumably much easier to decide than the substantive issue in the dispute. The courts must also be relied on to enforce the decision reached by the arbitrator. This issue does not raise difficult questions either in most instances.

In the absence of a mechanism leading to arbitration, parties to a dispute must choose between agreeing to settle it or putting it before the courts. If the legal rules applicable to the dispute are perfectly clear and the court's decision certain, a trial is normally superfluous and would occur only if one of the parties persisted in disregarding the law, in particular, if he refused to perform a clear obligation. Courts in this case assume, as Macaulay puts it, "a bureaucratic role . . . as part of the debt collection process."[97] His observations suggest that this role may be substantial as a proportion of all litigation.

A more important role for the courts concerns disputes that occur because the law is uncertain and parties disagree as to the likely decision. Of course, where the disagreement stems from a frivolous belief on the part of one party, one reverts to the "bureaucratic role" just mentioned. The decision merely emphasizes existing law and may serve as a deterrent for other "shirkers." But there is surely a class of cases in which parties for nontrivial reasons disagree about the likely outcome or in which the law is genuinely uncertain. If the disagreement is about facts, the institution of "discovery before trial" and of pretrial conference may contribute at low cost to bringing the parties' versions of the facts and estimates of the outcomes closer together and, thus, to avoiding trial. This is a genuine social gain.

If the dispute goes to trial in spite of these preliminary procedures, the court's decison may be expected to clarify the law. The courts are assuming here the second of the two roles mentioned at the outset of this section — namely, that of creating legal rules. This question has been given considerable attention in the law and economics literature in recent years, as attempts have been made to explain the observed tendency in the common law toward efficient rules.[98] Initially, these attempts focused on the personality of the judge or his previous experience in law practice. This line of reasoning was abandoned because of its implausible assumptions.[99] A new series of models were based on the idea that the parties' choice of which cases to take to court is at the root of the tendency toward efficiency. In the first attempts, associated with the names of Rubin and Priest, it was assumed that expected cost savings would lead parties to litigate "inefficient" rules until they were overturned, but not to litigate "efficient" rules.[100] While these models allow one to demonstrate in a formal manner a trend toward efficiency, it leads to the curious result that no one has an interest in litigating on the basis of an efficient rule in his favor rather than settling such disputes out of court. A very recent model by Landes and Posner seeks to overcome this counterintuitive result. It assumes that parties have an interest in "defending" favorable lines of precedent, in that decisions confirming them will put the rules in question on even more solid footing.[101] The model implies that inefficient rules will be left dormant, whereas efficient ones will be reaffirmed and extended, thus expanding the proportion of efficient rules in the common law. Whether the "dormant inefficiency" result in this model is less implausible than the "dormant efficiency" in the earlier models is a question on which the debate is open.[102] It should be stressed that in either type of model the trend toward efficiency does not require the courts to support this development, or even to be aware of it; indeed, they may well pursue different, though not diametrically opposed, objectives for such a trend to be possible.

A different source of efficiency exists in areas where parties can "contract around" inefficient rules — in contract law, as opposed to many instances of torts. In these cases efficient rules will be formulated in the course of business negotiations and will become part of trade customs and standard contracts if these are used. It may then be expected that, where judges accept reference to trade customs in their decisions, a trend toward efficiency will be observed.

Conclusion

This section has provided further evidence for Posner's thesis of a trend toward efficiency in the common law. Moreover, we encountered attempts to model the mechanisms that would account for such observations, assuming that they are accurate. The basic trade-off pervading procedure in an economic analysis concerns the quality of information on which the courts can base their decisions; procedural costs should be increased up to the point where the higher quality or quantity of information they entail is just equal to the reduction in error cost resulting from that information. This idea will be of particular interest in Part II.

Conclusion

The summary of some common law doctrines, and in some cases of civil law doctrines of equal venerability, as they are analyzed in the economic world view of the mainstream position in law and economics, justifies, we believe, the conclusion that there is substantial support for Posner's thesis that much of the common law is formulated as though it were meant to promote or contribute to the efficient allocation of resources. We also encountered some rules that Posner and others tend to brand as "inefficient," but of which, in a strictly descriptive perspective and accepting Becker's precept, one could say only that their contribution to efficient allocation could not be made apparent with the types of cost and benefit admitted in the mainstream view. Among these, recent doctrines designed to protect consumers are paramount. "Inequality of bargaining power" and jurisprudential development of product liability were mentioned as examples. Similar reservations are voiced by mainstream authors with respect to other consumer protection measures, such as regulations on the marketing of drugs,[103] on professional services, [104] on advertising,[105] or on safety features.[106]

In addition, we saw that inalienable entitlements do not conform to Posner's thesis. Prohibition on slavery was cited as an example; here too, we can find a voice that appears to regret this restriction on the "free market."[107]

The discussion in this chapter should have made apparent the unity of the common law,[108] the underlying principle of minimizing costs or maximizing gains. This testifies to the generality of the economic approach to law, which in Chapter 1 was advanced as one of its virtues. On the opposite side of the spectrum, the approach was also shown to lead to very specific analyses of particular rules. Together these findings establish, in our view, the economic analysis of law as a plausible and promising theory of law, in which one can justifiably invest time and effort.

The main task is now to learn to recognize costs and benefits in their legal disguises in order to explore the applicability of the theory more widely and in more detail. Or, to put it in accordance with Becker's precept, we must determine how far the set of costs and benefits admitted until now will take us and what other costs and benefits we might propose when we reach the limits.

CHAPTER 4

Economic Analysis of Major Common Law Doctrines:

The Critics

Introduction

The Focus of the Criticism

Among the critics of the mainstream view of law and economics, one can distinguish, as we argued in the previous chapter, a first group that remains within the neoclassical tradition but seeks to enrich the framework of analysis; a second group judges that framework as altogether too narrow in that the idea of "efficiency" covers too little of what society pursues in choosing among allocations of scarce means. Typical of the first position seems to us to be the work of V. Goldberg, who argues that neoclassical analyses take insufficient account of the fact that information is costly to acquire and to process.[1] In other articles, however, he focuses on the distributional effects of the Coase theorem, which are, in his view, inseparable from its allocative consequences.[2] On this account one would have to classify him in the second group.

The mainstay of the second group is the view that objectives other than allocative efficiency are important to society and would explain institutions dismissed as "inefficient" in the mainstream view. In this group one finds, besides Calabresi, authors like Ackerman,[3] Michelman,[4] Samuels,[5] Mishan in some of his writings,[6] and others.[7]

Calabresi's work incorporates the concerns of both these groups. Though it addresses itself to only a few areas of law and is in this sense specialized in comparison with Posner's writings, it considers explicitly objectives other than efficiency as well as information constraints; in *this* sense it is more general than Posner's work. In what follows we draw mainly on Calabresi's work as exemplary of where the critique of neoclassical law and economics may lead.

Calabresi's Work

Calabresi's main interest seems to be the problem of accidents or, more generally, tragic events. Any legal regime dealing with accidents reflects a choice by society, and Calabresi's purpose is to examine how such choices are made. He analyzes in particular what society's objectives in the areas concerned are likely to be and wonders what the appropriate means of pursuing them would be.

It is in these choices that the question of information becomes important. Social choice of the kind just mentioned requires the integration or ranking of values, which is not easy to accomplish. It also requires factual knowledge and insight in the links between means and ends, i.e., information that is costly to acquire and sometimes not available at all. Rather than writing these problems off as unanalyzable or simplifying the problem unduly, Calabresi proposes to study the ways in which society itself simplifies the decision problem to make it manageable and, for normative purposes, to make the best possible guesses.

An informaton problem exists not only at the level of the design of the legal system, but also for the participants in the economy and for the judges who adjudicate their disputes. Calabresi asks, for instance, whether it makes sense, as a free market philosophy proposes, to leave with consumers the choice between a safe, costly product and the hazardous, but cheaper, variety of it, *if one can foresee* that they will systematically misperceive the value of the safety features to them because of people's deformed intuitive perception of hazards with minute chances of occurring, but catastrophic damages where they do.

Furthermore, let us assume that it is indeed society's objective to minimize the cost of accidents, as Posner and other mainstream authors think it is. It must then be decided which party, between injurers and victims, can contribute most to this objective. To whom can this decision best be entrusted? Not necessarily, Calabresi would argue, to the judges, given the limitation of case-by-case rule development and the restrictions on the information they can gather under existing evidence rules. Neither should it be left in all cases to administrative agencies or the legislature, which may have no such restriction on admissible information but may face problems in attempting to tailor their rules to individual needs or to needs that change over time.

These are, in crude outline, the types of consideration one finds in the core of Calabresi's work on accidents from 1961[8] on until its major statement in *The Costs of Accidents*[9] in 1970. Around this core he has made several studies of particular problems: fault and no-fault or strict liability,[10] causality concepts.[11] Two publications deal with similar problems in other areas: product liability[12] and medical malpractice.[13] The choice of entitlements is examined in more detail in two articles[14] and in the recent *Tragic Choices*.[15] The question that preoccupies Calabresi in these writings is how the risk of error or abuse by decisionmakers would affect society's choice of how and by whom decisions of great momentum are to be made.

Tragic Choices focuses on a few situations in which the consequences of an erroneous choice are particularly burdensome or even fatal to the persons subjected to them, such as the allocation of scarce life-saving devices, the distribution of the right to have children, and the choice of personnel for the military. Pure market solutions will not always necessarily lead to solutions that most citizens find satisfactory; in particular, it is felt that wealth alone should not settle such issues, as it would in a market. The importance of values other than "efficiency" becomes most obvious in these cases. Information problems also become acute in these cases in that values must be ranked and detailed knowledge of people's preferences is crucial and yet not readily available. Thus, *Tragic Choices* focuses on the situations in which the critique of the neo-classical position in law and economics should be most clearly justified.

Objectives of Law

Calabresi's View in The Costs of Accidents

The principal goals of any system of accident law are, as Calabresi sees it, justice and the reduction of the costs of accidents.[16] By justice and other moral values he means such things as equity between parties to an accident — injurer and victim — and consistency among all injurers, or all victims.[17] The value is used negatively, as a constraint on blatant *in*justice in the pursuit of the other primary goal, the reduction of costs.

The principal function of accident law is "to reduce the sum of the costs of accidents and the costs of avoiding accidents."[18] This formulation sounds compatible with the negligence theory in the mainstream view, but the compatibility turns out to be illusory upon further analysis. Calabresi breaks the costs down into three large categories, which he terms primary, secondary and tertiary.

Primary-cost reduction relates to the number and the severity of accidents. This first subgoal is really the objective in the mainstream view of negligence law. Calabresi indicates two large avenues open in the pursuit of this subgoal. The first is to rely on the market, i.e., to make accident-causing activities bear the costs of the accidents they generate and let individuals decide whether under these circumstances they find it worthwhile to engage in them. Calabresi denotes this approach by the term *general deterrence*. Alternatively, one may forbid activities thought to cause accidents or prescribe some that are believed to avoid them. This, in Calabresi's terminology, is *specific deterrence* or the *collective method*.

Secondary costs relate, not to the accidents themselves, but to "societal costs resulting from [them]":[19] economic dislocation or the aggravation of injury. Reduction of these costs can be attempted by "spreading" them over time or among people, rather than leaving them on one or a few persons. This subgoal comes into play only after attempts at reducing primary costs have not been fully successful. The second subgoal may be pursued by spreading losses — insurance — or by the "deep-pocket" method — that is, by putting the burden on the rich, who appear to be best able to absorb it.

The last kind of costs are those associated with administering the treatment of accidents. Under general negligence rules, these would include litigation costs, lawyers' fees, costs associated with the delay in arriving at a settlement or a verdict and so on. Under a social insurance regime, the tertiary costs are mainly those of running the compensation board.

While the division into three large categories is not watertight, as Calabresi readily admits,[20] it is useful in his view in order to make one aware of the tradeoffs among these goals. A scheme that substantially reduces secondary and tertiary costs — as some no-fault collective accident insurance regimes are thought to do — may entail an increase in primary costs, and one must wonder whether on balance it is preferable to a regime with lower primary costs, but substantially higher secondary and tertiary costs.

Posner's Criticism of This View

In his lengthy review of Calabresi's book,[21] Posner explicitly discusses the objectives Calabresi discerns in accident law by comparison with those he advances himself as fundamental to the law of negligence. At the outset he notes that, as he reads Calabresi, the "justice" goal "turns out to be rather unimportant"[22] and that hence the only relevant one is accident-cost reduction.

Posner approves of Calabresi's criticism of "accident-law reformers" who focus their proposals on ways of spreading losses or "taking from the rich," but completely ignore the effect of such schemes on primary costs. However, Posner goes on to question the concern with secondary costs altogether. The spreading that is sought here can be achieved through the mechanism of insurance, and since medical, life, and disability insurance are amply available in the market, there is no reason for concern or for interference with the market. If people do not take a service that is amply available at reasonable cost, one must assume that they do not value it sufficiently. This is simply a consequence of the postulate of consumer sovereignty.

The availability of insurance has, of course, not escaped Calabresi, and his reply to this observation would presumably be that, since people do not accurately assess risks — as we mentioned before[23] — they are unlikely to make the right decision about insuring against them. This argument would appear to be altogether unpalatable to Posner. His view is that markets must be presumed to provide people with precisely the information they need — not more, not less — to evaluate the costs and benefits of services offered. In support of this proposition, he gives examples from the consumer and labor markets. The conclusion to which this leads him is that the absence of relevant information must not be presumed. The argument about people's peculiar inability to appreciate small risks is dismissed as a "psychological quirk."[24]

More fundamentally, Posner argues that the entire concept of "secondary costs" is misguided: "[they] are not real costs in the economic sense and cannot therefore be compared directly with primary and tertiary costs, which are." What he means by "real costs"[25] emerges from the same passage: "it may be important to compensate accident victims but the economic costs of not doing so are *hard to pin down*. Perhaps they are normally zero."[26] Of course, to limit economics to considerations that are "easy to pin down" reflects, as should be evident from our discussions in Chapter 2, a rather narrow view of it.

Be that as it may, if there is any reason for concern about the factors that Calabresi calls secondary costs, it is, in Posner's view, that under current insurance systems "the accident costs of the most dangerous drivers are systematically shifted to the less dangerous."[27] We are, in his words, "subsidizing accidents," "permitting people to kill and maim without bearing the costs of such conduct."[28]

The upshot of Posner's argument seems to be that if one removes from Calabresi's universe the goals that Posner would consider unimportant or "noneconomic," the remaining objective of accident law is but an application of Posner's general principles of negligence law.[29]

The Foundation Revisited in 1977

It is enlightening to see where this discussion stands at present. In his new book, *Tragic Choices*, Calabresi, far from relinquishing the idea of including in his analyses societal objectives other than those that can be translated into efficiency, brings them to the fore by studying situations in which the efficient allocation of resources cannot be expected to play a dominant role.

Calabresi observes early in the essay that American society recognizes not only efficiency, but also honesty and equal treatment as fundamental values.[30] The recognition of some notion of equality comes as no surprise after the discussion in Chapter 2. The relevant question, and one on which the answer varies from society to society, is what kind and what degree of inequality, of discrimination, will be permissible.

To explain the role of honesty, we must make a slight detour. *Tragic Choices* is concerned throughout with the question of why the decision on the allocation of a tragically scarce resource will not be left to the market, even though the market is decentralized and follows more clearly than other methods of decision making — the accountable political process, lotteries and customary approaches are discussed — the expression of individual wants. The reasons for this reluctance are that market outcomes in these areas offend our concept of egalitarianism and that "it too clearly prices that to which we should like to ascribe infinite value."[31]

To be sure, such pricing cannot be avoided. For instance, we know statistically that the creation of the Mont Blanc tunnel will cost a certain number of lives. But much turns here on the way in which the pricing occurs. Illustrative is perhaps the following passage:

> Consider the different attitude we all share toward the failure of Congress to pass truly effective safety legislation, as against the attitude we would have were it unwilling to appropriate funds for the rescue of a trapped hostage. Lives may be discarded in both examples, *but the choice is less exposed in the first case and therefore less destructive of some of the basic values involved.*[32]

In these cases, the conflict of values is veiled by various *subterfuges,* as Calabresi expresses it.[33] Their advantage is to make choice effectively possible in such instances. But there are risks to them: risks of abuse, of arbitrariness, of bias.[34] It is against these eventualities that we wish to invoke the value of honesty.[35] This examination of *Tragic Choices,* however brief, should have convinced one that recognition of values beyond efficiency and their effective use in societal costs-and-benefits analyses is fundamental to Cal-abresi's thinking and not, as Posner's critique of *The Costs of Ac-cidents* might have suggested, a temporary aberration.

Posner's own work appears to display a trend toward greater concern for these other values. In the second edition of his *Economic Analysis of Law*, it is stressed at the outset that it must not be taken for granted that efficiency is necessarily socially desirable or, if it is, the only socially desirable feature. Posner also sees the role of the economist more in line with what one would expect in a broad conception of welfare:

> [His] competence in a discussion of the legal system is . . .
> strictly limited [to predicting] the effect of legal rules and
> arrangements on value and efficiency, in their strict technical
> senses, and on the existing distrbution of wealth.[36]

Yet the body of his text remains substantially committed to a much narrower concept of welfare and of the appropriate concerns for the economist. Thus one finds the statement that liability for negligence has the *"economic"* function of deterring *"uneconom-ical"* accidents;[37] or that "[t]he goal of the procedural system, *viewed economically*, is to minimize the sum of two types of cost [namely those of erroneous judicial decisions and the direct costs of the process]".[38]

These and other passages in Posner's book show that the main thrust of his analysis is still to recognize a fairly narrow notion of efficiency in a variety of legal disguises. H. L. A. Hart's observation on the first edition of the book seems equally applicable to the second:

> No one who has read Professor Posner's elaborate and refined
> work and the large literature which has grown out of it,
> designed to establish these utilitarian underpinnings of the
> law, could fail to profit. This is not, I think, because it
> succeeds in its ostensible purpose, but because its detailed
> ingenuity admirably forces one to think what else is needed ·
> besides a theory of utility for a satisfactory, explanatory, and
> critical theory of legal decisions. It becomes clear that in
> general what is needed is a theory of individual moral rights
> and their relationship to other values pursued through law, a
> theory of far greater comprehensiveness and detailed
> articulation than any so far provided.[39]

Conclusion

In his *The Costs of Accidents*, Calabresi saw two goals for accident law — namely, the pursuit of justice and the reduction of accident costs. Justice, in his view, means equity among the parties, consistency of decisions. Accident costs are of three kinds. Primary accident costs are those on which Posner focuses in his theory of negligence: the direct costs as well as those associated with their prevention. Secondary accident costs are those associated with economic dislocation and aggravation of injury following accidents. Tertiary accident costs are those incurred in the administration of the accident-compensation scheme. These costs resemble those of the procedural system in the mainstream view.

Posner's criticism of this view is that all the objectives that do not fit into his own frame of reference are either figments of the imagination or not within the purview of economics. This leaves him with only primary and tertiary accident costs, and, reduced to these, Calabresi's philosophy amounts to no more than the mainstream view.

Posner's criticism reflects a narrow concept of welfare and of the scope of economics. Far from heeding this criticism, Calabresi, in his recent *Tragic Choices*, maintains his view that goals other than the efficient allocation of resources may be considered important. This is illustrated for tragically scarce resources, i.e., those where our choices involve human lives. Posner too, in the second edition of his *Economic Analysis of Law*, appears to move closer to a broad concept of welfare. He admits that the pursuit of efficiency need not be society's only goal. Yet his subsequent analyses are limited to efficiency calculi.

Information Constraints

While Calabresi recognizes several objectives for accident law, much of *The Costs of Accidents* is concerned with consideration of ways of reducing primary accident costs. Two large avenues are explored for accomplishing this: market, or general, deterrence and specific deterrence. The first approach is based on decentralized decision making; it leaves the choice between accidents and their avoidance to individuals on the assumption that, if they are made aware of the costs of each option, they will make what is socially the best choice. Specific deterrence is based on a collective decision that specific acts or activities are undesirable and hence to be proscribed or, on the contrary, desirable and therefore to be made mandatory.

Accident law in most countries is a mixture of the two approaches. Before analyzing its main component, the fault system, Calabresi examines market and specific deterrence in the abstract. In each he finds essential limitations; many of these have to do with assumptions they make about the availability of information and the ease of communicating and processing it. It is these information constraints that will interest us in what follows. Since the basic philosophy underlying the fault system is market deterrence, we first examine this approach.

A system consisting of negligence and contributory negligence rules has the effect of letting accident losses lie where they fall, unless it is determined — by a court or some other forum — that someone other than the victim could have prevented the mishap at a cost below that of the accident and that the victim himself could not have done so. Such a system would achieve optimal reduction of primary accident costs if several, in Calabresi's terms "incredible,"[40] assumptions are made. One must assume:

1. That the classes to which victims and injurers belong can accurately make the decision as to whether "prevention, even if costly, is more desirable than bearing the risk, and occasionally the actual cost, of such accidents";[41]

2. That they can give effect to their decision by undertaking preventive measures or, under circumstances, for victims, by transacting with injurers to do so;

3. That they are motivated to decide and act upon it;

4. That the determination required to shift the accident burden can be accurately made.

Each of these assumptions is unrealistic in Calabresi's view. We shall examine the first, third and fourth, as they clearly bear on information problems. The second assumption refers to the fact that individuals are not always capable of controlling individual acts as opposed to patterns of behavior[42] and to the familiar question of nonnegligible transaction costs.

In what follows we examine first the question of the evaluation of risks. This subsection should convince one that the first of the just-mentioned assumptions is unrealistic. We then move on to the question whether, even assuming that people can evaluate risks accurately, they have an incentive to act upon their judgment. It will be seen that in practice insurance may well interfere with the motivation to prevent accidents. The fourth assumption that in Calabresi's view underlies the negligence system is that the rules can be accurately formulated and applied. Calabresi contends that, because of the problems with the first three assumptions, it is not obvious that what he terms "the cheapest cost avoider" must necessarily be found among injurers and victims. Sometimes a third class may be in a better position to reduce total accident costs. The problem is then how to choose the cheapest cost avoider, given our generally limited knowledge about the cost-avoiding potential of various groups linked in some way to the accident. A further question must be asked in this context: Are the courts under all circumstances the best institution to make the choice of the cheapest cost avoider, given the characteristics of their decision-making procedure? This question will be addressed in another subsection.

The arguments advanced in the first four subsections are meant to show how information problems undermine the simple and elegant negligence rules advanced in the mainstream view. It might be thought that this discussion casts doubt on the marked-deterrence approach to accident-cost reduction in general. Against such a conclusion it must be said that the alternative, the specific deterrence approach, is beset with information problems as well. These are discussed in the fifth subsection.

The Evaluation of Risks

Calabresi fundamentally doubts that individuals will correctly decide whether prevention is worth its cost because of their relative inability to assess small risks — and hence the discounted accident costs — accurately. The reason for this is in part that they "do not have the data necessary to determine how great the risk is, how large the losses are apt to be if they occur, and how serious the secondary results of such losses would be."[43]

But Calabresi asserts, even if they had the data, individuals would be psychologically unable to make the correct evaluation, to see themselves as victims; accidents are always thought to happen to "the other guy."[44] He refers to psychological evidence for this proposition.

In contrast, these drawbacks, the limited availability of data and their inaccurate assessment, should not affect those who can deal with accident figures *in aggregate, as statistics.* Hence, this group should be able to make more accurate choices between prevention and the assumption of risks than those who face them individually. One would therefore expect that, for instance, manufacturers of dangerous products would generally be better able to make such decisions than consumers, a conclusion at which Calabresi in fact arrives.[45]

Calabresi draws a second conclusion from these observations. It is that individuals would tend to misperceive the value of insurance to them and hence that, even in the absence of market imperfections in the insurance industry, autonomous market forces would not lead to the optimal amount of insurance of small hazards. Where underinsurance is the result, the issue of secondary costs arises.

The problem is even more acute where individuals who fail to insure do not themselves bear the costs of that decision. Calabresi cites the example of the "judgment-proof driver"[46] who has no money to pay for damages he causes and offers no recourse in bankruptcy. His victims or, more likely, society in general through social insurance schemes — medicare, disability pensions, unemployment benefits or welfare — will bear the costs. This problem will be further analysed below as a form of "externalization." Calabresi's conclusion is that "it is not hard to see why society, which bears the costs of noninsurance, frequently compels insurance."[47]

Insurance and the Motivation to Prevent

The function of insurance is to spread the risk of losses over time or over different persons. If all risks were simply pooled and the insured charged the same fee, spreading — secondary accident costs reduction — would have been accomplished, but the incentive for individuals to minimize accident and prevention costs would have disappeared; no initiative in this sense by any one individual would significantly reduce his premium.

This situation is unlikely to last, since the more careful among the insured will press for lower rates. In much the same way as the differentiation among debtors according to credit-worthiness,[48] insurance companies will establish categories of insured according to their accident proneness. If the differentiation could be made without cost, each insured would be in his own category and pay a premium equivalent to the discounted accident risk he creates. He would face the precise social cost of his behavior and could thus decide accurately whether his preventive efforts were worth their cost in savings on the insurance premium. If he changed his pattern of activities and created larger risks, he would face higher insurance premiums.

In reality, of course, the differentiation is a costly process. There are the costs of gathering and analyzing facts to establish the categories, of assigning the insured to particular categories, and of ensuring that their behavior continues to conform to that required for the assigned category.[49] One would expect that insurance companies will find it profitable to differentiate so long as the increase in differentiation costs is smaller than the reduction of premiums it achieves for the better risks.

The problem is complicated by the fact that the features that are easy to measure and hence likely to be used for differentiation are not necessarily those that provide optimal incentives. Thus, it might make good sense for insurance companies to differentiate drivers by age and marital status; it may well be true that the highest accident costs per capita are generated in the group of nonmarried drivers, aged eighteen to twenty-four. But high premiums for this category, independent of actual driving practices, may unduly discourage careful drivers within this group and yet may not induce the less careful ones to adopt safer behavior patterns, such as driving cars in good state of repair or not driving at high speeds or through orange lights, all features that are costlier to monitor. Of course, once an individual has been classified in a category, and given that monitoring his behavior is costly, he has no strong interest in being careful, beyond the prospect, in case of an accident, of being reclassified into a higher risk category: the problem of "moral hazard," further discussed in Chapter 8.

Calabresi notes the difference between walking and driving with respect to the question of who can best insure against pedestrian-car accidents.[50] Walking, being an unorganized but common activity, would be insured without differentiation as part of the general cost of life; driving, on the other hand, could be readily differentiated according to the likelihood that it would cause injuries to pedestrians. Hence, as far as incentives toward primary-cost reduction are concerned, driver insurance would be preferable to pedestrian insurance. All in all, it seems clear that the availability of insurance is likely to change the incentives toward primary-cost reduction that the market deterrence approach could otherwise be expected to provide.

Choosing the "Cheapest Cost Avoider"

The central question of accident law is on whom liability for accidents should be put. If reduction of costs is the objective, it would be put on the party who, if liable, will achieve the lowest costs. Calabresi terms this party "the cheapest cost avoider."

If transactions were costless, it would not matter, as regards the reduction of primary costs of accidents, on which party, injurers or victims, one would put liability for the costs of accidents. Indeed, liability might be put on a third party, who would, under the stated assumption, bribe the party who could prevent the accident or insure for it at the lowest cost.

Obviously, transaction costs are not negligible in practice and may vary from one party to the next. Calabresi illustrates this with the following example.[51] Suppose car-pedestrian accidents currently cost $100. They could be reduced to $10 if spongy bumpers, which cost an additional $50, were installed. In a purely "Coasian" situation the bumpers would be installed, regardless of who bore liability initially.

But assume now that any allocation other than leaving the cost of accidents where it falls — that is, on the pedestrians — entails $5 in administrative costs. Assume also that the costs for pedestrians to bribe anyone is $65 because of the costliness of bringing them together and overcoming free-rider problems.

Assume finally that as a further option one considers the possibility of putting liability for the accidents on an apparently unrelated group, such as television manufacturers, a concentrated group, whose transaction costs for bribing would be only $30.

Consider now the outcomes as liability is placed on different groups. If the car manufacturers are liable, the bumpers will be installed since $50 plus $10 plus $5 is lower than $100 plus $5. If pedestrians are liable, the bumpers will *not* be installed; accident costs of $100 are lower than the cost of bumpers ($40) plus that of bribing ($65) and the remaining accident costs ($10). Notice now that this solution at the cost of $100 entails a loss of $35 in comparison with what would be possible if transactions were costless or if manufacturers were held liable in the first place. Finally, if the television manufacturers are made liable, the bumpers will be installed; $100 plus $5 is more than $50 (bumpers) plus $30 (transaction costs) plus $10 (remaining accident costs) plus $5 (administrative). But, in comparison with the first solution, this result has been achieved with $30 in "unnecessary" transaction costs. Clearly, one would expect the manufacturers to be made liable if primary cost reduction through market deterrence were the objective.

In practical situations the choice of the best cost bearer is likely to be more complicated. Calabresi notes that the relevant information is frequently unavailable or available only at too high a price.[52] He expects therefore that the choice will be made by relying on an initial rough guess and a series of guidelines.

The Rough Guess.   The rough guess is, in Calabresi's words:

> designed to exclude from consideration as potential loss
> bearers all those activities that could reduce costs only by
> causing losses which are clearly much greater, in terms of
> meeting individuals' desires as expressed in the market, than
> would result if one achieved the equivalent or greater
> reduction in accident costs by burdening other activities.[53]

The rough guess serves to delineate a class of "causes"[54] of accident not to be considered as loss bearers. Such a judgment might seem "fuzzy" in economic discourse such as one finds in Posner's work, but Calabresi points to its analogy with the decision to ignore, or not to attribute to a given activity, all sorts of external costs and benefits.

Consideration of Administrative Cost.   The first guideline counsels to consider the administrative cost of finding — or allocating costs to — the cheapest cost avoider.[55] If these are very high, it may be preferable, in his view, to allocate costs to a slightly more expensive cost avoider. Thus, "if placing accident costs on drivers according to miles driven results in nearly as much car-pedestrian accident cost avoidance as a charge on drivers according to age and accident involvement, and if the latter costs much more to administer, in practice the cheapest cost avoidance may well be achieved by the first method."[56]

Avoiding Externalization. The second guideline is to avoid externalization. This occurs when the group that initially bears liability passes the burden of it on to a different group, which would not have been chosen as the risk bearers. Externalization may, in Calabresi's view, come about in at least three ways. It may be due to *insufficient subcategorization.* If teen-age drivers were responsible for a disproportionate number of car-pedestrian accidents, allocation of car-pedestrian accidents to driving in general (through a tax on all drivers) would be externalization. Similarly, if liability were placed on pedestrians, it would most likely be externalized to the cost of living in general.

In a more extreme form, this phenomenon is found in externalization by *transfer.* An example of it are the "judgment-proof drivers" mentioned earlier. If these drivers are held liable, the burden of the costs they generate through accidents will not touch them, even in the form of general insurance, but will be borne instead by various social insurance schemes and perhaps the private accident insurance of victims.

Finally, externalization may be the result of *inadequate knowledge.* If liability is placed on a party who does not accurately assess the actual risk of accident — for reasons mentioned earlier — it would not affect his behavior and, as Calabresi notes, "would have as little effect on accident control as scattering the cost would."[57]

Finding the "Best Briber". The third guideline Calabresi gives is to "allocate accident costs in such a way as to maximize the likelihood that errors in allocation will be corrected in the market."[58] He terms this finding "the best briber." If we are unsure of who the cheapest cost avoider is, this guideline urges us to put the costs on the party who can most easily enter into transactions to correct the initial allocation. This requirement in itself covers other features, such as awareness of risk, ease with which one can discover whom to bribe, and possibility of coercing potential free-riders.

Hard Cases. If the forementioned guidelines do not allow one to make a clear choice, one has what Calabresi calls a "hard case." In these situations he counsels to make "educated guesses," to divide the costs among the restricted group of parties identified in earlier steps, or to use other goals.[59]

Refinements. In a series of articles that have appeared since *The Costs of Accidents*,[60] Calabresi has brought to the fore a slightly different approach to the minimization of costs, which he terms "strict liability." It order to decide on which party the burden of accident costs should be put, one asks not "Who is the cheapest cost avoider?" but "Who is in the best position to make the cost-benefit analysis between accident costs and accident avoidance costs and to act on that decision once it is made?"[61]

Strict liability in this definition means that one of the parties makes the decision that, under ordinary negligence rules, the court would make. Such a shift may indicate that the issue is technical and that the court finds itself in the awkward position of determining whether preventive action was worth its cost. It implies, as Calabresi notes, "a lesser degree of governmental intervention than does either of the Hand type tests."[62] Moreover, he believes that in practice it requires a judgment that is easier to make than under the negligence rule.

At present one finds strict liability in the areas of industrial accidents (workmen's compensation legislation), ultra-hazardous activities, manufactured goods (product liability), and no-fault automobile plans. There is empirical evidence that at least in the area of industrial accidents, primary costs have been reduced below their level under the previous, negligence regime.[63] It should be noted here that the tendency to introduce strict liability on the injurer's, rather than the victim's, side reflects an empirical judgment, not theory.[64]

With this refinement, Calabresi now formulates the problem of deciding on liability rules in the field of accident law.

As an overall guideline, efficiency requires the most refined cost-benefit analysis of social choices. This implies that one should aim for knowledgeable choices among social benefits and the costs necessary to attain them, or among social costs and the costs necessary to avoid them. Entitlements should be defined so as to favor such choices. This guideline is particularized as follows. If it is difficult to ascertain in general whether an activity yields a net social benefit, the costs associated with that activity should be imposed upon the party best able to make the cost-benefit analysis. In contexts such as accidents or pollution, this implies that the social cost of the accident or of the pollution should be charged to the party who can most cheaply avoid it. Where this does not allow one to arrive at a solution, the costs should be imposed upon the party who can most cheaply, that is with the lowest transaction costs, correct a mistaken initial assignment of entitlements, by inducing someone else to avoid social costs. Finally it should be realized that, as most of these difficulties arise in contexts where markets do not function perfectly, it will frequently have to be decided whether the imperfect market or collective decision making with its attendant drawbacks is likely to bring society closer to an efficient allocation of resources.

The Appropriate Forum

In a market deterrence approach, would the choice of the cheapest cost avoider best be made by the courts, in case-by-case fashion? Calabresi answers this question in the negative, and his reasons have to do in part with information constraints.

In the first place, because the proceedings take place between parties to the accident, courts are likely to ignore the danger of externalization due to transfer and, indeed, other forms of externalization as well. The same constraint would prevent the courts from considering which category of party can bribe most easily.[66] Moreover, by focusing on the individual, unusual event, courts may not be in the best position to modify recurring, ordinary behavior, which should be the mainstay of cost reduction.

Case-by-case allocation of losses in the courts further requires a description of events long after their occurrence and by parties who have an interest in the nature of that description. Such a description is likely to be rather unreliable, less reliable at least than statistical compilations based on observation at the site of the accident, which would be required in a system seeking to influence broad categories of behavior, rather than to solve unusual accidents.[67] Finally, Calabresi contends that the court system is a comparatively costly way of issuing rules of accident law.[68]

Information Constraints on Specific Deterrence

Given the limitations of attempts to reduce accident costs by means of collective deterrence — that is, by making the cheapest cost avoider choose between accident and avoidance costs — one might expect substantial interest in specific deterrence, which is the issuance of rules specifically requiring certain preventive action (wearing seat belts or installing fire alarms) or forbidding dangerous acts or activities (driving beyond speed limits, without a licence, or with a car in poor state of repair).

The weaknesses of this approach to accident-cost reducton are in many respects similar to those discussed for market deterrence. Information constraints are a troubling aspect here as well. In what follows we discuss what appear to be particular pitfalls for the specific deterrence approach.

In the first place, to determine which is the cheapest cost-avoiding activity, policymakers must rely on facts that are not freely available and must be collected at substantial cost. In this context Calabresi notes that "the market is often by far the cheapest fact-finding device available."[69] One would expect that in many cases leaving problems for the market to solve may well be a useful first step, even if specific deterrence is ultimately intended. Notice, by the way, that policymakers need not be worse informed than insurers,[70] who, as we saw earlier, substantially affect the outcome of the market approach toward cost reduction.

Aside from the question of access to information, it is surely very costly to make minute decisions politically or collectively. In Calabresi's words:

> the collective process lends itself to dramatic choices (war or peace, legal prostitution or not), even when fairly detailed behavior (drunken driving or not, seat belts or not) is involved. It does not lend itself to such prosaic choices as those between one type of shoe and another, or between driving 20 miles a day and 40 miles a day.[71]

One might say, borrowing microeconomic terms, that the collective process functions at high starting costs, but with substantial economies of scale.

A further problem arises where the collective deciders, though they have an idea of what they wish to prevent, cannot define it precisely before its occurrence. If only fuzzy descriptions can be given of it, the relevant question is whether the individuals subjected to such a rule can understand it well enough to apply it to specific situations. If they cannot, penalizing them after the fact leads to externalization resulting from inadequate knowledge.[72] Moreover, because of the uncertainty one may hesitate to use certain types of penalty.[73] If penalties are stiff, individuals, in order to avoid having to guess at the meaning of a rule in practice and being found wrong, may abstain from a broad category of activities far beyond those that the rule was meant to control.[74] Such disincentive effects must be weighed against the benefit of controlling the activities that were specifically intended.

Summary

It seems useful to summarize the types of information constraint examined in this section. Throughout, we have encountered the problem that fully adequate information for some decisions is not available, at least not at a price that it is worth paying, considering the improvement in the decision that such information would yield. We found this tradeoff for individuals assessing minute risks, for insurance companies setting up risk categories, for collective deciders in the advice to weigh the administrative cost against the improvement in their choice of cost avoiders, and in the decision to issue specific rules.

We also found apparently unrelated information constraints. Individuals were seen incapable of coping with information on small hazards. Collective deciders were advised (or expected) in the absence of information to work toward their decision by *eliminating* options, an inexplicable strategy at first sight. An important consideration at several stages in this strategy is the consideration of the *comparative* advantage or disadvantage that individuals have with respect to information. Courts were thought to have a disadvantage in the choice of the cheapest cost avoider because of the way in which they collect information — case by case. Finally, we saw that collective deciders are thought to have economies of scale in information processing and that the precision of the language in which rules are formulated reflects a subtle tradeoff between losses due to uncertainty and gains from the main effect of the rule. In the second part we hope to show how all these phenomena can be explained in a single underlying framework based on the costliness of information.

Conclusion

The criticism of the mainstream approach in law and economics parallels the more fundamental discussion in economics about the appropriate concept of welfare. The mainstream would view maximal welfare as equivalent to a Pareto-optimal state of the economy, or at least it restricts its analyses to this aspect of welfare, on the assumption that it can properly be dissociated from other aspects, notably the distribution of wealth. Critics find this position fundamentally inadequate.

It should be stressed that the critics in law and economics, no less than the mainstream, are committed to functional analysis of law — that is, to analyzing legal institutions in terms of their expected effect in society, as opposed to their internal logic or aesthetics, as a formalistic approach would.[75] Nor should it be assumed that the critics would deny the value of the kind of functional analysis that the neoclassical economic model represents. They recognize that, in our society, market processes, the focus of the neoclassical model, form the core of economic life.

Calabresi writes on this subject:

> Every time a system of allocation other than a pure market is established in a society in which the market continues to operate in other areas, there is danger that nonmarket allocations will be altered by market pressures. . . . In each case, those with money are tempted to buy the resource by bribing the deciders or by paying the recipients of the resource to sell it.[76]

Costly measures may be taken to prevent the undermining of the nonmarket scheme, but such action is unlikely to be fully effective and entails its own cost, material as well as, frequently, moral. Such considerations are likely, in his view, to increase the weight given to pure markets in society's choice of a mechanism for the allocation of its resources.

The dispute appears to turn fundamentally on the relative importance that one believes society attaches to the goal of allocative efficiency. This is more than a quarrel about principles. It is the choice between a very workable, but unrealistic, model and a more encompassing one, in which deriving precise propositions is more complex.

For our part, we would judge that what is termed "uneconomic" in the mainstream analysis, but which we would prefer to consider as unexplained in their model, is still rather substantial in comparison with the issues on which the model does provide new insight. More pressing still is the observation that several of these unexplained problems could be accounted for perfectly well in the richer model suggested by the critics. One might think here of the areas of strict liability mentioned earlier or of the rules proscribing or requiring certain behavior, which are found to coexist with the general negligence rules. We also find it intellectually pleasing that within the framework provided by *Tragic Choices* one can account for people's observed tendency toward formalistic — as opposed to functional — approaches to law and toward "process values," to which legal philosophers have drawn attention.[77] We believe that these phenomena could not be as easily accommodated within the Posnerian framework and are likely to be classified there as aberrations.

There is, in our view, reason, even accepting the gains afforded by the mainstream analyses, to widen the outlook on which they are based. Following Becker's precept, we should like to *extend the mainstream world by considering information as a scarce commodity, one for whose acquisition other resources must be given up.* We would now expect that individuals would acquire information only up to the point where its added benefit would no longer exceed the corresponding cost, which may be well before they have the amount of it required to make decisions of the quality assumed in mainstream analyses. As a result, one may expect that some choices will be predicted to be made differently from what the mainstream would anticipate.

The risk with introducing new costs and benefits in the neoclassical model is that much will be explainable, but less will be predictable. Information appears to be an acceptable choice in this regard. While it is frequently not tangible, its cost can be assessed or at least perceived in most instances, and crude comparisons of cost are usually possible. Information is also, as the discussion in the third section suggested, a ubiquitous phenomenon and the problems with it are pervasive. Finally, the addition of information is not a choice out of the blue; there is a sizable and increasingly active literature on the "economics of information."

In Part II we deal with the economics of information and its implications for the economic analysis of law. Chapters 5 to 8 follow divisions that are suggested by the economics of information. They are written at a high level of abstraction. Only occasionally, in particular in the conclusions, will attention be drawn to the legal applications. Chapter 9 focuses on one area of law where explicit consideration of information constraints promises, in our view, a more realistic economic analysis. The area we have in mind is consumer law. All in all, we hope that the second part provides the answer to the question that, itself, could be formulated as an information tradeoff: Are the additional insights afforded by making information a scarce resource worth their cost in loss of predictive power?

PART II

The Costliness of Information Introduced in the Economic Analysis of Law

CHAPTER 5

The Role of Information in the Economic World View

On the Nature of Information

" 'Information' in most if not all of its connotations seems to rest upon the notion of *selection power*."[1] Cherry, from whom this quotation is taken, writes elsewhere in his book *On Human Communication:* "Information can be received only where there is doubt; and doubt implies the existence of alternatives — where choice, selection, or discrimination is called for."[2] The role of information in the economic model is stated here in a nutshell: Information is the essential ingredient of choice, and choice among scarce resources is the central question of economics.

Lack of information impairs one's ability to make decisions of the fully rational kind postulated in economic discourse. Decisions must therefore be made in the presence of *uncertainty*. In many instances uncertainty will cause people to make decisions different from what they would have been under conditions of abundant information. As information subsequently becomes available, such decisions may appear in retrospect to have been erroneous. They entail a loss or a failure to obtain a gain that could have been avoided with better information. Uncertainty is generally a source of disutility,[3] and information is the antidote to it. In most instances efficiency will be enhanced by moves that improve the flow of information in society.

Uncertainty has many causes. Our collective knowledge does not allow us at present to control a variety of natural phenomena, such as the weather, and we must accept the whims of nature in this regard. Changes resulting from human choice or from inventions create uncertainty. With respect to human choice creating uncertainty, one needs only to think of the pricing policies of oil-producing nations and of ever-changing fashions to find examples. It is not surprising to find that Knight associates the intensity of the need for information with the rate of change in society.[4]

Uncertainty is used here in a very general sense. For the present purpose it does not seem fruitful to distinguish, as Knight proposed to do, between the kind of uncertainty where at least the statistical distribution of relevant variables is known (a situation he terms "risk") and the kind in which even this information is not available and one has to rely on intuitive values ("uncertainty," in his terms).[5] The distinction reflects but different degrees of reduced "selection power," and this continuity is recognized in modern decision theory. Nor is there an essential difference for the present purpose between uncertainty stemming from our "genuine" ignorance of nature and the situations in which we lack information because we find it too costly to acquire. Indeed, we may experience uncertainty, even where information is well within reach, as a result of our inability to combine and condense it into a form usable in the decision at hand.

The term *information,* too, is used here in a very general sense. The distinction sometimes made between "data," "information" and "knowledge" has no useful consequence for the discussion at hand. "Information" in that more limited meaning results from analysis or refinement of "data," which are the figures derived from observation. Information in this sense is thought to be more readily usable in decisions. "Knowledge" is best seen as a substantial body of information collated and systematized for repeated use in the future. Defined in this manner it can be analyzed as information in the form of a capital good, as will be argued in later chapters. For the present purposes all these phenomena will simply be treated as varieties or "grades" of information.

A last remark concerns the relation between information and the concept of transaction costs introduced earlier.[6] It is true that the acquisition of information of various kinds is a major component of transaction costs. For an ordinary purchase, for instance, one would want to know the identity of several suppliers, their prices, the quality of their products, terms and conditions on which they sell (for instance, warranties or return privileges), and perhaps even whether shortage of the product in question is likely in the near future. Transaction costs will be reduced and market functioning enhanced if this information can be made available more cheaply. But transaction costs also consist of other factors, such as the physical accessibility of the suppliers. Inversely, not all information acquisition is directly aimed at transactions. For professionals and scientists the acquisition of knowledge is undertaken in preparation for a productive service. Information processing which judges do in order to reach their decisions does not directly pertain to a transaction, unless this term is given a singularly wide and unusual meaning. Hence, while the notions of transaction and information costs substantially overlap, they do not coincide. The latter notion is useful because we believe that there are economically relevant features common to all situations in which information must be acquired at a cost.

The Information Tradeoff

Uncertainty, we argued earlier, is a source of disutility in the sense that people would feel better off if they could make it disappear or at least reduce its impact. Two broad strategies are available to do this. First, one may bear the risk but reduce its effect by *pooling* it with other similar risks. An individually uncertain event thus becomes part of a larger set in which the incidence of loss can be statistically predicted. One may also share a large risk with others so that for each the portion he bears is manageable. In all these instances there is scope for trades, in which all or part of an uncertain large loss is exchanged for a much smaller, but certain, payment or decrease in expected gain.

The second strategy in the face of uncertainty will be termed *search* here. It consists of attempts to acquire information as an antidote to uncertainty. Search may consist of individual efforts to acquire information through observation. But information may also be acquired in collaboration or through trade with others. It may entail the search for, and the introduction of, ways to compile and integrate information that is available but could not, without such processing, be brought to bear upon the decision at hand.

The difference between the two strategies is that in the first society continues to bear the risk, though differently distributed, whereas as a result of the second strategy society eludes it, at least in part. It should be added that while in the first strategy the risk has not been dissipated for society as a while, for the individual who is its initial bearer, pooling or sharing may make a great deal of difference and in some cases be the dividing line between undertaking a venture and forgoing it. Uncertainty is to him an autonomous source of disutility, and he is willing to pay to have it removed from him, as is obvious, for instance, in insurance. The insurance premium exceeds the (mathematically) expected value of the loss that is covered.

If information were costlessly available, one would surely always opt for exhaustive search. Indeed, the problem of search would not even arise since, in this hypothetical world, the mere effort of thinking of the problem would make one instantaneously informed and have the appropriate decision at one's lips. In the real world, where information must be acquired at a cost, there is a problem of how much search should be performed. In the neoclassical tradition the optimal amount of search would be determined, as in the case of other goods and services, by the rule that marginal cost should equal marginal benefit.[7] Hence, individuals would be expected to compare the cost of search and that of bearing the risk (under the best formula as discussed above) and to devote resources to search up to the point where the cost of an additional effort to acquire information would exceed the benefit one could derive from it in the form of reduced loss from uncertainty. It can readily be shown that at this point the difference between the total benefits and costs of search is maximized and that the sum of uncertainty and search costs is at its minimum.[8] This is graphically illustrated in diagrams 5–1 and 5–2.[9]

Several interesting conclusions can now be drawn. It is obvious that *in general it is not optimal to inform oneself exhaustively on*

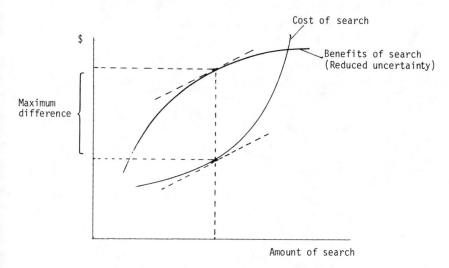

Diagram 5.1. **Maximize Net Benefit of Uncertainty Reduction over Search Cost**

a given problem.[10] Downs stated this proposition in 1957, in his classic *An Economic Theory of Democracy.*[11] It is the basis for a refined sense of rationality, in which the ideal of looking for what is substantively the best solution is abandoned as unrealistic. Instead, to be rational in this sense means to look for the best solution *that it is worth looking for.*[12]

A second interesting conclusion is that while the impact of the costliness of information will be reduced, and hence one will move closer to the economist's model of full rationality both by a decrease in uncertainty and by a reduction in search costs, these changes are not equivalent. The former will lead to a drop in the amount of search, whereas the latter will have the opposite effect of stimulating information acquisition and processing. The difference would appear, for instance, with respect to buyer uncertainty with regard to the quality of used cars. Prescribing minimal quality features or mandatory warranties has very different effects from obliging vendors to publicize warranties or known defects in standardized form.

If information is costly, even the best tradeoff between search and uncertainty entails a real cost for the decisionmaker. This cost should count as part of the cost of the venture on which one makes the decision. Thus, in the purchase price of an object, one should include the cost of the search necessary to decide on this one over

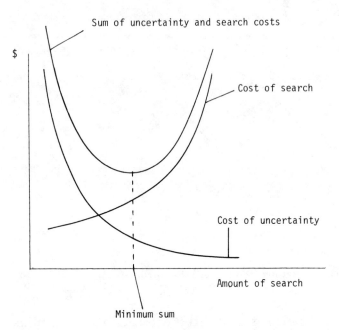

Diagram 5.2. Minimize the Sum of Uncertainty and Search Costs

others as well as the cost of the residual uncertainty pertaining to its true quality. For this reason it is not surprising to find, as Kronman shows, that the law treats differently a rare object with a market price of $10,000 and a currently available new car of the same price; specific performance would be granted for delivery of the former, while for the latter damages would have to do.[13]

The introduction of information cost considerations in substantive decision making leads to a refined concept of rationality. The principal can be easily stated: One must choose the least-cost or best-return option (which takes into account the cost of uncertainty) *net* of search costs. The hard questions begin when one attempts to locate the two cost functions underlying the information tradeoff. Search cost, for instance, depends no doubt on information — of the second degree — about how information of the first degree is best found. Second-degree information might refer to possible sources of information on the reliability of primary information. Whatever its nature, second-degree information may in turn raise a tradeoff problem of the kind discussed before and give rise to even higher-order tradeoffs. Do we face an infinite regress, as McKenzie believes we do?[14]

The answer to this question lies perhaps in its reformulation, such as March proposes in a recent article: not how much human behavior is rational, but how can one adjust, stretch, engineer models of rational choice to provide a better fit of observed ways of decision making "where goals are unstable, ill-defined, or apparently irrelevant"?[15] March's earlier work was in the theory of organizations and operational research, all relativley "hard" subjects. His recognition that what is at issue here is akin to "some classical and modern questions in literature and ethics . . ."[16] is both indicative of the vastness of the problem and perhaps of the most fruitful way to address it. Accordingly, we shall deal mostly with information tradeoffs of the first order, taking higher-order choices for granted. We hope to show that even this modest step adds substantial realism to the neoclassical model.

Information as a Commodity

The term *search* used in the preceding section for efforts to acquire information may have suggested a strictly personal activity. Information would be produced, extracted from the surrounding world, and distilled by reflection by the very person who intends to use it to push back some uncertainty that he faces. While this is indeed in many circumstances the most appropriate way of gathering information, in many more instances information produced by one person can be used by another. One is therefore tempted to ask the economist's usual question about the advantages of specialization and trade in information. Why, in other words, is information not a commodity like other goods and services available in the market?

This question is certainly worth asking since, as Knight observed over fifty years ago:

> The outstanding fact is that the ubiquitous presence of
> uncertainty permeating every relation of life has brought it
> about that information is one of the principal commodities
> that the economic organization is engaged in supplying.[17]

A commodity information certainly is, for it takes resources to produce and it can usually be bought and sold. But it is a peculiar commodity. For one thing, it is frequently hard to put a price on it because of the difficulties of measuring the quantity of the commodity, as Boulding has observed.[18] The "bit," which information science uses, does not correspond to what is an economically relevant denomination to the user. Yet information is easily sliced where one buys information on one's health from a doctor or access to a series of lectures in a department of continuing education, or where one buys a map of a foreign city or a book explaining how to perform a difficult operation.

A prerequisite for trade in a commodity is that use of it can be controlled or, to put it differently, that property rights can effectively be maintained on it. From our discussion in Chapter 3, it should be obvious that in the absence of that possibility, the commodity would be overused, if available, and generally no supplier would find it worth his while to put it on the market. The appropriability of information is susceptible of degrees. The diagnosis of a patient can be fairly readily controlled by the doctor who poses it, and he can ensure that he is effectively paid for it. But now think of the student who, at great cost and risk to himself, has gained access to the question that will be put to him and his 600 classmates at the forthcoming exam with Professor X, who has a reputation for severity. Suppose for simplicity's sake that the value of this information is the same for all students, namely v. If the informationholder sells to student A for v, how can he prevent A from underbidding him in his dealings with other students? Of course, the problem could be solved by a collective agreement among the students, but under the circumstances this is likely to reveal the leak to the administration. Should the initial holder charge $(n-1)v$ (where n is the total number of students) to his purchaser, who, in turn, can sell it for $(n-2)v$ to his buyer, and so on? This would solve the underbidding problem, but again would not appear feasible under the circumstances.

A further problem with information as a marketable commodity is its inspection prior to purchase (in the same way in which one judges apples before buying them). Normal inspection reveals the information and in many cases would make the transaction superfluous. Sometimes one can judge on the basis of samples. Where one deals repeatedly with the same supplier, a series of future transactions gives that supplier an incentive to provide the promised quality (reliability) of information. But clearly this is a peculiarity of the information market.

All in all, property rights in information are not always feasible and are usually imperfect in comparison with those that exist in most physical commodities. It would seem that property rights are most nearly viable with respect to information that is extensive and complex or highly individualized to the prospective purchaser.

Information also has in many instances the peculiarity of being a public good, in the sense that its use by one person does not curtail its usefulness to another.[19] For example, one has only to think of the information made available through public broadcasting. The example points to another interesting aspect of information, namely, that in many instances it can be disseminated at very low marginal cost. The mass media dissemination shows large economies of scale, and this would lead one to expect substantial concentration in this industry and even a virtual "natural monopoly" in extreme cases.[20]

In sum, while information is in some respects a marketable commodity, its peculiar features in many instances would lead one to expect distortions in the markets for information. What these distortions might be and what effect they might have will be discussed in later chapters.

Information as a Capital Asset

The creation of information takes money, effort and time. In many instances the expenditure of these scarce resources can produce benefits not just once, but several times, indeed repeatedly over time. In such cases it is worth considering whether information should be accumulated in a form amenable to such repeated use. Information in this form is like a capital asset, and the decision to acquire it can be analyzed as an investment problem.[21]

Information that has been systematized for repeated use is usually referred to as *knowledge*. We might include in the term not only figures or facts to be extracted from a store of similar information, but also procedures for solving certain kinds of problems or finding certain types of information. Where knowledge is held in a person's memory, it is termed *human capital*.[22] As with other capital assets, human capital can be increased or allowed to depreciate or to become obsolete. It is a peculiar asset in that its value does not usually decline as a result of use. Moreover, it appears to be irreversible and inalienable, although knowledge can of course be "copied" and transmitted to other people.

As in other investment problems, the decision to acquire knowledge will be governed by the rate of return on resources invested in this allocation relative to that which could be expected if they were used otherwise. Costs and benefits considered in such a decision will vary according to the context, and only some general remarks can be made here. On the cost side it should be considered that individuals vary in their ability to transform time, effort and money into productive knowledge. They may also differ in the degree to which they can accurately assess such ability. One needs only to think of decisions to acquire professional knowledge to find examples of such differences.

Benefits may be monetary as well as nonmonetary. Nonmonetary benefits might be the pleasure of carrying on stimulating conversations with people having similar knowledge or of appreciating subtle differences, which knowledge of art or music makes possible. Such diverse benefits, as well as the various kinds of cost, must be integrated in some fashion in order that a net return can be determined and compared with that of other activities. How such a task might be accomplished will be discussed in the next chapter.

Since knowledge produces benefits to its holders over time, the decision to invest in it must take into account the likelihood that such knowledge will cease to be useful before one would normally have abandoned it. This corresponds to what, for physical equipment, is known as economic obsolescence. Thus, one would hesitate to spend time learning tricks to facilitate calculation of some complex mathematical formula if standard programs to do the calculation were likely soon to appear in hand calculators. Of course, the investor in knowledge must also in other respects be assured of the yield on his investment, and the limited effectiveness of property rights in information noted earlier could be a substantial impediment here. Uncertainty about future yield would normally be reflected in a higher required return, as portfolio theory indicates.

Once a decision to invest in knowledge has been made and executed, the investment is a "sunk cost." This means that even if an unexpected event renders the knowledge obsolete, continuing to produce information from it may be preferable to setting up a new capital asset. In general, an existing capital asset should be replaced by a new one if the yield on the new one net of its average *total* cost is higher than that of the old one minus its average *variable* cost. For information, fixed (or investment) costs are usually high relative to variable costs. This has several interesting consequences.

Arrow argues, for instance, that it will be difficult to reverse an initial commitment in the direction in which information is gathered: ". . . even if subsequent information suggests that the initial choice was wrong, it would not pay to reverse the decision later on."[23] It also explains why an individual finds it "easier to explore new areas near to those he has already covered,"[24] and "to communicate with other individuals with whom one has a common approach or a common language, literally or metaphorically."[25] Habits, customs, particular ideosyncratic search heuristics, or "ways of looking at a problem," all appear on balance to be rational devices in this light.[26]

The capital nature of knowledge makes it rational for individuals to ignore or even suppress incidental pieces of information discordant with their current knowledge. There is ample evidence that such tendencies in fact exist.[27] Yet it is equally obvious that these tendencies could be very damaging if carried too far. One has to have procedures leading one to discard existing knowledge at the right time.

Conclusion

Information was defined in this chapter as "selection power." It is the essential ingredient of choice and for this reason of interest to the economist. Information was seen to be the antidote to uncertainty, which invades the economy from many sides. Since information is costly, one must decide how much of it to acquire. This problem can be addressed initially with the "marginal cost equals marginal benefit" rule, but it reappears at a higher level where one must decide how much information to obtain with respect to primary information, and so on. As a solution out of this infinite regress, it was proposed to consider only the first-level information tradeoff and to take the higher levels for granted. Given the ubiquitous role of information, one is led to ask whether markets in information exist. After all, one might expect advantages from specialization and trade in information as there are in the production of other commodities. Our analysis shows information to be a peculiar commodity. It cannot be as readily divided and measured in an economically relevant way as other commodities. It is not always amenable to the exercise of property rights, with the consequences set out in Chapter 3. In some circumstances information behaves like a public good. And in many cases, while the initial gathering of information is rather costly, there are vast economies of scale in duplication and dissemination, such that there would be a tendency toward a "natural monopoly" in the market for the information in question. For all these reasons it would seem interesting to study markets in information in more detail.

Information can also be accumulated for repeated use in the future, as knowledge. Knowledge can be analyzed as a capital asset; it takes scarce resources to produce and is expected to yield revenue over time. Acquisition of knowledge can be treated as an investment problem, and several interesting inferences can be drawn from such an analysis. One is that people will seek to resist the unanticipated obsolence of their knowledge, which would appear to explain such conservative traits as exploring new areas near those one already knows, adopting customs or habits and so on.

In the next chapters we study the terms of the information tradeoff. The next two chapters will deal with search, the third one with risk bearing. Chapter 6 covers search as the activity of information processing. Scarce (mental) resources impose constraints on the ways in which we can hope to cope with information. Chapter 7 deals with information acquisition in markets and is perhaps at the center of what is known as the economics of information. Where uncertainty cannot be avoided through search, one must find the best way of assuming it and this is the topic of Chapter 8, risk bearing.

CHAPTER 6

Search:

Human Information Processing

Rationality

One of the central postulates of economic analysis is the rationality of *homo oeconomicus*. In Becker's words, this assumption "simply implies consistent maximization of a well-ordered function, such as a utility or profit function."[1] It means that "people respond to incentives — that if you change a person's surroundings so that he could increase his satisfactions by altering his behavior, most of the time he will do so."[2]

As a first approximation of human choice in most current situations, the postulate seems to be unobjectionable. One wholeheartedly agrees with Posner where he writes that:

> [The rationality] assumption is no stronger than that most
> people in most affairs of life are guided by what they

119

conceive to be their self-interest and that they choose means
reasonably (not perfectly) designed to promote it.

> Although the assumptions of economic theory are to
> some extent, certainly, oversimplified and unrealistic as
> descriptions of human behavior, there is abundant evidence
> that theories derived from those assumptions have
> considerable power in predicting how people in fact behave."[3]

The interesting question is why this should be so. Becker, in
his article on "Irrational Behavior and Economic Theory,"[4] formulates an evolutionary argument to account for it. His reasoning
is essentially that where individuals or firms are tempted to choose
irrationally, resource constraints (budget lines) would force them
in the direction of consuming less of a good whose price rises in
relation to other commodities. As a result their behavior could in
aggregate be represented by a negatively sloped demand curve. The
argument is analogous to those made with regard to the effect of
income changes, of which economists have long been aware:

> "regardless of the decision rule used . . . , a decrease in real
> income necessarily decreases the amount spent of at least
> one commodity, and the average percentage change in
> expenditures on all commodities must equal the percentage
> decrease in income."[5]

Becker argues that "a change in opportunities resulting from a
change in relative prices also tends to produce a systematic response, regardless of the decision rule."[6] The survival argument
advanced by Alchian as a basis for the assumed rationality of firms
is shown to be an instance of this general line of reasoning.[7]

The argument is seductive as far as it goes, for it suggests that
we can dispense with the study of individual decision making. But
it supposes that individuals accurately recognize the options facing
them and their prices, and that assumption is plainly unrealistic
in a number of circumstances. This is the reason why, even for the
purpose of economic analysis, the study of decision making, nor-
matively as well as descriptively, is still relevant.

The Theory of Decision Making

Introduction

The economist's idea of rational choice has traditionally been translated by what Kirsch[8] calls *closed models*. This term is used where within the framework of the decision model no consideration is given to how the decision problem arises, how information is acquired, and how the environment influences the unfolding of the decision-making process.[9] Closed models are typically focused on the identification of the optimal choice in situations where the conceivable alternatives, the likelihood of uncertain contingencies, and the preference structure of the decisionmaker as well as his decision rule are given.

While this approach might seem to suppress some real problems in what it assumes to be given, it has allowed mathematicians to develop a theory of decision making of considerable generality and with great promise for practical application in a normative sense. It has also enabled those concerned with its descriptive accuracy to pinpoint their doubt more precisely and to conduct experiments about the nature and the degree of the discrepancy between theory and observations.[10]

A Simple Model Without Uncertainty

In the simplest situation the individual is faced with a choice from among a series of possibilities (such as purchasing various commodities at their respective prices), each of which procures him a certain net benefit (or satisfaction or profit). The decision model assumes that under these circumstances he can compare any two options, that he can systematically express a preference for one of them (consistency) and that these preferences are transitive (i.e., that if A is preferred to B and B to C, then A is preferred to C as well). The three assumptions combined imply that all possibilities can be ranked in a simple order. The decision rule is simply to choose the highest ranked one.

Unobjectionable though this model may appear, its accuracy as a description of how humans choose is questionable. Psychological studies have shown that people's preferences are not always consistent or transitive.[11] Initially, it was thought that these objections could be met and the theory preserved by introducing the so-called just-noticeable-differences (j.n.d.). People have difficulty in distinguishing between closely similar items, and it was thought that this would lead to inconsistency and by extension to intransitivity. For differences exceeding the level of a j.n.d., the theory would still hold.

A further objection to the model is that it will handle only unidimensional comparisons. In comparing two houses we might, for instance, take into account that one is close to work but has a small garden, whereas the other has a large garden but is much farther away. The model assumes that for the purpose of the comparison, we can resume the two dimensions in a single index. Support for such a view is provided by N. H. Anderson's information integration theory.[12] Shepard,[13] in a classic article on the subject, believes that this is plainly unrealistic, and Slovic et al., in their review article, consider Anderson's theory as a descriptive approximation only.[14] An integration of profit considerations with, let us say, human-relations aspects in a business decision is "uneasy" for the decisionmakers involved, as many empirical studies have shown. Be that as it may, the model might still be useful as a norm for dealing with those values that are more readily amenable to a common denominator, typically money.

The Introduction of Uncertainty in Decision Making

A last and important practical limitation of the model is that it does not handle uncertainty, typically the key question in daily life. The problem is how to make an optimal choice among options, some of which depend only on one's own actions, while others are affected by uncertain contingencies as well. Over a large number of repetitions, one might be indifferent between the success multiplied by the probability of its occurrence and an immediate payment in the same amount. But in practical situations one faces the unique rather than the repetitive case. Under those conditions most people prefer a sure (certain) payment over a contingent one, a lottery, whose expected value is the same or even slightly higher. Conversely, they prefer as a rule a certain small loss (such as an insurance premium) over the risk of a catastrophic one, even if the expected value of the latter is smaller than the former.[15] Technically this is expressed by the statement that the utility of an uncertain gain or loss is generally not the same to people as that of a certain payment of an amount equal to the expected monetary value of that gain or loss.

The Subjective Expected Utility Model

The solution to the problem of handling certain as well as uncertain options in decisions consists of replacing the uncertain events by their certainty equivalent, in terms of expected utility to the decisionmaker or, at the limit, of expected monetary value. Once such substitutions have been made, the choice problem reverts to a straightforward, though possibly elaborate and technically complex, question of identifying the best of various courses of action in a riskless world. This procedure is the basis for the so-called S.E.U. (subjective expected utility) model of decision making.[16] The S.E.U. model underlies many of the practical procedures designed to help business people to make better decisions.[17] In such a context it raises operational problems, for instance, how to elicit the expected utility functions of decisionmakers and how to assess the probability of various contingencies;[18] both of these issues introduce substantial amounts of subjectivity in the procedure. Furthermore, the decision problem must frequently be simplified to bring it to manageable proportions. The choice of contingencies to be ignored is another tricky problem in practice. We need not go into these problems here.

The S.E.U. model can be enriched by allowing for the possibility of considering sequences of acts by the decisionmaker and natural events outside his control. Suppose, for example, that a farmer has the choice of planting one of two kinds of wheat, the first rather valuable but tender, the second more sturdy but less valuable. Under normal conditions the first crop will fetch 100, but if there are cold spells only 40; for the second kind these figures are 80 and 60, respectively. If nothing can be said about the probability of cold spells, one chooses among such strategies as minimizing conceivable loss or, on the contrary, going after maximal gain.[19] If some indication of the probability of cold spells is available, one may replace sequences involving uncertainty by their certainty equivalent. If the cold spells occur one year out of ten, the expected monetary value of growing the first kind of crop is equal to 94

(.9 × 100 plus .1 × 40). The corresponding figure for the second crop is 78, and the best choice is therefore the first option.

The interesting thing is that this entire decision problem in its turn can be thought of as part of a larger one in which the farmer considers whether to stay in farming or go into some other trade for that year. Here the global value of the farming option is that associated with the best choice within its range, in this case 94. A similar value can be calculated for the other option(s) and the best one retained. Generally the model allows one to solve quite intricate decision problems by breaking them down into smaller units. The problem is mapped out as a tree, at the root of which is the initial decision to be made. Each option (branch) gives rise to a series of possible states of nature, each represented by a branch. Upon each such contingency, i.e., at the terminus of each state-of-nature branch, the decisionmaker faces a new choice, each option of which is represented by a branch; each of these branches, in turn, at its terminus may give rise to a further range of contingencies (branches), and so on until the analysis stops.

In time the world will evolve according to one of the possible scenarios represented by a sequence of branches, going from the root to the side of the tree that is fully branched out. The analysis proceeds in the reverse direction. One first determines the best choice for each of the decisions that occur latest in time, then determines the expected value or utility of the contingency immediately preceding that decision; this value in turn serves to determine the optimal choice among options at a yet earlier state, and so on until one reaches the root of the tree. It is important to note that the procedure used for analyzing the decision at the root of the tree has been applied in all stages leading up to it. The tree can be partitioned into subtrees and these again into subsubtrees without loss of quality in the analysis. The analysis is, in other words, fully decomposable, and this is a very powerful feature of the model.

Descriptive Inadequacy of the S.E.U. Model

In analyses of this kind, it frequently happens that events at one stage of the sequence are related to some that were known earlier. If the farmer, in the example above, had at his disposal an expert long-range weather forecast or if he knew that a mild winter, such as occurred that year, would be followed by a cold summer half of the time, the likelihood of a cold summer in his calculations and hence his decision would be different. In fact, the prospect of a different decision after expert advice might in itself justify an analysis to see if its cost was compensated by increased expected utility. In all these cases initial information about probabilities is revised in the light of subsequent new sources. To make optimal use of the new information to correct the old, the S.E.U. model prescribes the so-called Bayesian rule.[20] The mechanics of this rule are somewhat involved, and the only reason to mention it is that psychologists have found repeatedly that people, left to their intuitive devices, systematically violate the Bayesian rule: They do not "learn" as much from experience as the rule would allow.[21]

This finding is especially disturbing, since the subjective probabilities that people use — we noted earlier that objective values are frequently unavailable — are observed to deviate from their objective values, where these are known. They tend to overestimate low probabilities and underestimate high ones.[22] These tendencies should be explained, according to a recent review article, in the light of the more general finding that "people appear to prefer strategies that are easy to justify and do not involve reliance on relative weights, trade-off functions, or other numerical computations."[23] The S.E.U. model can no longer be maintained as a fully realistic description of decision making, although it is still useful in a normative way for designing procedures that improve decision making by limiting the extent to which human "biases" can affect the decisions.[24] Since we are investigating the tenability of the rationality assumption, we must turn now to other attempts to seek descriptive realism in the study of human decision making.

Theories of Bounded Rationality

In the decision theory exposed so far, the central problem is to determine which of several options facing the decision maker is optimal. The question of how he knows these options and acquires all the information required to determine the best choice is left untouched, presumably because in most circumstances the information-acquisition problem is thought to be negligible in comparison to that of optimization. Increasingly, however, it is realized that this aspect of decision making cannot generally be taken for granted and that decision theory should be extended to account for the fact that decisions are frequently made with far less than full information simply because it is exceedingly costly to acquire, or even not available at all.

Early Attempts to Introduce Information Cost in the S.E.U. Model

The first step in the direction of what Kirsch would call "open" models of decision making was taken within the S.E.U. paradigm, in the study of optimal sampling decisions in statistical theory.[25] The question of whether to draw a further sample or of how large a sample to draw should be decided according to that theory on the basis of a comparison of the expected precision gains in the solution of the substantive problem and the marginal cost of further or larger samples. If samples include not only strategically spread observations of members of some population, but also expert opinions, the methodology developed for sampling decisions is applicable to such questions as whether to consult an expert in our farmer's problem above.

Two important assumptions are made in this procedure. The first is that one can compare the cost of drawing the sample and its benefits in increased precision. Practically, this means that these two factors must be amenable to a common denominator, usually money. It is open to question whether such a conversion can always be undertaken without substantial loss of precision, especially in cases involving personal effort or gains.[26] Moreover, the procedure makes another, be it more modest, information assumption: The decisionmaker must know the cost and the possible outcomes and reliability of the sampling process. Yet in many circumstances we adopt an information-gathering strategy whose promise we could express not nearly so specifically.[27] A more fundamental revision of decision theory with regard to information acquisition is therefore in order if it is to maintain descriptive adequacy. Attempts to revise decision theory in this sense have moved the subject increasingly away from the formalization of the idea of the rational man of economics and studies of the discrepancy between this and observed decision making to the psychological underpinnings of the latter.[28] One of the earliest moves in this direction was made by H. A. Simon.[29] His name is associated with the term used as the title of this section, *theories of bounded rationality*, by which he means those theories of decision making that incorporate constraints on the information-processing capacities of the actor.[30]

Simon's Critique of Classic Decision Theory

Simon's objection to conventional decision theory is twofold. Humans cannot in general be expected to hold the information necessary to construct the entire decision tree proposed by the theory, and, even if they did, the task of constructing such a tree would in many cases far exceed their mental capacity and could at any rate not be accomplished in the time available in practice for reaching a decision.[31] It is unrealistic to presume that in complex problems humans will be aware of all options open to them and of the consequences that might flow from each and their likelihood, that they will be able to value the outcome of such sequences appropriately by anticipation, and that they could integrate all these pieces of information in anything like the fashion prescribed by S.E.U. decision theory. Simon argues this last point in reference to chess. If on average there are 30 legal moves at any given position in a game of chess, then there are for a move and its replies close to 10^3 possible continuations to consider. An entire game of 40 moves would have some 10^{120} possible sequences. Obviously, it is impractical at any given stage to consider the 10^{12} possible sequences that cover only four moves ahead. Thus, while the environment, in this case the position of the pieces on the chessboard, is perfectly certain, the chess player nevertheless faces uncertainty as a result of the inability to scrutinize all the implications of the situation at hand. Simon concludes: "But the result of the uncertainty, whatever its source, is the same: *approximation must replace exactness in reaching a decision.*"[32]

Key Features of Simon's Ideas on Bounded Rationality

In constructing a descriptive decision theory, we must therefore "conceive processes which are within the powers of human computation under the circumstances and within the time limits in which decisions are ordinarily made."[33] Simon submits that where complexity and uncertainty exclude global rationality in the traditional sense, people resort to two broad strategies to reduce the problem to manageable proportions. The first is approximate optimization. Here, "the description of the real-world situation is radically simplified until reduced to a degree of complication that the decision-maker can handle."[34] Features of the situation are selectively ignored until the remaining problem description agrees with a known procedure. This approach follows what Simon calls "Gresham's law of planning,"[35] which states that humans attempt to, or tend to, replace nonprogrammed activity with programmed or routine behavior. To predict how humans will make decisions, one must study how they solve the problem of finding an appropriate approximation for the problem at hand, i.e., which procedures are most likely to occur to them in their effort to simplify the problem. Such procedures may be individual or collective, conscious (deliberate) or not; they may have been developed by the decisionmaker himself or learned from others in some way. One must assume that in the "library" of such procedures that an individual builds up over time, only the most effective ones would be retained. Such an implicit selection would create a trend toward rationality in much the same way as Becker's evolutionary mechanism discussed in the first section.

The second strategy employed in the face of complex problems is to abandon the idea of finding a "maximizing" solution altogether, settling instead for "satisficing." In this case the decisionmaker sets an aspiration level, searches until an alternative that is satisfactory by that criterion is found, and selects that alternative.[36] The crucial element in this approach is the search process. Since the decision tree in these complex situations is not known a priori and would, at any rate, be unwieldy, the decisionmaker must have at his disposal procedures to conceive possible sequences selectively and evaluate them as they appear. Such a process of sequential evaluation does not admit extensive comparisons among options; a few at best can be remembered, and most must be disposed of (forgotten) after summary inspection. It is obvious that "best" under such circumstances can mean only "best found so far" or "first to exceed some rather demanding criterion" (aspiration level). Further rules are necessary to decide when to stop "looking in a certain direction" where no satisfactory solution appears and generally when to stop searching altogether, i.e., when no satisfactory solution can be expected to appear or when the prospect of finding a better one is too small to be worth the effort or the cost. Simon observes that, theoretically,

> A satisficing procedure can often be turned into a procedure of optimizing by introducing a rule for the optimal amount of search, or, what amounts to the same thing, a rule for fixing the aspiration level optimally. Thus, the aspiration level in

chess might be adjusted, dynamically, to such a level that the expected improvement in the move chosen, per minute of additional search, would just balance the incremental cost of the search.[37]

The adjustment process poses, however, some delicate measurement problems, and the effort required to optimize decision making in this sense would probably, in Simon's view, not be as worthwhile as an equivalent effort spent on improving the selectivity in methods that generate moves and evaluate them.[38]

We need not go into the nature of these methods for generating and evaluating sequences of actions and events, which Simon calls "heuristics." In general, they are rules that offer some promise of arriving at an improvement or a solution (in theorem proving), without guaranteeing such a result, as an algorithm does.[39] Simon submits that we have a variety of general heuristics at our disposal, but develop more specific and effective ones in each problem area of particular concern. People vary in their ability to develop such heuristics, and Simon observes in this regard that one may not always discover for oneself clever strategies that could be readily taught.[40]

One very general strategy we follow in dealing with complex problems is to break them down into smaller problems to which we then apply our arsenal of problem-solving methods anew. We have already encountered this phenomenon of decomposition of complex situations in the discussion of partial optimization in the pursuit of an overall improvement and in the breakdown of decision problems in the S.E.U. model. Decomposability of this kind is an essential feature of hierarchical systems. Simon argues, drawing examples from organizational design, empire building, problem solving and evolutionary biology, that such systems are the most effective method for structuring complexity,[41] in the sense that their functioning requires minimal communication among components and offers the best guarantees for survival when there is a failure in any of the subsystems. Hierarchical systems would be the choice of a rational designer where the process to be accomplished is decomposable.

Bounded Rationality in Political Decision Making

Hirschman and Lindblom have studied the implications of bounds on rationality in the area of policy making. Apart from the information problem to which reference was already made, the complexity here may stem from the pursuit of several, possibly conflicting, objectives at once.[42] Substantial departures from comprehensive understanding are both inevitable and desirable on specific grounds. Hirschman and Lindblom argue that "exposition of [such departures] serves . . . to formalize our perceptions of certain useful problem-solving strategies often mistakenly dismissed as aberrations in rational problem solving."[43] The collection of strategies noted by Hirschman and Lindblom have become known as "disjointed incrementalism." Among them are these:

> Attempts at understanding are limited to policies that differ only incrementally from existing policy.
>
> Instead of simply adjusting means to ends, ends are chosen that are appropriate to available or nearly available means. . . .
>
> Problems are not "solved" but are repeatedly attacked.
>
> Analysis and policymaking are remedial — they move *away* from ills rather than *toward* known objectives. . . .
>
> Analysis and policymaking are socially fragmented; they go on at a very large number of separate points simultaneously.[44]

Linblom notes also that:

> Individuals often agree on policies when they cannot agree on ends; . . . attempts to agree on ends or values often get in the way of agreements on specific policies.[45]

Bounded Rationality in Bureaucracy

A further extension of the idea of bounded rationality is given by Downs in his study of bureaucratic behavior. It is perfectly rational for a bureaucrat not to limit his search to the occasions when a problem must be dealt with urgently. A continuous, moderate search of the environment without focus on a specific problem allows the bureaucrat to set his aspiration levels appropriately and may provide him with useful heuristics to be applied in the context of a specific problem. Focused search of substantially increased intensity becomes necessary when a change in the environment creates a "problem" for which the existing approach is inadequate or when the general scan reveals the possibility of substantially improved solutions.

In general, search is directed first at possibilities similar to familiar ones. Only if no satisfactory solution is found will less familiar areas be examined. As time constraints become severe and no satisfactory solutions appear to be forthcoming, the individual is faced with a conflict situation that he can solve by a variety of forms of emotional behavior (aggressiveness, repression and other neurotic postures)[46] or by adjusting his aspiration level. This last option, while allowing the individual to arrive at a decision in the short run, exposes him to the risk of conflicts after the decision (remorse), which Festinger designates with the term *cognitive dissonance*.[47] Efforts to reduce such conflicts tend to be biased in that they are meant to justify the actual choice and reduce the importance of discordant information.[48]

How the aspiration levels are set is of central importance to the quality of decision making and problem solving. Simon believes that in the long run, aspiration levels are adjusted to actual performance.[49] The question has been studied independently by experimental psychologists.[50] No clear picture emerges from this literature. Kirsch, in summing up his review of it, states that the decisionmaker seems to take into account not only past experiences (as in reinforcement learning through success and failure) but also his expectations about the future and information gathered during the current search process.[51]

Recent Assessment of the Idea of Bounded Rationality

A "Festschrift" for Herbert Simon published in the Fall 1978 issue of the *Bell Journal of Economics* has been the occasion of an overall review of his work, in particular in the area of bounded rationality.[52] March's article and Simon's own are of special interest in this light.[53] The issue as a whole makes clear how varied are the fields in which consideration of bounds on rationality leads to interesting refinements of the analysis. There are contributions on the size of business firms, on the forces generating and limiting concentration, on obligational markets and the mechanics of inflation, as well as references to work in organizational theory. Simon himself reviews the fields where his idea of bounded rationality has led him — operations research and management science, artificial intelligence, computational complexity, cognitive simulation — and the effect that it is creating there. Clearly, the idea of bounded rationality appears to capture something of consequence in human intelligence. In spite of the interest generated by Simon's ideas, March observes that twenty years after their initial presentation, there is still no unified, widely accepted theory of choice.[54] Nonetheless, research sparked by Simon's early publications has certainly broadened our understanding of decision processes, and the idea of bounded rationality is, in March's view, accepted as a description of how people choose.[55] It has stimulated a good deal of research, most of it by psychologists, but some by economists and others as well. The interest of the concept of bounded rationality is that it does not imply a radical rejection of classical decision theory, at least not if one views, as Simon does,

> the differences between perfect rationality and bounded
> rationality as explicable consequences of constraints [namely,
> on the availability of information and on human beings as
> information processors and problem solvers].[56]

Simon believes his ideas on bounded rationality to be most consequential in fields that are "too complex, too full of uncertainty, or too rapidly changing to permit the objectively optimal actions to be discovered and implemented."[57] In these areas the relevant focus is not the optimal solution (which cannot be determined), but rather the procedures used to reach decisions: What basis do we have to believe that these procedures will generally lead to the best available solutions and to adopt them in practice? This leads logically to the notion of "procedural rationality," which Simon describes as:

> the rationality of a person for whom computation is the
> scarce resource — whose ability to adapt successfully to the
> situations in which he finds himself is determined by the
> efficiency of his decision-making and problem-solving
> processes.[58]

We believe that this line of thinking might well be fruitful to the analysis of law. Procedural considerations are paramount in law; the relevant questions would be whether particular procedures can be shown to be justified by the need to reach a decision in limited time in the face of information input that is overly abundant or, on the contrary, not available or not reliable.

In his contribution to the Simon issue, March has extended the idea of bounded rationality to cover not only the calculation of the consequences of actions, but also the goals themselves. There is ample evidence that people tend to adopt imperfectly specified goals, goals that are inconsistent or that change over time. Moreover, such "oddities" are maintained even when attention is drawn to them. How could such observations be accommodated in a theory of rational behavior? March's answer is that these phenomena could be explained as rational adjustments to limitations on human memory organization and ability to process information. People appear to make the best of the endowments provided by nature. Very succinctly March states the point as follows:

> Human beings have unstable, inconsistent, incompletely evoked, and imprecise goals at least in part because human abilities limit preference orderliness. If it were possible to be different at reasonable cost, we probably would want to be.[59]

From here he goes on to draw some consequences of his thesis, such as that one must guess future preferences and that tastes are continually developed or constructed. This leads to familiar conundrums, such as:

> How do we act sensibly now to manage the development of preferences in the future when we do not have now a criterion for evaluating future tastes that will not itself be affected, by our actions?[60]

Inevitably one is drawn to prescriptions of moral philosophy.

All in all, it would seem that the ideas of bounded rationality allow one to bring within the purview of scientific study aspects of human choice of which one is intuitively aware but that cannot in an obvious way be accommodated within classical decision theory as it is usually applied. Bounded rationality pinpoints as critical some aspects of choice that are likely to be neglected in traditional decision-theoretic analysis. While in Simon's view bounded rationality can be fitted in a generalized theory of perfect rationality, it is important to stress its advantages in comparison with the S.E.U. model. The problems of inconsistency and intransitivity, fatal in the latter, are perfectly understandable in the former. The requirement that all conceivable options be comparable (on a single scale) and reduced into a single rank order is abandoned under bounded rationality. Thus, objects with multiple attributes can be handled comfortably; for each attribute aspiration levels are set, and search continues until an object satisfies them all. Of course, if no such object appears, aspiration levels for some attributes may have to be adjusted, and this involves some comparison among them. But that is a less strenuous assumption than a comparison of *all* attributes required to produce a single scale for *all* options. Finally, the manner in which in the S.E.U. model one "learns from experience" requires substantial and sophisticated information processing that is unlikely to take place in human minds, as will be argued in the next section. In all, then, bounded rationality seems to add realism to standard decision theory. But it should be added that this realism is bought at the price of reduced predictive power. No longer shall we able to infer from a few simple postulates how people will decide in reality when problems are complex or unwieldy.

Recent Observational Evidence on Bounds of Rationality

Intuitive Assessment of Probabilities

In their review of the literature on decision making since 1971, Slovic, Fischoff and Lichtenstein state that "almost every descriptive study of probabilistic thinking has attempted to determine how the underlying cognitive processes are molded by the interaction between the demands of the task and the limitations of the thinker."[61] Many of the ideas for this new emphasis in the psychological literature are due to Tversky and Kahneman, who demonstrate three judgmental heuristics that determine intuitive assessment of probabilities in a variety of circumstances. The three approaches, labeled representativeness, availability and anchoring, and the evidence supporting their postulation are lucidly summarized in a recent article by these two authors.[62]

In judging probabilities such as the chance that object B belongs to class A or that process A will generate event B, humans rely on the extent to which B is *representative* of A — that is, the degree to which B resembles A.[63] Asked to judge the likelihood that a person of whom one is given a short description belongs to a certain profession, humans tend to find this all the more probable as the description resembles the stereotype of the profession. In reaching such a conclusion, they are typically *in*sensitive to the prior probability — that is, the overall frequency of that profession in the population — a factor that, according to the decision models reviewed above, ought to affect their judgment. Similarly, people appear to be insensitive to sample size and the associated reliability considerations, where the outcome of the sampling procedures tends to confirm the conclusion they expected. They are also subject to the "gambler's fallacy"; after a series of "heads" on the throw of a fair coin, they expect the likelihood of a "tail" on the next throw to be much better than 50 percent. These peculiarities are not limited to uneducated people. Research psychologists were shown to have unwarranted confidence in the evidentiary value of small samples if they appeared to be representative of the populations from which they were drawn, a phenomenon termed the "law of small numbers" by Tversky and Kahneman.[64]

Availability refers to a heuristic as a result of which people judge an event to be more likely or frequent if it is easy to imagine it or to recall relevant instances. Tversky and Kahneman give the following two examples:

> . . . one may assess the risk of heart attack among middle-aged people by recalling such occurrences among one's acquaintances. Similarly, one may evaluate the probability that a given business venture will fail by imagining various difficulties it could encounter.[65]

While the actual frequency of occurrence substantially determines availability in most cases, other, irrelevant factors may also affect it. Among these would be familiarity with the event, salience and recency of its last occurrence. To see the power of this last factor, recall that most drivers become more careful when they see a car overturned by the side of the road. Similarly, the risk of a dangerous expedition is assessed by imagining contingencies with which it is not equipped to cope. Macaulay's observation that most businessmen prefer not to spell out all but the most common contingencies — much to the horror of their legal counsel — must no doubt be explained in this light.[66]

By *anchoring* is meant an approach to probability assessment whereby some value is set as an initial approximation — anchor — of that probability, which is then adjusted in subsequent steps on the basis of additional information. Obviously, the way in which the problem is initially presented will affect the "anchor"; its adjustment will, similarly, much depend on the order of presentation of the additional information and is in practice insufficient by standards of the S.E.U. model. In an experiment, subjects were asked how many African nations were member of the U. N. As an introduction they were asked to state whether the number was higher or lower than some initial value, suggested by the experimenter, which for one group was given as 10, for another as 65. The average estimates made by the two groups were 25 and 45, respectively. Similarly, when asked to give a quick estimate of $8 \times 7 \times 6 \times 5 \times 4 \times 3 \times 2 \times 1$, subjects typically gave a higher number than $1 \times 2 \times 3 \times 4 \times 5 \times 6 \times 7 \times 8$; moreover, both estimates were substantially lower than the actual value. Tversky and Kahneman submit that imperfections due to anchoring explain why subjects overestimate the probability of conjunctive and underestimate that of disjunctive events, tendencies that have been observed in other experiments. They believe that these biases may significantly affect planning of complex sequences of events. Since the success of some enterprise depends on a sequence — a conjunction — of events, the tendency to overestimate would lead to undue optimism. Conversely, a complex system, such as a nuclear reactor or a human body, may fail if any of its components do, a disjunction of possible events. Anchoring would here lead to underestimation of the actual risk of failure. Tversky and Kahneman also show that the anchoring heuristic will make people state overly narrow confidence intervals, which reflect an unwarranted degree of faith in the accuracy of those values, for their estimates.

Slovic et al., in reviewing other psychological studies supporting these findings, conclude that people tend to be overconfident in their judgments.[67] The puzzling question is why they maintain this confidence in the face of incongruent reality. Slovic et al. suggest that the environment is often not structured to show people their own limits; many decisions are relatively insensitive to past errors in estimation, and most people extract from reality little or no feedback allowing them to correct those errors. Tversky and Kahneman write that:

> statistical principles are not learned from everyday experience because the relevant instances are not coded appropriately. . . . It is not natural to group events by their judged probability.[68]

Why, then, do we use these heuristics at all? It is tempting to introduce irrationality, but Tversky and Kahneman offer an explanation that unwittingly reminds one of Becker's precept: "These heuristics are highly economical and usually effective."[69]

Intuitive Choice Processes

The decision models reviewed in the second section of this chapter focus on the ranking of alternatives as a preliminary step to choice. Slovic et al. argue that psychological research moves away from the idea of ranking and focuses on less demanding forms of information processing for choice.

One of the better-known models advanced along these lines is Tversky's theory of *elimination by aspects*. The theory states that, faced with complex choices, people may resort to a strategy of choosing by eliminating all but one of the conceived options. The process of elimination is accomplished by successively selecting features that a desirable solution should have and eliminating options that are unsatisfactory on any one of these. Which features are selected for this purpose is, of course, of critical importance to the ultimate choice. On this subject, Tversky has the following to say:

> For virtually any available alternative, no matter how inadequate it might be, one can devise a sequence of selected aspects or, equivalently, describe a state of mind that leads to the choice of that alternative.[70]

The process of elimination by aspects may therefore on occasion be quite hazardous. Advertising and, generally, sales efforts can be designed to induce the desired state of mind by stressing certain features of the commodity and suggesting their use as criteria in the elimination process. Yet, as in the discussion of their heuristics, Tversky stresses that in the face of an overwhelming amount of relevant information, it is in aggregate quite efficient to employ a strategy of elimination. It generally provides a "good approximation to much more complicated compensatory models [i.e., as were discussed in the second section] and could thus serve as a useful simplification procedure."[71] In reviewing similar work by other psychologists, Slovic et al. state that:

features of the task that complicate the decision, such as
incomplete data, incommensurable data dimensions,
information overload, time pressures, and many alternatives,
seem to encourage strain-reducing, non-compensatory
strategies. . . . In general, people appear to prefer strategies
that are easy to justify and do not involve reliance on relative
weights, trade-off functions, or other numerical
computations.[72]

Thus in an experiment in which subjects were forced to choose between alternatives that were of equal value to them, rather than choosing at random, they would follow the easy and defensible strategy of selecting the alternative that was superior on the more important dimension. Considerations such as these are highly relevant if one is to forecast how people should be expected to choose among various insurance policies, offering coverage of different risks and with different deductibles,[73] or how they will react to various infinitesimal but serious risks in "hazardous" products.[74]

Conclusion

The rationality postulate in economic theory serves to attribute to people a predictable line of conduct and allows one to anticipate the unfolding of their interaction. Traditionally the postulate was held to mean that people would make their decisions so as to maximize their utility or satisfaction. Mathematical decision theory allows one to determine which decision will maximize utility under given circumstances and hence is rational in the just-mentioned sense. Because of its generality, the parsimony of its assumptions, and the precision of the inferences it allows, decision theory must count as a major scientific accomplishment.

In spite of its obvious qualities, decision theory has recently become the subject of doubts. These doubts touch both its descriptive and its normative use. Descriptively it has become obvious, as psychological evidence has been amassed, that humans frequently do not make the decisions the theory would predict and that even where they do, they arrive at that result in ways other than those prescribed by decision theory. And even the normative use of the theory has come under fire, on the grounds that it requires people to state their preferences, order them, and use this information in their decisions in a manner well beyond what humans can be reasonably expected to accomplish.

In both instances the reservations about classical decision theory stem from its implicit assumption that there are no constraints on human ability to process information (for the purpose of making decisions) and to provide information on personal preferences. This is, in different disguise, the assumption of the costlessness of information discussed earlier. The central thesis of this text is that this assumption is generally unrealistic and that its abandonment will lead to significant changes in the predictions drawn from economic theory. In the field covered in this chapter, that of information processing, the thesis implies that limitations of human memory impose "production costs" on information. As a result, fully rational decisions of the postulated kind would frequently not be "cost effective" in terms of the tradeoff proposed in Chapter 5. The literature on bounded rationality can be seen as a refinement of decision theory in the light of the costliness of information. Recent psychological studies seem to lend support to such a refinement.

Acceptance of the idea of constraints on rationality does not entail rejection of classic decision theory. In many circumstances this theory is used to describe collective phenomena for which, as a result of aggregation over large numbers, it still provides a good fit. Yet where the choices of individuals are to be predicted and the substance is complex or unwieldy or where it involves small probabilities, deviations from perfect rationality must be expected. What form such deviations will take cannot always be as easily predicted as rational choice can be inferred from decision theory. Bounded rationality is quite varied in the manifestations recognized so far, and more theoretical and empirical work is yet to be done.[75]

Preliminary though the theory of bounded rationality may be at present, we expect it to affect the economic analysis of law at several points. In Chapter 4 we referred to Calabresi's observation that the cheapest cost avoider is not always the person who can physically control the incidence of accidents at the lowest cost. Where small probabilities or complex variables are involved, the quality of information processing may vary substantially between the parties, and this factor alone could determine our choice of who should bear the accident burden. It is quite conceivable that between individuals on the one hand and companies on the other, a substantial difference of this kind would exist. Further observations will have to settle the issue, but consideration of the information constraints alerts us here to what the relevant questions are.

We also expect a role for considerations of bounded rationality in areas where consumers face choices involving complex issues or small probabilities (hazardous products, for instance). The presence of such features does not *necessarily* mean that consumers will make seriously nonoptimal choices, as Schwartz and Wilde argue persuasively,[76] but the possibility is there and merits study. This question will be raised again in the next chapter.

Bounded rationality ideas should also be useful in the study of what one might call complex decision making. In the economic analysis of law, two outstanding examples of it come to mind, namely, decision making by regulators and by judges. With regard to regulation it has frequently been observed that it is not clear what objective it seeks to achieve in terms understandable to economists. "Promoting the public interest" may refer to objectives derivable from efficiency (such as correcting market failure) or to redistribution of wealth. Where more precise objectives are stated, the administration of the area in question is frequently left within the executive responsibility of government.[77] One must conclude that regulatory structures are created primarily where the activities to be regulated are not in this sense "programmable." Since regulation is instituted by political authority, one must infer that the problems to be dealt with are of a political nature and yet more cheaply dealt with outside the political sphere.[78] Why this is so could be the object of an analysis focusing on the cost of balancing the power of interest groups per industry (in a regulatory agency) or across many industries at once (in the political sphere). This analysis might lead to the type of consideration suggested by March's article discussed in the third section. More mundanely, it should be noted that the "information-processing capacity" of the political sphere (Parliament) cannot be easily expanded, whereas one can readily create such capacity in the form of new regulatory agencies.

It has been observed that it is difficult to formulate meaningful performance standards for regulatory agencies.[79] Yet, if one accepts that the agency seeks to avoid its own uselessness or abolition in the presence of fuzzy objectives, one would expect it to set itself the task of arbitrating among the various interest groups in its domain in a way that avoids having a problem "bounce" into the political sphere.[80] From this it follows that it must hear all groups that could make themselves heard in the political sphere, and that it must hear them on all issues that to any one group weigh sufficiently that it would make itself heard politically if it felt wronged by the regulators. Such calculations are, of course, too complex to perform, and simplifying procedural rules will be adopted instead. Moreover, the acceptance of the compromise between opposed interests no doubt requires persuasion by the regulators, if March is correct in his thesis of how bounded rationality affects the formation of tastes.[81] This aspect of their activity would be reflected in procedural rules, such as the required motivation of decisions, open hearings, the publication of decisions, and a certain degree of consistency from one decision to the next.

Other aspects of bounded rationality may be expected in the ways in which the regulators cope with complex information or information regarding small probabilities. The recent FAA decision to ground all DC-10 aircraft for a substantial period of time smacks of the "availability" heuristic discussed in the fourth section. All in all, the functioning of regulatory agencies would seem to be fruitfully amenable to the type of analysis proposed in this chapter.

The last-mentioned area in which ideas of bounded rationality may be expected to be enlightening is that of judicial decision making. In Posner's analysis of law, this question is treated rather unsatisfactorily. The literature on judicial reasoning is not accounted for in his analysis, and to the question — central in his view — of what judges maximize, his answer that they "seek to impose their preferences, tastes, values, etc. on society"[82] rings somewhat hollow. Nowhere does one sense that judicial decision making is a difficult and delicate task, imposing a variety of not easily perceived constraints, as accounts of it tend to present it.[83]

We believe that judicial decision making should be analyzed somewhat along the lines proposed above. It may be useful to divide the arguments into two analytical steps, the first being the question of why judges would want to contribute to the creation of a relatively coherent, yet adaptable web of rules and the second why they should perceive their task as the pursuit of various values subject to canons of interpretation and other constraints formulated as rules of thumb.

To answer the first question, one must consider what sets courts apart from other dispute-resolving agencies. Historically, according to Posner and Landes, courts were clearly in competition with other, arbitrationlike institutions.[84] It was not until later in their development that courts were granted a monopoly on some aspects of dispute resolution, initially the enforcement of decisions.

Where courts compete with other dispute-resolving institutions, they can be expected to reach decisions that will not indispose their clientele. Landes and Posner, in "Adjudication as a Private Good," show that under such contraints decisionmakers are likely to issue fuzzy rules rather than clear ones by which parties can guide their future conduct.[85] Yet substantial certainty and precision in the law became valuable to private parties as commercial organizations grew more complex and investments had to be planned over longer periods. Hence one expects pressure from these parties on the political authority for law with these qualities. As the political body itself could not issue specific rules in the quantity required by commerce and trade, it was only natural that ways should be sought to enable the courts, among dispute-resolving institutions, to assume this role.

For courts to issue relatively precise and certain rules, they must be effectively shielded from pressure by parties to the disputes they have to resolve. This condition is satisfied by judicial independence. Moreover, parties who stand to lose by the court's decision must not have the power to escape its jurisdiction. The courts must have monopoly of dispute resolution in the last resort. The requirements of independence and monopoly have been granted by political authority.

The courts, to play their role effectively and to maintain their powers, must now avoid dissatisfaction among parties to the disputes that they resolve beyond a threshold at which these parties will seek political curtailment of judicial powers. The curtailment may take the form of special legislation changing the case law or the creation of parallel dispute-resolving agencies.

The key question, therefore, is to avoid letting dissatisfaction reach the threshold for political action. Of course, where the costs of going to the courts rise very substantially, it may well become cheaper to seek law through the political authority. But this should be the exception. On substantive grounds dissatisfacton might grow in two, diametrically opposed ways. Where the law was too uncertain, it would hamper trade, and it would be to the advantage of all to seek greater certainty.[86] On the opposite side of the spectrum, one can imagine that developments in society or in the technology it uses make it advantageous to have a change in the law that the courts cannot produce in time. Again there is a Pareto gain for all to be made by seeking change through political channels.[87]

We can now address the question of why judicial reasoning should be couched in terms of the pursuit of various values, such as certainty, justice and others, subject to a variety of canons of interpretation. The constraints under which the courts act in the hypotheses set out in the two previous paragraphs define a very complex optimization problem, for which the basic data — on the different kinds of dissatisfaction — must be gauged intuitively. It is only natural that this problem should be simplified and codified in practices and rules of thumb. Even the pursuit of the goal of certainty in law is itself a question fraught with complexity. To maintain the coherence of legal rules over large areas of law is no mean task and may itself call for the sort of procedures we associated earlier with bounded rationality. To weigh the results obtained in the pursuit of this goal against at least minimal respect for other objectives, such as justice, is even more complex. Perhaps this task is simplified by setting intuitive standards for what are *not* acceptable decisions, a strategy akin to what was earlier discussed as "elimination by aspects." If this thesis is accepted, it is not at all surprising, nor irrational, for lawyers to say that in most disputes several, possibly opposed, decisions could be validly taken. The idea of a form of reasoning that is "noncontraignant" (not binding) is explicable in a theory of bounded rationality.[88] So is the idea of a set of generally — but not always — convincing arguments, such as is advanced by proponents of the "topoi."[89] There is room for further work here. All in all, we conclude that bounded rationality is a fruitful idea for the economic analysis of law.

CHAPTER 7

Search:

Information Acquisition in Markets

Kinds of Information in the Market

There are several things one might wish to know before purchasing some object. First, one might want to know the identity of one or more sellers who have the object in question for sale. For each seller further relevant information would be his price; the quality and other properties (features) of his ware; accessories that come with it; the terms on which the sale will take place (in particular for complex or costly items); in some cases, facilities for maintenance and availability of parts after the sale; delivery mode and date; and so on.

This enumeration is not meant to suggest that for any transaction the purchaser will want to acquire all this information. If he were applying the information tradeoff proposed in Chapter 5, he would inform himself only on those aspects for which the cost of his ignorance (a subsequent disappointment, for instance) exceeds what he has to spend to research them. It is obvious that the greater the amount involved in the transaction — or series of transactions — for which the search is undertaken, the higher the optimal amount to spend on searching and the more aspects to research. This perhaps explains why the economic literature on search has focused to a large extent on comsumer problems rather than, say, those of professional buyers for department stores. The substantial stakes involved for the latter justify measures to avoid the common information-deficiency problems that consumers face.

Inspection and Experience Features

The kinds of information identified above are not usually distinguished in the economic literature. Instead, one author, Nelson, distinguishes between what he calls "search" and "experience" goods.[1] By search goods he means those whose relevant qualities can be detected by inspection prior to purchase; experience goods, in contrast, reveal their qualities only in the course of normal use — that is, after purchase. The distinction appears to be fruitful since Nelson concludes his empirical study as follows:

> (1) There will be more monopoly for experience goods than for search goods, and more monopoly for durable than non-durable goods. (2) The recommendations of others will be used more for purchases of experience goods than search goods; advice will also be used more for durable than non-durable goods. (3) Stores that sell search goods will cluster more than stores that sell experience goods. (4) The ratio of retail advertising to national advertising will be greater for search goods than for experience goods. (5) Investory-sales ratio will be higher for stores selling search goods than for stores selling experience goods.[2]

While these results are interesting, the distinction they are thought to justify appears to be rather crude. Is it useful to propose a dichotomy where the study itself already recognizes a gradation of possibilities between the two polar cases? The problem is that many commodities are search goods in some respects, experience goods in others. It would therefore seem more fruitful to attach the qualification to the individual properties of the object. Thus one would distinguish "inspection" features and "experience" features of objects.

Credence Features

A further concept proposed in the literature is that of "credence" features — defined as properties that cannot be assessed even through prolonged normal use.[3] Only unusual circumstances would make them discernible. The value of safety features in cars, flammability of fabrics, likelihood of explosion of bottles, side effects of drugs, and dangers of toys to children are examples.

Since credence features frequently center around very unlikely contingencies, they raise special problems. Left to their own devices, people tend to misestimate the accurate values of the probabilities involved, as we saw in Chapter 6. If, in spite of this risk, people rely on their intuitive judgment of credence features, they will make nonoptimal choices. Yet if they are aware of the limitation and seek outside help, there is also a problem: Who can provide an adequate assessment, which involves large samples or even population statistics, and how can one ensure the trustworthiness of these assessments?

Diagnostic Information

Darby and Karni, in their classic article in this field,[4] cite as examples of "credence" information the services provided by a repairman who recommends that some part of a car or of a television set be replaced or by a surgeon who suggests that an appendix be removed. The client or patient cannot readily verify the appropriateness of such recommendations, as he is unfamiliar with the intricacies of the object on which the service is to be performed.

While there is clearly a problem for the client or patient, the analysis is hasty. It seems to us that, following Trebilcock et al. in their study of professional regulation,[5] one should distinguish in these and in other professional services between two phases or aspects. In the first the object is to identify the problem and the best way of dealing with it. The second phase is aimed at solving the problem itself. The first phase concerns information as a tradable commodity, the second a technical service comparable to others separately available in the market.

The joint provision of these two services is not a necessary condition. One can, for instance, have his car diagnosed by an agency that will not make the repairs. Physicians leave to pharmacists the provision of the drugs they prescribe, and ophthalmologists do not provide the spectacles they prescribe for their patients. Yet there are frequently good reasons for the joint provision. The diagnosis of a car's problems may require so much dismantling of the motor that the actual replacement of the defective part would be only a minor addition. The joint provision of diagnostic and surgical services may be justified by the great overlap in the knowledge required for each and by the difficulty of specifying the result of the initial analysis in sufficient detail for an independent surgeon to undertake the operation without repeating the analysis himself.

While the technical services may have a credence character and raise problems for that reason — consumers would not normally become aware of the quality of the repair work or the surgery for which they contract — it is the joint provision of information with the service itself that may lead to a conflict of interest. As provider of information one may have an interest in recommending technical services beyond what is strictly necessary. There exists a potential for "demand generation" where consumers cannot fully appraise the professional advice they receive. Whether this potential is in fact exploited only empirical work can tell.[6]

Trustworthiness of Information in the Market

The distinction between kinds of information made in the first section focuses on the degree to which a purchaser can rationally dispel his ignorance with respect to important features of the commodity whose acquisition he contemplates. In many instances the purchaser will not rely only on his own means of search, but will use information provided by others. This may be advantageous because of economies of scale and useful specialization in the production of information. But while such moves appear to increase the purchaser's search powers, the fruit may be poisoned if the information on which he relies is distorted by the supplier for the purpose of promoting the sale of some commodity. This risk is, of course, particularly great where the supplier provides the commodity itself as well as information on it. To be sure, where the distortion is too great, the purchaser will abandon this source of information and rely on other means of search, perhaps his own effort. But surely this point, disadvantageous to sellers and buyers alike, will not be reached. Thus, while there may be incentives to distort information in the market, there are opposite incentives not to exaggerate the distortion. We might now ask: Is there an "optimal amount of fraud,"[7] or, to look at it through the purchaser's eyes, an optimal level of credulity?

The Supplier's Incentive to Distort Information.   For a supplier to distort information in his favor — stating that prices are lower than they really are, promising quality that is not really there — the prospective gains must be higher than the prospective losses.[8] The gains are increased sales or profit; inflated promises increase demand beyond what it would have been for accurately informed purchasers. These gains are, of course, possible only if the purchaser does not immediately detect the "puffing" of which he is the victim. Immediate detection would make such a distortion ineffectual.[9]

The prospective losses to a supplier who distorts the information on his ware would seem to depend on three factors:

1. The likelihood that purchasers will discover the distortion,
2. The likelihood that they will cease to buy the product and encourage others to do the same,
3. The amount of business lost in the latter case.[10]

A few remarks will be made about each of these factors.

The third factor, which one might term future business, explains why fly-by-night operators have little incentive not to defraud their unsuspecting customers, whereas firms that have steady relations — "repeat business" — with their clients will very much hesitate to do so. One might think that those who sell to tourists fall into the first category, but tourists can communicate their bad experiences to other tourists via travel columns in newspapers and also through the intermediary of travel agents and travel guides.

The likelihood of discovery of the distortion depends on the amount of independent search that purchasers undertake. This depends in turn on the search-uncertainty balance that purchasers adopt, about which more will be said presently. It should be noted that the supplier's calculation of gains and losses does not depend on each purchaser's ability to discover distortions. Schwartz and Wilde have shown in a recent article[11] that even if most consumers are ill informed, sellers cannot exploit this ignorance, provided that a few customers do inform themselves (in their study, "shop around") and that suppliers cannot at reasonable cost distinguish informed from uninformed customers. Their argument, it seems to us, can be carried over to information concerning aspects of commodities other than their price.

If purchasers could readily identify those of the various sellers who distorted information, they could "punish" them by ceasing to buy their products and switching to honest suppliers. But if they could not easily make such distinctions, those sellers who would like to be honest would simply make less profit or have less business than their competitors.[12] Surely, they will heed competitive pressure and distort as much as the others. As a result the level of distortion would be fairly homogeneous among competitors. Purchasers would presumably treat this phenomenon as "noise" in their information channel. The upper limit to the noise would be reached where the information channel provided by the sellers had lost its comparative advantage — in terms of the search-uncertainty tradeoff — over other ways in which purchasers can inform themselves.

Will supplier information necessarily deteriorate to this minimal level? In a recent paper[13] Klein and Leffler suggest a way out for honest suppliers. Suppose, they argue, that some purchasers were willing to pay for the assurance that the supplier would honestly represent the quality of his ware to them. The price of this "insurance," which to the supplier takes the form of supracompetitive returns, should be set just so high that cheating would never be profitable for the seller; the loss of superprofitable repeat business would always more than offset the possible gains from cheating. The authors submit that substantial investment in advertising may signal to potential purchasers that the firm makes substantial profits, which in turn suggests that it offers quality insurance against payment. To put it differently, the image or reputation built up with the advertising acts as a capital asset with which it is possible to realize higher-than-competitive profits in the market. The seller will want to avoid its premature obsolescence, which would occur if consumers lost confidence in the quality of his product (or generally in the accuracy of the information he supplied about it).

The Purchaser's Incentive to Rely on Information Supplied by Others. For the purchaser to rely on information supplied by others, or more generally, to adopt a new mode of searching — a different information channel — in preference to his current ways, the new channel must allow him to reach a better search-uncertainty cost balance than the old one. This is simply an applicaiton of the theory proposed in Chapter 5.

The change may be advantageous in various circumstances. For instance, one information medium may be as readable and accessible as the other, but provide more reliable information. In terms of the tradeoff suggested in Chapter 5,[14] one would say that while the search-cost curves for the two media are the same, the uncertainty-cost reduction per unit searched is greater for the former than for the latter — that is, the uncertainty-reduction curve for the former lies below that for the latter. Similarly, two media may provide equivalent information, but one is cheaper or easier to find or more readable than the other. The search-cost curve for the former lies below that for the latter, with the same uncertainty-cost reduction curve. Hence the first medium would be preferred to the second. More complex combinations can be readily imagined.

It seems useful to consider information, or rather the informative medium, as a commodity itself. The usual considerations with respect to the choice among commodities then apply to it; one can shop around for it, and the amount of shopping around would vary with the value of the purchase. Where one intends to rely for a substantial period on a particular medium — a subscription to a trade journal or, for a newspaper, a contract with an existing network of foreign correspondents — more search is justified before the agreement is concluded. Once in place, the agreement is like a capital asset with the consequences discussed in Chapter 5.[15] One would rather tolerate some quality deviation than to break the contract and reinvestigate all the options.

Of the various properties of the information medium on which one would do research, the trickiest is perhaps its reliability. Supplier's identity, price and ease of access are easy to ascertain before purchase and to monitor subsequently. The quality of information — its reliablity — can be verified only at substantial cost, and, what is more, variations in it over the course of a long-term agreement can be concealed with ease. To assess the quality of information requires its comparison with information from an independent source.[16] Hence someone who intends to rely on information provided by someone else must decide how much to spend on "backup" information from a different source.[17] The choice involves a tradeoff between the cost of this second-level information and the reduction in uncertainty it makes possible with respect to the quality of the primary information source. This second-level uncertainty reduction depends on the (decreased) likelihood of deception by the primary source, multiplied by the cost of such deception where it occurs. Of course, one could imagine even higher-level backup provisions, but for reasons exposed in Chapter 5 with regard to McKenzie's point of an infinite information regress,[18] we will leave these out of consideration. Notice that even in the hypothesis advanced by Klein and Leffler, where one pays a higher price to a supplier in return for quality assurance, the need for backup information has not disappeared, but only decreased substantially. But at that level relatively common and inexpensive means of search would be adequate.

The foregoing considerations allow us to situate the earlier distinction between inspection, experience and credence features. Inspection features are those for which personal search can provide immediate backup for the information supplied by the seller. For experience features this same source of secondary information will also yield satisfactory results, but only over time. Hence some other source of information or of secondary information, if the supplier provides primary data, will have to be relied on. What these sources might be will be discussed in the next section. Credence features, finally, are those for which personal search is not an appropriate source of information. Outside sources will be essential here as well.

The immediate visibility of inspection features requires further comment. It is true that the price of a product or its color can be immediately ascertained upon inspection. Yet this does not mean that the potential for distortion in information provision is absent. A seller may well misleadingly advertise particular prices or colors that are interesting to his customers if, once they are in his store to buy, it is costlier for them to go to a competitor who has advertised a higher, but true price. And, who guarantees that the competitor has been honest? There are, of course, limits to this kind of trickery, which we explored earlier. But occasional deception on some products might well be profitable.

Some Modes of Information Acquisition

The topic of this section might be called somewhat fancily the structure of the information market. Several groups might act as producers in this market: the information user himself, alone or in collaboration with others, independent information providers, sellers of goods who inform on their wares, as well as the government. It seems fruitful first to consider in a general way the comparative advantages and disadvantages that each of these groups might have in supplying information for market transactions. This comparison sets the stage for an analysis of some of the forms or institutions through which information is made available in practice.

A General Comparison of Information Providers

In Chapter 2 we referred to the postulate of consumer sovereignty in economic analysis, which one might paraphrase crudely as the idea that ultimately individuals know best themselves what is good for them. Applied to the present context, it means that the last stage of the decision-making process, that in which options are compared and the best one is chosen, must remain with the individual.[19] But it would seem that delegation could take place in the other stages, such as gathering data, selecting from them the relevant information, formulating the different options and determining their implications for the decisionmaker, and so on. Since nature provides individuals with personal searching ability to deal with problems of information acquisition, delegation is worthwhile only if it is expected to outperform this base mode.

Cooperative Efforts by Consumers. Perhaps the easiest form of delegation occurs where one divides the field (or the stores) to be surveyed with some neighbors. Pooling of efforts makes it possible for each to cover for given effort a larger area than he could on his own. Since all members of the cooperative have an interest in accurate information, there is no problem of deception as discussed in the previous section. Yet the scheme has other weaknesses — namely, that as the number of participants increases, it becomes more and more difficult to ensure that all use the same standards for information gathering, especially where relatively "soft" information is at stake. A more serious problem, common to all cooperative ventures, is that with growing numbers some participants will be tempted to shirk — that is, to free ride — at least in part on the efforts of others.[20] This is perhaps why such ventures are relatively rare in reality.

Independent Agencies.   An independent agency avoids the free-rider problem. It collects the information in anticipation of trade and sells it to interested parties. Provided that it can control access to the information, free riding is excluded. The independent agency may also be advantageous when the kind of information to be provided is more easily collected or assembled by some than by others or if a division of labor promises economies of scale. Professionals and consultant agencies are examples of the first, data-processing departments in large firms instances of the second. The considerations that make a specialized independent agency viable are the same as apply to the production of ordinary physical commodities. Competition among agencies would insure the quality of information; there would be no problem of a systematic deceptive bias.

In reality, independent information-providing agencies are not always viable. In part the problem is the appropriability of information, already mentioned in Chapter 5. If, for instance, numerous consumers are interested in comparative tests of some commodity, such as cars, stereo equipment, or household appliances, the information can usually be generated at a reasonable cost per customer, but it is often not feasible to extract this cost from each consumer who actually acts on it. This problem is absent for the seller who provides both information and commodity and recovers the cost of the former in the price of the latter.

Sellers Providing Both Information and Commodity.[21]   There are several other reasons militating in favor of combining provision of information and commodity, in spite of the risk of deception discussed in the previous section.[22] In some instances the supplier already has the information available, and the cost of adding an intermediary turns out to be not worthwhile in extra benefits to the consumer. This explains perhaps why price advertising is generally undertaken by the supplier rather than an independent agency. Some newspapers produce lists of comparative prices, but this source of information seems marginal in comparison with what suppliers themselves provide. Since suppliers in these instances can take advantage of the scale economies involved in mass media, independent agencies are discouraged on this ground as well. Where sellers operate on a small scale or even an individual basis, there is ample scope for an intermediary, as the housing market seems to demonstrate.

In other instances the supplier, though he does not generate the information as part of the normal trade process, has a comparative advantage in generating it because he is the manufacturer of the product. Such would be the case for characteristics like the durability or the average energy consumption of a commodity. In other instances the very size of the manufacturer's enterprise allows it to undertake research that on a smaller scale could not be justified. This might be true for information on the hazardous qualities of drugs, for instance.

The Government.   The government, in intervening in the information market, has several potential advantages. It can attain economies of scale in research of the kind just mentioned. It operates at reduced transaction costs as it can impose uniform rules on numerous parties who in private agreements could not come nearly as easily to such a result. The government may thus induce uniform pricing methods, uniform grading, and other forms of standardization.

The government may also force suppliers to divulge information that they would have kept from private agencies and use this information to certify the presence of qualities or features. Darby and Karni submit that this information is unlikely to be very reliable, since government officials are subject to bribery as much as private agencies would be.[23] Firms would be tempted to offer such bribes in anticipation of the higher profits that a favorable rating would allow them to make. Whether this perverse hypothesis is in fact justified will have to be settled by empirical work. For the moment, we retain that the government has a comparative advantage in creating uniformity and in its enforcement powers. Besides, it can afford to produce information even where the cost cannot be recovered through prices in the market, but where there are social benefits to having it available.

Forms of Information Provision

It seems useful to regroup the observations to be made here under two — somewhat arbitrary — headings: the information channels and their content. The discussion focuses on the purchaser's problems and is meant to be illustrative, rather than exhaustive.

Information Channels. The purchaser's difficulty in gathering data can be alleviated by improved information channels. Foremost among these is advertising, but one might also consider personal canvassing of potential customers by (traveling) salesmen or by mail on the basis of mailing losts.

The term *advertising* covers, in the words of Comanor and Wilson in their important book on the subject, "a vast variety of kinds of messages, which have in common the characteristic that they are provided by the sellers of the product."[24] Advertising, in the view of these authors, aims at "providing a summary of the product to prospective customers."[25] The advertising message may give information on various product attributes and on its price. But most important, these authors add, "the messages provide information that the product is being advertised."[26]

True though these observations may be, we believe that advertising should first and foremost be seen as an improved information channel. Improvements in the content of what is to be communicated, such as the use of labels and brand names, would not normally as such be qualified as advertising, although advertising messages may stress this kind of information. As a mode of communication with potential customers, advertising distinguishes itself from personal canvassing in that its messages are uniform across the intended audience. This has two consequences. First, only information that need not be personalized can usefully be carried through advertising. The advertising medium will thus promote industries whose products have features with this characteristic. Moreover, one may expect — because of the great advantages of advertising as a channel — that advertisers will look for messages that, though uniform on the surface, can be interpreted by each client to his personal taste. The prevalence of "fuzzy" qualities in advertising must perhaps be explained in this manner. The second consequence of the uniformity of the advertising message across a large audience is that one expects to find it in particular in media with substantial economies of scale in dissemination. The risk in these economies of scale is that they give established firms, who enjoy the full extent of them, a competitive advantage over newcomers and thus help to create a "barrier to entry" in the industry.[27]

This in turn reduces or even stifles competition. This issue will be further discussed in the next section.

Given the low cost of advertising compared with *personal canvassing*, one would expect this last mode to be used only where the former will not have the desired effect. This would be the case where the service offered must be individually tailored to the customer or where the customer has difficulty using advertising because it is inaccessible or because of his low intelligence, language problems, or other handicaps in search. The aim of the traveling salesman is to conclude the agreement during his visit with the prospective customer. This puts the customer to the task of deciding in very short order whether the advantage of dispensing with further search for the commodity being offered outweighs the chances that such searching would reveal better deals. The salesman has, of course, an interest in downgrading this possibility, and the customer may on his own misperceive his potential for finding better deals, for reasons exposed in Chapter 6.[28] The "cooling-off period" introduced by consumer legislation may allow him to make a more accurate assessment of the pros and cons of the proposed purchase. It should be noted that the cooling-off period does not apply to purchases made by salesmen in stores or by those who come to the house on the customer's request. In these cases one would assume that the customer has been able to do enough preliminary searching to avoid being lured into an inconsidered deal.

Content. The most direct way of facilitating search by purchasers is to provide them with the information they seek. To the extent that such a move is also in the seller's interest, ways will be found to disseminate this information through advertising, through salesmen, and on the labels of products. Yet in the previous section reasons were discussed why the seller may perceive it as against his interest to divulge certain kinds of information accurately. In these cases the legal *obligation to disclose* information — assuming that it can be established that what is disclosed is indeed what the purchaser wants to know — is a means of facilitating search. In law the issue comes up at many points in such questions as whether one must inform the opposite party in a negotiation so as to avoid his contracting under the spell of an error, whether the seller must disclose apparent defects in his product, and how banks and other lenders must divulge the total cost of credit. Apart from the problem of reliability of what is divulged, discussed in the previous section, the two hard questions here are whether the purchaser in fact desires and can cope with the information brought to his attention and whether the obligation to divulge deprives the seller of the revenues (made at the profit of the purchaser's ignorance) that made it worthwhile for him to generate the information in the first place.[29] Where this last question must be answered in the affirmative, mandatory disclosure amounts to killing the goose that lays the golden eggs.[30]

Where information is disclosed, one can further facilitate search by its *uniformization*. Price comparisons are made easier by unit pricing.[31] The comparison of complex warranties or insurance contracts is greatly facilitated, indeed practically feasible, only where the options are expressed in standardized categories by the various suppliers.[32] Uniform grading of meat and of eggs is another example. Uniformization may create problems where the qualities involved are not readily inspectable and suppliers themselves have a hand in the assignment of categories, problems discussed earlier.

A major task in the information market is to find devices through which qualities that are not inspectable by the common customer can yet be made sufficiently transparent to him that he will agree to purchase the product in question. As we saw earlier, if this task is left in the hands of the suppliers of products, there is a risk of deception, whereas independent agencies that provide such information are not always viable.

Certification is a statement about a product or service in which a party independent of its supplier attests that it has certain minimal qualities. Certification is known in some professional disciplines (the certifying authority being the professional association), but also with respect to weighing scales in stores (certified by government inspectors) and documents declared to be in conformity with the original (the certifying authority here could be a notary or an other semipublic official). Of course, the supplier himself can issue what he terms a "certification" with respect to his product, but the truthfulness of such a statement is not guaranteed in the same way as that of independent sources.[33] It should be treated as part of the supplier's own arsenal of devices to inform on experience and credence qualities.

In some cases where the product as a whole is not inspectable, *samples, proxies or indicators* that are can be offered to customers.

Pictures outside movie houses, the text on the dustjacket of a book, and tastes of cheese or wine are examples of it. The risk in this practice is that sellers manipulate the indicator to their advantage without improving the underlying quality of the product. Thus, if the "redness" of meat is used by customers as an index for its freshness, one would expect a temptation for sellers to inject some red coloring chemical into their cuts. In a different form this tinkering with indices is thought to be at the root of "signaling," a term used by Spence to designate what he believed to be excessive investment in higher education.[34] His argument goes as follows. It is difficult for employers to detect in a short time the usefulness of a candidate for some of the higher positions in their enterprise. Education, in particular higher education, provides a reasonable proxy for the candidate's talents and by extension his usefulness to the firm. Employers will therefore start to use formal education regularly as an index. This practice in turn makes it interesting for everyone interested in employment to seek further education, and where this movement sets in, the value of education as an index to distinguish the talented from the less talented diminishes. This will lead the talented to seek even more education, and the inflationary process that now begins may well lead, in Spence's view, to amounts of formal education far in excess of society's real needs. We shall deal with this argument in the next subsection.

Samples and proxies, however useful, are not the most used, nor the most ingenious device through which invisible qualities can be made visible. More interesting is the phenomenon of *brand names* and *reputation,* in which a name that is usually not inherently informative, comes to represent noninspectable qualities of a product or set of products. One can analyze the phenomenon as an implicit contract between a supplier and his customers, similar to that which Klein and Leffler assume with respect to quality insurance. The agreement here provides that the supplier will substantially maintain the qualities of his product over time in return for steady patronizing by his customers. To the customers the arrangement is advantageous in that the search, which they undertake initially, with respect to experience features of the product and its competitors will be useful over an extended period of time. In due course they can make their purchasing choices without new searching; the comparative information about experience features has become to them a capital asset that reduces their average decision costs over a long series of repeated purchases. To the seller the agreement is interesting because repeat purchasing reduces his business uncertainty, which is normally a cost, as we shall see in the next chapter. Of course, once the trust relationship has been established, the seller may be tempted to "water down" the quality of features that are not directly observable. This temptation should be held in check by the capital asset he holds in the form of steady customers; the larger the proportion of repeat purchasers and the longer the period over which they remain faithful to him, the less it should be attractive to deceive them. The argument here follows the general logic set out in the second section.

It is not hard to see that a firm's reputation follows the same logic, but with respect to all its products or services at once and, of necessity, in a fuzzier manner. Reputation should carry over from the commodities on which it was originally based to new ones. Notice that one can establish a reputation for having low prices in comparison with one's competitors.

Since the name used as a brand or to convey one's reputation represents in fact a valuable capital asset, it is only natural that the law should recognize property rights in it. Trade names can be bought and sold. Their unauthorized use gives rise to an action in damages.

Return privileges and *warranties* are sometimes thought to convey information about the quality of a product. An initial analysis would see these schemes as means of reducing the purchaser's uncertainty, in the first case with respect to his general satisfaction with the object that has been purchased, in the second with regard to the possible presence of defects. Of course, such privileges are not costless to the seller, and the entire scheme could best be seen as an insurance bought by the purchaser in the price of the commodity. It would remain to be shown why purchasers prefer the insurance to bearing the risk themselves, a subject for the next chapter. The relevant point here is that very liberal warranties for a moderately priced object normally indicate good quality of the product. For a poor product the cost of the "insurance" would be very high and could not be justified in the moderate price. The association of liberal warranty or return privileges with a limited class of traits is now generalized to the quality of the product as a whole. Liberal return privileges becomes a proxy for high quality in general.

Market Imperfections Attributed to the Costliness of Information

For its optimality conditions to hold, the neoclassical model assumes fully informed actors. Since we have argued earlier that in general it is not rational to inform oneself exhaustively on any subject, we must now ask ourselves how this modifies the analysis presented by neoclassical theory. In particular, we must ask whether market imperfections that might justify government intervention will now arise. It should be stressed here that an imperfection does not in itself justify intervention, since the intervention, too, is subject to information constraints and may indeed be further from perfection than the situation it is meant to correct.

Monopolistic Tendencies

To the extent that purchasers limit their search because they believe that the marginal cost of further search exceeds its benefit, a seller enjoys a moderate form of protection against his customers' switching allegiance when a competitor offers a better deal. The costliness of search, in other words, will stop consumers from exploiting all price and quality differences. As a result, the relevant model for analyzing such situations from the viewpoint of sellers is thought to be that of monopolistic, and not perfect, competition.[35]

Against this view, Nutter and Moore argue that this very friction provides an incentive for sellers to undertake strategic initiatives. In a world of perfect information and instantaneous switching by consumers, any such move would be met immediately with retaliation, and there would be no prospect of gains to price cutting.[36] But the argument is incomplete. In a fully enlightened world, while competitors would be fully informed about each other's moves and on this ground might be thought to reach a "quiet understanding," consumers too would presumably be fully informed about their price structure, in particular about their supracompetitive profits, and this in due course would drive prices down.

Be that as it may, it would seem that in our imperfect world improved circulation of information might strengthen competition.[37] How much of an effect one might expect is an empirical question. Yet, on the faith of Schwartz and Wilde's argument that the presence of even a few comparison shoppers and the impossibility for sellers to distinguish them from other shoppers would be sufficient for healthy competition, one would not expect a very large effect.

Advertising

A second source of monopolistic tendencies is thought by some to arise from the advertising medium. The economies of scale in it are so large that the firms that have reached the size to take advantage of them are thought to have an insuperable advance over newcomers. This is a form of market imperfection and would lead in particular to a decrease in the influx of innovative forces to an industry.[38]

The defenders of advertising would consider this as too pessimistic a view.[39] They would argue that in spite of the economies of scale, advertising is merely information and will protect the advertiser only if his product is truly better. If not, prospective competitors will find it worthwhile to invest in huge advertising in anticipation of the substantial returns to be made once they penetrate the market. Moreover, these authors would argue that restrictions on advertising as a remedy are worse than the disease. Since consumers are confident that the truthfulness of advertising is policed by the government and hence that they can believe the content, those sellers who dare to publish deceiving messages will find it even more profitable than without such intervention.[40]

From our reading of the literature, we conclude that the empirical evidence to decide this issue is not yet in. Most significant to date seems to be the conclusion at which Comanor and Wilson arrive:

> The evidence presented in this study supports the view that advertising enhances market power through its effects upon entry barriers and upon the relative positions of large and small firms in the market.[41]

While there are thus net welfare losses associated with advertising in the view of these authors, it is not clear in their view that other solutions in our imperfect world would not lead to equally great losses. For what it is worth, they propose studies to see how impartial information could be effectively circulated in the market. They also propose government regulation to impose products standardization and limits on advertising expenditure.[42]

Hazards of Information Controlled by the Seller: The Lemon Effect

The term *lemon effect* was proposed by Akerlof for situations in which "the presence of people who wish to pawn bad wares tends to drive out the legitimate business."[43] We saw earlier that various devices are used to make visible to customers traits that are not directly inspectable. The lemon effect comes about where sellers of lower-quality goods can adopt indicators normally associated with better ware and thus extract higher prices than fully informed consumers would pay for their goods. Of course, the producers of higher-quality products — presumably with higher production costs — who are unable to distinguish their merchandise from that of their imitators will face lower profits than the latter and will in due course follow suit or disappear from the market. The market has deflated the information medium on which consumers relied.[44] Akerlof illustrates the phenomenon in the second-hand car market, the market for private health insurance for elderly people, credit markets in underdeveloped countries, and other markets.

One must wonder whether this is indeed a significant feature of Western markets. Where customers accumulate quality information in due course after purchase, brand names and reputation should prevent the lemon effect, even more so where there is substantial repeat purchasing. Such feedback should also discourage low-quality producers from imitating high-cost quality proxies such as return privileges and guarantees; they would not be able to maintain their low prices.

One can well imagine that imitation would be attempted for other features. American automobile producers have recently taken to imitating some stylistic features of the better European cars in their higher-priced models. Whether such action can effectively deflate the quality confidence associated with makes such as Mercedes Benz and Rolls Royce is open to question. If it can, one would expect these automakers to try to innovate in the features that, as a result of imitation, have become part of the public domain. There have also been attempts to imitate the very aggressive advertising campaign in North America undertaken for Volkswagen. But the attempts have not persisted, presumably because in the long run quality feedback must confirm the advertised message.

Hence, we see no evidence that the lemon effect leads to pervasive market imperfection. Where there is evidence of it, as undoubtedly in the used-car market, one may wonder whether government intervention will improve matters. For instance, the mechanism of warranties on used cars, which would substantially alleviate the problem, is available for sellers to introduce. If it has not come about in a rather competitive market, the conclusion comes to mind that customers find it better to assume the quality uncertainty themselves than to transfer it to the vendor and see the prices increased. The vendor may prefer this arrangement because he fears abuse of the car on which he offers the warranty, a problem called moral hazard in the insurance literature and discussed in the next chapter. Where warranties are offered but vary greatly in form and content, government intervention may ensure uniformity, with the benefits discussed above.

We argued earlier that one should expect modest amounts of misrepresentation in the messages given by vendors about their products. One might see this as the lemon effect applied to honesty in information supply. If all sellers could somehow agree to be honest in their messages, increased consumer reliance on that information would surely be beneficial to each.[45] Yet agreements to that effect are notoriously unstable. Once such a cartel is in place it is very profitable to cheat.

Could government intervention improve matters? Enforcement of honesty in advertising would have much the same qualities as a private agreement. The difference lies in the enforcement. The government can make cheating very costly by imposing penalties, whereas penalty clauses in private agreements would not be admissible, as we saw earlier, assuming that the agreement itself is considered valid. The problem with government enforcement lies in the incentives to search for violations and to prosecute them. Budget limitations may play havoc with good intentions here.[46] The overall comparison that we now face is between a situation in which consumers are moderately mistrustful of seller messages with its attendant welfare loss[47] and one in which the welfare loss consists of the cost of enforcement and the cost of the — now very profitable — deceptions where they succeed. Nelson would rather see a third option installed: the possibility for (dis)abused consumers to sue for misleading advertising in the courts.[48] It is true that private initiative is in a better position to detect violations. Whether it has also better incentives to prosecute and how damages or penalties should be set in those cases are questions not so easily answered.[49]

Hazards of Information Controlled by the Seller: Signaling

In the previous section we introduced the notion of signaling and discussed the fear expressed by some that there is overinvestment in signals. The most talented people would continually seek more education in order to distinguish themselves from lesser talents who acquire degrees, and thus society as a whole would invest in education well beyond social needs. But will it happen? Our discussion in the second section suggests that the process of increasing investment in signals will go on to the point where the next-best source of information will be cheaper. Surely the investors in education expect on average to recover subsequently at least the cost of their investment in higher earnings. This directly affects the employer's cost. Hence if a cheaper mode of information is available in the market, he will prefer it.

Barzel suggests one such arrangement.[50] It consists in a contract covering the entire period — perhaps several years — necessary for the employer to discover in the work environment the true quality of a person in the category with which we are here concerned. Suppose that, where true quality is known, salary would be equal to the marginal contribution the employee brings to the enterprise. The contract now offers each employee of the category discussed the same salary, the amount of which is slightly more than that of the least productive workers in this category. At the end of the contract, salaries are adjusted to conform to the true productivity of the person.

Each person who has been paid less than his true productivity over the course of the initial contract receives a bonus covering the difference (including accumulated interest) minus some sum that is less than the cost of the (superfluous) formal education in which he would otherwise have invested. It is easily seen that for both parties this arrangement would be preferable to education to the extent that the education contributes nothing to productivity.[51]

Of course, it can be argued that contracts as lengthy as the one proposed by Barzel would be rejected for other reasons: the risk of personality clashes, uncertainty about the future of the business and its ability to pay the bonus, preference for flexibility to take advantage of as yet unforeseen possibilities and so on. These are costs — associated with uncertain events — that would have to be accounted for by the parties to Barzel's agreement. However this may be, the upshot of the argument is clear. The potential for over-investment in signals is limited by the availability of other sources of information, and, while it is true that there may be some waste in comparison with the case of a fully informed world, it is not clear that in our imperfect one this waste can be reduced.

Overinvestment in education may stem from another cause, namely, the fact that education is subsidized. The subsidy may have been introduced as part of a redistributive policy or to better exploit a society's intellectual potential. But the issue in this case is the subsidy rather than some perversity in the information market; any subsidy will encourage purchase of the subsidized commodity. Overinvestment in education would cease if people faced the social cost of their choice. Whether education at that cost would make politically acceptable social policy cannot be discussed here.

Moreover, people may invest in education not only because of its signaling qualities, but also because they consider it a pleasurable activity or because they believe that it can provide nonmarketable productive skills.[52] Consider also that in practice it is much cheaper to acquire a university education in one's late teens and early twenties than later in life.

Misperception of Features

We are concerned here with situations in which people, even in the presence of adequate information, cannot appropriately assess some features of a commodity. Typically such features involve small probabilities, for which human intuitive assessment is an unreliable guide, as we saw in Chapter 6. Examples would be the value of safety features in cars or airplanes, the risk of explosion in glass bottles or the risk of side effects in drugs.

Colantoni et al. study the problem of the consumer's choice in the face of such minute hazards.[53] They assume, after Lancaster, that goods are perceived as bundles of features and apply this analysis to safety devices in cars, where the relevant aspects or features are given as the "quality of life" and the "probability of noninjury." Any particular combination can now be represented as a point in a two-dimensional space with these two aspects as axes. The consumer's budget sets a limit to what he can actually afford, reflected by a region in the space. The actual choice depends on the point where the highest preference curve touches a point on the outer-bound of the budget region. The interesting conclusions of this study are that even small distortions in the perception of the risky aspect may cause shifts in the perceived outerbound of the budget region and hence in the actual choice, *independent* of variation in taste, and that the consumer may thus well believe that he has acted rationally, even though he has not in fact maximized his preference subject to his real budget.[54]

If this argument is correct, the consumer may buy more or, on the contrary, less risk than he would had he been fully informed. Why does the market not correct the problem? Presumably, producers, to whom such problems are a statistical fact as they deal in large numbers, would prefer not to assume an uncertain cost — which will put their prices up — unless asked to by consumer demand, i.e., unless they can offer the consumer something that he clearly values. Why would consumers as a group not insist on having information on the problem or on shifting the risk to the producer? The explanation might well be that the experience feedback on which most people rely to decide whether risks are "worth bothering with" would suggest to the vast majority that they are not; occurrence of the problem is extremely infrequent, and most people would not "know of cases."

Yet to the unfortunate few who do fall victim to the unsafe product, the outcome is catastrophic indeed. Will their cases suffice to sway the opinion of the majority of consumers so that in due course the market will autonomously solve the problem, either through safer products or through independent accident insurance? Chances are that their cases will be thought of as part of the "risks of life," all the more so if skill or caution in manipulating the object can reduce the hazard. It would seen that the normal market regime — contract rules — in which one gets what one bargained for leads to a nonoptimal situation here. This would be true, one may presume, even where labels on the various objects detail the hazards, assuming that producers would make the expenditures necessary to estimate them.[55]

Ordinary private law treats these features differently from the normal conditions about which people bargain and also from unforeseen contingencies. It allocates this risk to the seller who is a producer or specialized vendor of the product.[56] The reason can be no other than that these two groups have a clear and systematic advantage in informing themselves about the danger and, if they choose not to, in deciding that assuming the risk is preferable to informing oneself on it and perhaps avoiding it in part. The costliness of information clearly has an effect on the substantive law here, as Calabresi thinks it should.

Yet matters are not usually left there, and one frequently sees the government intervene with rules stipulating minimal quality standards. The argument against such a move is that it deprives those who have a taste for risk of a variety of the product that is cheaper, but more hazardous. Oi, in discussing exploding glass bottles in this light, feels that the intervention is unwarranted.[57]

Several arguments could be advanced for government intervention of this kind. First the liability of the manufacturer may be imperfect; in some cases proof is not possible and hence he will not be sued. In other cases compensation covers only part of the actual damages because of difficulties in proving them, because of lawyers' costs, or because certain types of damage (moral damages) are systematically undervalued by the courts. As a result the manufacturer faces a biased tradeoff between the cost of assuming a risk and avoiding it.[58] The argument that "a suffocated child cannot be brought back to life by court action" is simply a variety of the problem of damage awards that do not fully compensate: If the manufacturer were made to feel the full social cost of such deaths, he might well find it worthwhile to avoid them in anticipation of potential lawsuits. Admittedly, this argument really addresses the imperfection of the damage-recovery system and would lose its weight as a result of high damage awards, small-claims courts and class actions.

Another line of reasoning advanced to justify government intervention is that the victims of hazardous products either directly or indirectly fall back on various collectively provided services — medicare, financial assistance to the victim and his family — and that, in buying hazardous products, people may create more than their proportional share of these collective expenses without being made to feel the social cost of their choice. It is possible that some people who use the product so control its use that this would not be true, but in other cases people may believe that they are similarly careful, while, objectively speaking, they are wrong. Since it is too difficult to discriminate among these groups (an information-cost problem!) and together they create more expenses to society than they pay for, a uniform standard for their hazardous product seems the lesser of several evils.

Goldberg has developed a different argument for explaining the prevalence of standards.[59] If consumers delegated part of their information-processing task to an agent, if there were economies of scale in collective provision, and if they requested results in a form simple enough for them to apply, it is not unlikely that the outcome would include general rules of thumb ("buckle up for safety") as well as specific prohibitions and requirements. Constraints in the conveyance of information to people of bounded rationality might well, in his view, dictate the use of such apparently unrelated forms as product bans and liability rules to achieve for the consumer a situation in which, on average, the choice made for him is most nearly that which he would have made himself, had he been fully informed and perfectly calculative.

Conclusion

Effective exchange in the market economy presupposes knowledge of trading opportunities on the part of economic actors. Such knowledge could in many cases be acquired through the effort of those who need it — that is, through personal search. But usually less-expensive modes of acquisition exist, and the ordinary forces of specialization will work toward making their benefits available through trade.

The obstacles in this process are that information is imperfectly appropriable and that it has a fiduciary component; its quality cannot be perfectly checked, at least not without undoing its economic viability. Limited appropriability will frequently cause information to be supplied by the seller of the commodity. Yet the fiduciary nature of information would make it preferable to have it supplied independent of the commodities on which it supposed to inform. In practice the economies of joint provision outweigh the risk of biased information for most commodities.

This observation has led us to examine in a general manner what determines the trustworthiness of information in the market. This question has two aspects, namely, the incentive for the information supplier to distort it and the incentive for the information consumer to rely on it nonetheless. Information suppliers have an incentive to distort information if there are gains to be made from the practice. Such gains must be expected for sellers who also provide information on the commodities. Other sources of information for the consumer would not have such an incentive, unless of course they were paid by the sellers of the commodities on which they inform. The potential for gains is not by itself sufficient to make information distortion profitable; the gains must outweigh the expect losses. These losses are a function of the likelihood that customers will detect the distortion and switch suppliers and the loss resulting from these switches. This explains, for instance, why sellers who rely on steady relations with their customers have less incentive to distort information than do fly-by-night operators or stores selling to tourists.

It is also the basis for an interesting suggestion of an "insurance premium against cheating." If the seller can charge a higher price in return for his promise of honesty, the stream of extra profit or rent that he can thus expect would make it less worthwhile for him to try to cheat. To eradicate cheating, according to this suggestion, the premium should be set just high enough that its present value would offset the gains from cheating. This model would explain why high price can rationally be thought to be associated with higher quality. Whether such a scheme can be realized in practice will depend on whether consumers are willing to pay the price in order not to have to be mistrustful of their source of information.

The consumer's choice of relying on a particular information medium should be analyzed in terms of the tradeoff proposed in Chapter 5; the total cost of search and uncertainty is presumably lowest for that medium. Since it is costly to investigate the reliability of an information source, there are advantages for the consumer to be able to undertake such an investigation if he can rely on the results for a substantial period. Research regarding the reliability of an information source is like a capital asset to the consumer. This means that even if slight distortions are noticed, the consumer will not put his reliance on the information source into question. It also means that where one relies on one source, a second, much less costly one must be maintained so that one can decide when to reinvestigate and possibly abandon the primary source. The choice of such a secondary source — possibly one's own experience and sample inspections — is presumably made on the same basis as the primary one. The idea of even higher-level backup information was abandoned as it leads to an infinite regress. The cost of the secondary source must be included in the cost of relying on the primary source, in particular when it comes to comparing different suppliers of primary information.

Similar considerations apply with respect to the suggestion that the government step in to guarantee the truth of information supplied by sellers. While it is true that if all sellers were honest, there would be gains for each of them, there can be no question either that in such circumstances cheating would be very profitable. Hence, to see if the government's intervention will improve matters in the information market, one must compare the gains resulting from increased consumer confidence in information with the losses in the form of the cost of law enforcement and the cost to consumers of the deceptions that do occur. Studies of the economics of law enforcement show that it implies itself an information tradeoff: the cost of search for violations against the likelihood that as a result of such policing the social loss due to violations decreases. Budget limitations may impose on enforcement agencies practices that do not lead to the optimal amount of enforcement, as this calculus would suggest it. Hence it cannot be said in the abstract that government intervention to ensure honesty in information will lead to a net social gain, even though it may. The foregoing considerations should suggest the relevant factors in an empirical study of the question. To put it differently, whether legal rules requiring honesty in advertising and other information supplied by the seller will improve on market forces in the same direction is an empirical question.

This conclusion holds for what was discussed under the broad heading of the lemon effect, but also for the variety of it known as signaling. It may be true that people acquire more "education signals" than would be necessary in a world in which quality is transparent. But competing information sources set a limit to this wasteful practice, and it is not clear that government intervention to ensure reliable signals (entry restrictions into universities, into professions?) would not lead to more serious waste.

Another potential market imperfection due to the costliness of information we called misperception. It concerns features that people relying on intuitive thinking, as most consumers would, tend to misestimate as a result of information-processing peculiarities discussed in Chapter 6. The result is that people believe they have made optimal choices, while objectively by their own standards they have not. As a result the demand in the market, which reflects the aggregation of these individual preferences, will not represent the optimal quality of the commodity in question. Hence one cannot rely here on the central principle of contract law according to which effect should be given to agreements freely made by informed parties. In practice, various mechanisms are used in the law to impute liability to manufacturers and specialized vendors for hazardous features: breach of contract or latent defects in contract law, liability with presumed negligence or strict liability in torts.

We also discussed ways in which the costliness of information might create monopolistic tendencies in markets. While it may be true that the cost of search makes competition less fierce than it would be in a fully transparent world, it is not obvious that the model of perfect competition could not be an adequate representation of reality in many markets. With respect to advertising, more pointed conclusions were reached. There is evidence that this medium can significantly affect entry into markets and hence provide power to established firms to the detriment of competition. This finding has led some authors to recommend a study of ways in which impartial information could be effectively circulated in such markets. They also recommend for consideration limits on advertising expenditure and product standardization (where excessive product differentiation is accomplished through advertising).

The incidence of the foregoing on the economic analysis of law has already been hinted at in various places. Some aspects of competition law (advertising, agreements concerning common standards), consumer protection law, and even traditional civil law principles were touched upon. Calabresi's analysis of the law relating to accidents, which was summarized in Chapter 4, relies in part on principles discussed here under the heading of misperception. His analysis also introduces information-processing limitations — such as were discussed in the last chapter — with respect to judges and political decisionmakers, who have to allocate accident burdens without being perfectly informed on comparative costs and benefits. Risk bearing, the subject of the next chapter, is part of Calabresi's analysis as well.

CHAPTER 8

Risk Bearing

One of the recurring aspects of human life is uncertainty. The uncertainty may be due to the caprice of nature and reflect our ignorance or inability to control it, or it may stem from our lack of information on a subject that is well within the range of human knowledge, but on which we find it too costly to inform ourselves. This chapter deals with ways in which people handle uncertainty other than by doing nothing and letting losses fall where they will.

Uncertainty may come in the form of gains and of losses. The former may appeal to our gambling or risk-taking instincts. Yet it is usually against the prospect of an uncertain loss, in particular where it takes catastrophic proportions in comparison with one's current wealth, that special measures are taken. Uncertainty in this context is an unpleasant aspect of life.[1] We look for ways to reduce its impact on us.

In the literature on decision making, this observation is reflected in the more precise statement that people are to most purposes *risk averse.* They would prefer to have a certain sum rather than a lottery with the same expected value: $100 rather than a lottery with a 50 percent chance to win $1,200 and a 50 percent chance to lose $1,000.

But would one still prefer the certain sum if it were $50, $25, $10 or even less? Let us assume that someone is indifferent between the sum of $10 and the lottery ticket whose expected value is $100. The discrepancy between these two values, i.e., $90, reflects the degree of risk aversion. Risk aversion depends on a variety of factors, one of which, an important one, is the amount of the loss risked in the lottery in comparison with one's current wealth.[2] A very rich person might, on this account, be indifferent between $100 and the lottery ticket. The intensity of one's aversion for a particular risk will determine how hard one will look for ways of reducing its impact.

Coping with Risk Autonomously

Avoidance

The most obvious way to cope with uncertainty is to search for information that allows one to reduce or eliminate it. The risk of fire in a dwelling can be reduced by installing proper electrical wiring and using less wood and more concrete in construction. In this case the remedies are common knowledge. In other contexts they are not, and costly search must be undertaken to develop them in the first place (proper safety measures for nuclear reactors and evacuation plans where a leak occurs) or to discover them in the market. Once a possible remedy against risk has been discovered, one must decide whether the benefits in reduced uncertainty outweigh the installation and maintenance costs. Obviously, in some cases remedies may not be available at all or not at a viable cost and other means of coping with risk must then be sought.

In some cases flexibility is a means of reducing the effect of uncertainty. Hirshleifer and Riley discuss this possibility under the heading of "emergent public information."[3] Suppose that one must make an investment in securities or in some new productive process. Suppose, moreover, that one expected that in the near future information might become publicly available with some possibility of opportunities for investment with higher yields or more productive equipment, as the case may be. Rather than making the commitment immediately and living with the uncertain possibility that in retrospect one has missed a better opportunity, one would like to suspend the decision until the emerging information has become public. The suspension may be costly, and this cost must be weighed against the expected gains from a better decision. In reality, such choices must be made at times; the willingness of some investors to hold short-term securities in preference to longer-term ones with a higher yield is surely evidence of this phenomenon.[4] Liquid or flexible investments are thus a substitute for immediate information about future opportunities; they are complementary to "emergent information" that will be publicly available in the future.

Loss Reduction

In some instances where it is not possible to eliminate the source of the uncertainty, one may yet reduce its effect by limiting the extent of the loss where it occurs. For instance, a sprinkler system in a building reduces the cost of a fire where one takes place. A general mechanism with this purpose is inventory; where one is uncertain of the demand or the supply of a commodity, it may be worthwhile to build up a stock sufficient to "ride out" the worse conceivable contingency. A store, uncertain of the demand for some commodity in the near future, may build up a stock of that commodity — at a cost, of course — rather than running the risk of losing customers who will be disappointed when the item is not available. Consumers will invest in a larger than usual supply of some good when they fear that the supply of it will be irregular. On similar grounds one can explain extra food taken on a yachting trip; while the trip should take no more than its expected duration, one provides for the contingency in which it lasts longer, given that resupplying at sea is practically excluded.

Diversification

The term *diversification* is used by investors for a policy in which the capital to be invested is spread over various independent projects rather than concentrated in a single larger venture. The reason for diversification is that a misfortune in one project is expected to be offset by good fortune in another, so that on the whole and considered over some time, the investor can treat each project as equivalent to its expected monetary value, rather than a smaller amount as in the example discussed at the beginning of the chapter.

The essence of diversification is the pooling of risks that tend to cancel each other out, i.e., that are in a statistical sense independent. If, for instance, a real estate investor is worried about fire hazard, he is better off with a variety of buildings scattered through a city or region than with a row of houses on the same street.

The question of how to choose a set of investments that are appropriately diversified is known in the literature as the *portfolio selection problem*.[5] The theory has applications in many areas, such as securities investment, capital budgeting, insurance, acquisition policies by conglomerates, "investments" by recording companies in young singers or song writers.[6]

Markets in Risk

The foregoing discussion should have made it obvious that uncertainty must usually be treated as a cost, something that people would pay to have removed from them. It should also be clear that people and institutions differ in their ability to cope with uncertainty, and the question then arises whether trade in risk is possible. The answer is generally affirmative, with qualifications to be discussed.

One may transfer risk to various kinds of people and for different reasons. One transfers the risk of theft of one's valuables to a bank where one rents a safety-deposit box. The reason is presumably the bank's superior ability to avoid this hazard. The risk of fire is transferred to an insurance company because of the pooling of risks that it makes possible. Some of the risk of a business venture is transferred to the person with whom one forms a partnership for that venture. Implicitly, some of this risk is also borne by creditors; in case of bankruptcy, they stand to lose part of their claim against the partnership.

The viability of these and other modes of risk transfer depends on the absence of perversities of various kinds. These perversities are best discussed in the context of insurance and risk sharing.

Insurance

Insurance is a mechanism through which the insurer, against payment of a premium, assumes a risk normally borne by the insured. The premium is equal to the sum of the expected monetary value of the loss due to the risk and the cost of the transaction. Transaction costs include here those of estimating the expected loss and those of writing the agreement, as well as general expenses incurred in finding and attracting potential clients. The crucial element here is the estimation of the expected loss. There are two problems with it. The first is that making perfect measurements is generally not worthwhile, for reasons set out in Chapter 5. The second, related problem is that once the parties have agreed on a premium, the insured, in cases where the size of the risk depends in part on his caution, which is costly to him, has an incentive to reduce his level of care. This problem is known as moral hazard.

Rate Differentiation and Adverse Selection. Since it is costly to determine the precise expected monetary value of the loss associated with a given risk, insurers will in practice group "similar risks" and charge a uniform premium within each group. Such groupings are made on the basis of features that are easily assessed. Suppose that on this basis the fire risk for city houses is treated as uniform and that all owners pay the same premium. If one insurer discovers that these risks can be further differentiated by means of easily assessed features, such as the presence of sprinkler systems, recent installation of electrical wiring, or the material of which the house was built, he might offer lower premiums for those houses that rate favorably on these criteria. Owners of such houses would switch companies, and the initial pool would be left with a lower proportion of low risks. As a result the average expected value of the loss, and hence, in due course, the premium charged would go up. Further customers might leave, and this process would go on until the insurer who initially did not differentiate is left with the worst risks in terms of the classification of those who find it worthwhile to make the differentiation.

At first sight this result might seem paradoxical. Insurance is thought of as a means of spreading risk over all members of a group. Yet those insurers who set out to spread it evenly will end up with the worst risks in all instances where differentiation among insured can be economically made. The "full equality" insurer is put in this position — and in practice may be eliminated as a result — through what is known as "adverse selection" by the insured. To put it differently, within each undifferentiated group, the better risks cross-subsidize the poorer ones. As in other sectors of the economy, market forces will seek to drive out cross-subsidization where that can be done economically.

How fine will the differentiation among risks ultimately be? This will be determined by the information tradeoff implicit in the search to differentiate classes. Suppose that there are two insurers, A and B, who have adopted the same classification and charge the same premiums. A thinks of further differentiating the risk class X into two subclasses, X_1 and X_2, and wonders whether this move will attract clients away from his competitor. He will attract customers from B if his premium for the better risks is lower than that of B, which is feasible if the additional measurement costs are less than the premium reduction he can offer. Of course, the poorer risks will initially find it worthwhile to switch to B. But B will have to raise his premiums under the impact of adverse selection, and in the end the premiums for A's clients in X_2 and for B's customers should be equal, provided of course that the group X_1 assumes the additional measurement cost necessary for the differentiation. Hence, the differentiation can be expected to go on until the additional measurement cost of further differentiation is just equal to the premium reduction that can be offered to the newly differentiated better-risk group.

The question of rate differentiation and adverse selection is frequently discussed with regard to the very high premiums that young drivers have to pay for accident liability insurance. At one level one regrets that these drivers, as a group, have to pay such high rates. Assuming that these rates accurately reflect the expected monetary value of the losses these drivers, as a group, incur, the problem may well be that the premium variation does not result in adequate incentives toward safe driving. If this is so, a demerit point system is a better inducement. But the argument can be continued at another level. It turns out that the high expected losses for these drivers as a group are due to a few of them causing many and very serious accidents. If this is so, one may ask whether it is too costly to distinguish the safe drivers in this group from those primarily responsible for the high accident rate. Since insurance companies do not differentiate, one must assume that they find it too costly to do, all the more so as a major measuring device, the length of the period of accident-free driving, will become effective only after several years, which is when the drivers in question leave the high-risk category in any event through age. Hence, a young driver who is particularly careful would yet pay substantially higher insurance fees than one with the same driving habits, but who is, say, in his thirties.

This result is thought to be unfair to young drivers, and in various nationalized car-accident insurance plans, such as the one in force in Quebec, the rate differential is reduced. Several remarks are in order here. The reduced differential would normally lead an economist to predict a higher overall level of accident costs. Such a development would not be observed if the link between rate level and care in driving were absent or if other accident-reducing measures — demerit point systems, mandatory safety belts and other features in cars, speed limits — were introduced at the same time as the nationalization of the insurance, as they were in this province. It should be clear that because of "adverse selection," the reduced rate differentiation would not be viable in a private market and that the system implies cross-subsidization from safe to unsafe drivers beyond what is inevitable as a result of the costliness of information. The system implies, in other words, a judgment about redistribution of wealth.

Moral Hazard. Moral hazard presents itself where the insured can affect the accuracy of the risk assessment by the insurer. It may occur through nondisclosure of relevant facts or because acts by the accused after conclusion of the insurance contract effectively alter the risk as the insurer could estimate it. Driving behavior is an example of the latter. Moral hazard is a problem because it gives the insured the incentive to try to transfer his risk for a payment below its expected cost — that is, to obtain a gift. Where this possibility cannot be controlled, risks become uninsurable. It is no doubt for this reason that one cannot insure against traffic tickets and other legal penalties, nor against business failure.[7]

There are two ways in which the insurer can react to the prospect of moral hazard. He can underinsure the risk or he can monitor the acts of the insured. Where the insurer underinsures, part of the risk is left with the insured on the presumption that since he has something at stake himself, he will be less tempted by behavior that is unduly risky from the insurer's point of view. The insured part of the risk is an ordinary insurance; the remaining, uninsured part makes the scheme somewhat similar to risk sharing such as occurs in a partnership, to be discussed below.

Underinsurance can take the form of "deductibles." A $250 deductible in car insurance, for instance, is interesting for the insured because he can "self-insure" these small amounts, but mostly because he can adjust his behavior in an attempt to avoid the small accidents for which he is now himself liable. Presumably, he would have an incentive to try to avoid the more serious accidents because of the risk to his own life and limb, whatever the insurance.

The insurer's second response to moral hazard is monitoring the behavior of the accused. This may take several forms. For instance, the insurer may specify that the policy does not cover damage following certain kinds of actions by the insured, such as driving under the influence of alcohol or arson. It goes without saying that beyond such clear cases, detailed description of behavior is cumbersome because of the difficulty of spelling it out in a policy and of establishing, after damage is done, whether the insured has followed the rules. The insurer's task is facilitated by legal norms prohibiting certain kinds of behavior, such as driving unsafe cars or while under the influence of alcohol, whose observance is monitored by public authorities. While the reasons for such intervention are usually the risk of the activities concerned, it may have the incidental advantages of economies of scale in monitoring.

In practice the pressure for rate differentiation is sufficiently strong that insurers accept monitoring the behavior of the insured by relying on his habits. Drivers are assigned to a risk category on the basis of their accident record as it is known to the insurer, a practice called experience rating. Periodic inspection of buildings for the purpose of fire insurance is another example of monitoring the behavior of the insured. The problem with these practices is that the insured have an interest in "scrambling" the monitoring process by exhibiting exceptionally cautious behavior during measurement and reverting to their habitual, more risky modes afterwards. This would leave us with a problem of moral hazard, albeit a reduced one. Obviously, the insurance premiums will reflect the actual accident rate. Where scrambling impairs the insurer's ability to differentiate high and low risks — and this restricton holds for all insurers alike, so that no adverse selection takes place against anyone — it results in cross-subsidization from the latter to the former group. It goes without saying that the insurers have an interest in searching for indicators that are discriminative among the various risk groups, are not easily scrambled by the insured, and are relatively inexpensive to assess.[8]

Risk Sharing

Risk sharing takes place where each of a number of people will pay part of a loss, if one occurs, against uncertain payment or gain. It is the uncertainty of the payment or gain that distinguishes this figure from insurance of a large risk by several insurers. Risk sharing occurs mostly in the context of business ventures: partners share business risk as stockholders do, and creditors share the risk of their debtor's failing. The reason for it is probably that business risks are uninsurable because of moral hazard, as we noted earlier.

It is important to stress here that the reduction of uncertainty accomplished through risk sharing — or through insurance, for that matter — constitutes a welfare gain in the sense that some ventures would not be undertaken if the initiator had to carry the entire burden of the risk. Some projects are, as the trade says, "too big to swing." This observation makes it plain that the way in which risk is borne is not indifferent to society's welfare. A risk constitutes less of a burden in some people's hands than in those of others. Hence, in a world in which people are — to different degrees — risk averse, shifts in the allocation of risk may bring about Pareto improvements.

Risk Sharing in a Partnership.   A useful starting point here is perhaps Umbeck's analysis of sharing arrangements during the California gold rush.[9] Miners formed groups that claimed plots of land as their own and defended these against nonmembers. Two arrangements for the exploitation of these plots were known. Under the first the spoils were divided evenly — with small exceptions to be discussed — among all members. For simplicity's sake we shall refer to this as a partnership. The second arrangement, which Umbeck calls the "allotment contract," consisted in dividing the territory claimed by the group as its own and allotting to each a parcel that he could work to the exclusion of all others.[10] The parcels were thus private property to each miner.

Since the talents of the miners were very similar and the equipment used for sifting gold from sand was rather elementary, one would not have expected a pooling of resources or a division of labor to have been interesting. Hence, one would have expected the division of the common land into private parcels to have been made from the outset.[11] But this is not what happened. Initially, the sharing contract or partnership was prevalent.[12] The explanation must be the great uncertainty about the yield of individual plots; sharing could reduce this uncertainty while not causing insurmountable problems itself. The actual yield could be easily supervised by all as gold had to be separated from sand in a common rocking cradle. Only large nuggets could be found by the naked eye, and these belonged to the discoverer, an exception to the sharing rule.

In later years sharing contracts disappeared in favor of allotment contracts. The reasons for this change are instructive. The change occurred as large numbers of adventure seekers moved into the mining area, making it impossible for an established group to defend its claimed territory against intruders. The absorpton of intruders into the group did not work either. The cost of reaching agreement within a larger group is higher, but most or all the enforcement of the contract — that is, the supervision of each group member by all others — becomes untolerably burdensome. Yet shirking becomes increasingly interesting for all with the growing number, since its effect would be seen as minimal on the efforts of the group as a whole. These disadvantages are similar to those of a "commons" discussed in Chapter 3 and, hence, one would expect that on balance the institution of private property rights would now have a comparative advantage over sharing. This development is confirmed by observation. It should be noted, though, that as more exploration had taken place, the uncertainty with respect to the yield of particular plots may have decreased, thus diminishing the advantage of sharing over property rights as a means of reducing individual risk.

The Principle of Limited Liability.   In a partnership the partners are fully liable for all the debts incurred in its name. For someone with capital to invest, this may be too much of a burden, even where he diversifies his placements. Instead, he would rather not participate in the running of the affairs of the partnership, but in return have his liability for its debts — in particular in case of bankruptcy — limited to the sum he invested. Such an arrangement is known as a limited partnership, or *société en commandite*.[13]

The scheme requires that publicity be given to the limitation of liability of the silent partner, in order that potential creditors can appropriately assess the risk-bearing capacity of the partnership. It is also obvious why the silent partner may not partake in the administration; there is a risk of something akin to moral hazard, since, if he administered it, he might be tempted to confer unto himself benefits for which his contribution would not fully pay. The silent partner may share in the profit of the partnership, but such payments must not consume his own contribution, again for obvious reasons.[14] Finally, the silent partner, though absent from the administration of the partnership, must have a say in the choice of managing partners[15] and be able to withdraw for a legitimate cause.[16] Of course, he must also be able to inspect the books of the partnership.[17] These last measures should be analyzed as means of preventing abuse — moral hazard of some kind — by the managing partners.

Stock in Companies. The idea of limited liability is further extended in stock in companies. The contribution to the enterprise is now made tradable; the denominations are sufficiently small that trade is in effect viable. For investors this facilitates diversification. But the tradability of stock gives a special coloring to this diversification. To illustrate, let us assume that while everyone expects some company to pay ordinary dividends, one of its shareholders knows that in fact it will do poorly. Rather than taking this unexpected loss as part of his diversified risks, this shareholder might sell the shares and buy into a company that is expected to do better. Where such foreknowledge is systematically available and used, the shareholder can expect to have higher returns on invested money than his competitors.

But what if one learns of the impending poor performance at the same time as most other people? At what price can the stock be sold? To analyze this question, we must introduce the notion of target or required yield on invested money, which shareholders set themselves. If the bank rate is at 11.5 percent, an investor who wishes to play the stock market must do better than this and would set himself the target of, say, 15 percent. This means that, whatever the nominal value of the stock, the return he expects on each dollar used to purchase it is fifteen cents. If dividend is lower than expected, let us say 7.5 percent per dollar that current shareholders have previously paid for the shares, new purchasers are interested in those shares only if the price is such that the (expected low) dividend will still give them a return of at least 15 percent on the new purchase price. But this means that the shares must sink at least to half their earlier value before purchasers will be found.

Of course, the calculation is slightly more complex in reality. Rather than the performance in the immediate future, one would take into account the entire stream of expected future dividends, discounted to the present. But the principle is the same. Poorer than expected performance of a company creates a capital loss — in stock value — for current holders. Once the loss has been taken into account, it yields normal returns on the depreciated value. It is also clear that early knowledge and quick action are very valuable in the stock market; they help to avoid those capital losses.

The discussion allows us to analyze more closely the value of the required return. It must include first of all the cost of using money in the absence of all uncertainty. This is presumably an amount close to the bank prime rate. It must further include an amount for the uncertain possibility that the company will fold and the investment will be lost. This second cost factor is common to bonds and stock. One might see it as a self-insurance premium on the capital. The return on stock contains yet another component, which sets it apart from bonds. Whereas the interest on bonds is fixed and is due barring bankruptcy, payments to shareholders come after those to ordinary creditors and only if earnings permit. It is this last uncertainty that requires an additional "insurance premium." Overall the share owner copes with uncertainty by diversifying his holdings, by investing in information that allows him to avoid or limit stock value losses,[18] and by requiring a higher yield than other moneylenders.[19]

This analysis points to some possibilities for false play. If share owners rely on information provided by company management, the latter might be tempted to release relatively pessimistic information ahead of the publication of the official results, or, what amounts to the same, they might withhold particularly favorable news. In all these cases they could buy stock at current prices and sell it at higher prices once the accurate information became public. Of course, shareholders, foreseeing this, will not rely only on such information, for the same reasons for which purchasers doubt seller information, as was discussed in Chapter 7. Be that as it may, prohibition of insider trading, publication of financial statements by independent auditors, and control of information on new share issues reflect concerns that privileged knowledge will be (ab)used to inflict losses on investors.

As in the case of silent partners, shareholders need to be informed about the company's performance. They also want a say in the appointment of the directors. This raises intricate questions due to the actual separation of ownership and control in modern companies. It would lead us to far afield to discuss these here.[20]

Risk Sharing by Creditors.   The insolvency of an enterprise usually means that creditors will be paid only part of what is owing to them. Hence, creditors share to some extent in the risk of such insolvency. The cost of assuming this risk is reflected in the rates or prices the creditor charges.

Once the creditor has established the "risk premium" he requires and agreement has been reached, the debtor has an incentive to increase the riskiness of the loan: the problem of moral hazard. Creditors may react to this prospect by charging higher rates — if the opportunity for moral hazard is circumscribed — and by monitoring the behavior of the debtor. In either case the additional cost is included in the rate or price set by the creditor. How much monitoring will be done depends on a tradeoff of the kind discussed in Chapter 5. Monitoring should be increased up to the point where an additional amount of it is costlier than the reduction in moral hazard it achieves.

The foregoing discussion provides an explanation for the unenforceability of the transactions made by the debtor on the eve of a bankruptcy, which reduce the assets available for distribution among creditors.[21] Lawyers would probably justify this rule by referring to the principle of equality among ordinary creditors. In an economic analysis one would argue that if creditors could contract on the subject while the debtor was still perfectly solvent — which in practice they cannot because of high transaction costs — this is most likely the arrangement they would come up with.[22] The reason for it is that if each creditor calculated that, in case of bankruptcy of the debtor, he would most likely recover nothing, but have an outside chance of being repaid in full — namely, if he pressed the debtor more quickly than the other creditors — he would increase his premium for uncertainty. Hence, even in good times the cost of credit for the debtor would go up.

Once the loans have been granted and the debtor's affairs seem to have taken a turn for the worse — he defaults on payments and so on — the creditors are locked in a prisoner's dilemma.[23] If all show restraint, it is possible that a consolidation agreement, which allows the debtor to turn around his affairs, may be reached. This is presumably in the interest of all creditors and of the economy at large; needless bankruptcies are a cost. Yet if one creditor decides ahead of the others that the debtor's business is irretrievably lost, he could press the debtor for payment immediately. This creditor would be better off under this arrangement than under a consolidation agreement; his money is not tied up for a long time. Of course, all the other creditors would now be worse off than under the consolidation agreement. This in turn leads one to the expectation that all creditors will spend more on monitoring the debtor to avoid being stuck after someone else has pressed the panic button and that on the whole more bankruptcies will be called — and each bankruptcy will be called sooner — than under a rule of restraint observed by all. The law voiding eve-of-bankruptcy transactions to the detriment of the creditors breaks the prisoner's dilemma here.[24]

Jackson and Kronman present an interesting argument about the reason for the institution of *secured creditor*.[25] At first sight it would seem to be an unjustifiable encumbrance of the principle of equality among creditors, a private agreement made to the detriment of other creditors. On further analysis, however, it emerges as an arrangement at which creditors would arrive among themselves if high transaction costs would not prevent them from doing so. The argument goes as follows. Let us abstract for the moment from monitoring costs. If one creditor obtains a security, his risk factor diminishes and hence he requires a lower rate. If one assumes only one other creditor, the risk factor for the latter increases since the assets available to cover his debt have shrunk in value. He would increase his rate. Standard theory of investment and risk analysis leads to the conclusion that these two changes offset each other. But now let us reintroduce the monitoring costs. If one of the creditors has a comparative advantage in monitoring the behavior of the debtor, one could give him an unsecured debt and the security to the other creditor. Monitoring the value of a security can be done at relatively low cost. Hence, one may expect for the second creditor a substantial saving, which is greater than the increase in monitoring cost for the first creditor. Taken together, the cost of monitoring has been reduced, and the resulting saving could be divided between the debtor and his creditors and reflected in the credit rates. The institution of secured loans thus allows one to make a Pareto improvement over a situation of unsecured creditors on an equal footing.

This analysis shows how one can take advantage of "specialization" in monitoring without an actual market for such services. Presumably, the sale of "monitoring" information by one creditor to others is not feasible because of the difficulty of recovering the fruits of this information from its various beneficiaries. Moreover, the other creditors would have reason to fear collusion between the monitor and the debtor to their detriment. The institution of secured loans offers a neat way to avoid these problems of "appropriability" and "reliability" of information.

Risk Transfer by Law

Contracts

In discussing markets for risk, we encountered several situations in which parties explicitly assign risks to one of them. They follow general principles of contract law in doing so. Yet contract law also contains specific rules with respect to the allocation of risk. These hold in the absence of agreement to the contrary and provide standard solutions on which parties can rely without having to take notice of them explicitly. If Posner's thesis of the efficiency of the common law is correct, the solutions proposed by these rules are those at which parties would have arrived themselves and that, in general, allocate risks at the lowest cost.

Impossibility and Force Majeure. An important set of such rules are those relating to impossibility and force majeure. They cover situations in which the promised performance is no longer feasible as a result of an unforeseen event (a promised rare painting has perished in a fire) or only at very much higher cost to the debtor (oil delivery from the Middle East after the blockade of the Suez Canal). Where the debtor could have prevented the contingency from occurring or have softened its impact, one might apply the Hand test discussed in the context of torts in Chapter 3. But even where prevention is not feasible, it may sometimes be efficient to hold the debtor liable. Posner and Rosenfield, in their article on the subject, state that in general the debtor (promisor, in their terms) should not be liable and, hence, the creditor (the promisee) should be saddled with the risk where:

(1) the promisor asking to be discharged could not
     reasonably have prevented the event rendering his
     performance uneconomical, and

(2)   the promisee could have insured against the occurrence of
the event at lower cost than the promisor because the
promisee
(a)   was in a better position to estimate both
(i)   the probability of the event's occurrence and
(ii)   the magnitude of the loss if it did occur, and
(b)   could have self-insured, whereas the promisor would
have had to buy more costly market insurance.[26]

The article from which this quotation was taken shows that
this general principle explains much of the case law on the subject
in areas as diverse as contracts for personal services or for the manufacture of specialized equipment, transportation contracts and
contracts for the supply of agricultural products.

Warranties.   Warranties give the purchaser of an object an action
against the seller or the manufacturer in cases of malfunctioning
of that object. When should warranties lie? As with unforeseen
contingencies, the answer should rest on a comparison of the two
parties with respect to prevention of, and insurance against, malfunctioning and the damages resulting from it.

With regard to prevention, one would expect that, if manufacturers were liable under warranty, the accent would be on design
improvement, whereas if purchasers were left with the burden, caution in use and careful maintenance would be promoted. How the
effectiveness of these avenues for prevention compares is an empirical question. One would imagine that in general, as objects become more complex, improved design contributes more to their
proper functioning — and absence of accidents — than caution and
care. Be that as it may, the combination of the two avenues would
be more effective than either one separately, and this might explain
why warranties by manufacturers are subject to an exception — a
defence — of abuse by the purchaser. Such abuse will now be recognized as moral hazard.

For damages that it is too costly to prevent, the relevant question
is which of the two parties is the better risk bearer. For mass-produced objects this may be the manufacturer. The manufacturer has
more accurate information on risks associated with the object he
manufactures than would the general insurer to whom the purchaser could go for insurance. The insurer would lump this particular risk together with a variety of others affecting his customer.

The cost of insurance for the particular object would be diffuse and not felt in the purchase of that object. Hence, the disincentive to acquire risk-generating objects would be less with purchaser insurance than with mandatory warranty by the manufacturer.

In recent times there has been a trend to impose mandatory warranties on manufacturers of mass-produced objects. It is plausible, on account of the foregoing, to believe that the manufacturer has a comparative advantage with respect to prevention as well as insurance, or at least for the two taken together. The intriguing question is, then, why the warranties had to be imposed by law. To an extent warranties are already offered by manufacturers, but the variety is such as to make them practically incomparable and unintelligible to purchasers. Government intervention would have created uniformity where it was lacking before and would have taken more time to emerge from autonomous market forces. But this answer is not entirely satisfactory. The mandatory warranties appear to have gone further than manufacturers would like in several cases. Misperception may be the problem here. Customers will not insist on features whose value they do not properly perceive, as we argued in Chapter 7. And manufacturers will not offer such features because of the risk of moral hazard.

Tort Rules

In Chapter 3 we saw that in the mainstream view the principle to be used in deciding whether someone is liable for damages or injuries inflicted on someone else is whether the injurer could have prevented such loss at less than its cost. If so, he should have prevented it and is liable; if not, the victim bears the burden. The victim also bears the burden of the misfortune — at least in some jurisdictions — if *he* could have prevented the accident economically, whatever the injurer's potential for doing so. It was argued that these rules favor arrangements that minimize the social cost of accidents — that is, as we then saw it, the sum of accident and prevention costs.

The discussion in this chapter affects these rules in several ways. Suppose that those who should prevent accidents according to these rules — injurers or victims — insure themselves against the liability or the losses they incur. If they are risk averse, the mere fact of the insurance will make the insured risk less burdensome (costly) to them. Hence, one might expect them to "consume more of it," — that is, to take greater risks. They will be all the more tempted to do so as the monitoring is difficult for the insurer. We are faced here with moral hazard.

The discussion in this chapter also affects the "unpreventable" accidents. Under the rules stated above, these are left where they fall, namely, with the victim, presumably on the ground that it is costly — lawyers, courts — to shift them. But what if the parties differed strongly in their ability to absorb risk? For instance, what if the injurer could more accurately assess the risk of loss and self-insure against it than could the victim? In that case overall cost to society would be lower if the injurer bore the burden of the un-preventable accidents, as we argued earlier with respect to warranties. The argument need not be restricted to insurance; any difference in the parties' ability to bear risk should affect our judgment as to who could best be burdened with the accident costs. If the parties could negotiate, they would presumably have put it themselves on the "cheapest risk absorber." We find here a justification for Calabresi's secondary costs, discussed in Chapter 4.[27] It should be stressed that these considerations are not to be confused with the consequences of liability rules on the *wealth* of injurers and victims; they are arguments of efficiency, albeit a refined version of it. A recent paper by Shavell argues that these considerations upset the conclusion put forward in the mainstream view that there is no difference between a negligence-liability rule and one of strict liability with a defence of contributory negligence.[28] For instance, strict liability for producers might be preferable to a negligence rule on the ground that the latter are less risk averse than consumers.

Conclusion

In most human affairs uncertainty is considered undesirable, and scarce resources are devoted to searching for ways to limit its impact. This can be done through prevention — that is, by trying to eliminate the risk of loss or to reduce the amount of the loss where it occurs — or through diversification. By this last term, borrowed from the field of finance and investment, one denotes a policy of combining a variety of independent risks so that losses occur at different moments or that losses in one instance are offset by gains in another during the same period. Diversification allows one to treat uncertain losses as equivalent to their expected monetary cost, whereas to a risk-averse person they would be much costlier.

People vary in their ability to cope with uncertainty in the ways just indicated, and this suggests the possibility of specialization in risk bearing and, generally, trade in risks. Two main forms of trading in risk — insurance and risk sharing — were discussed. In insurance an uncertain large loss is traded against a certain small one (the premium). The insurer himself diversifies his portfolio of risks or reinsures with others. While insurance may suggest the idea of "spreading" risks evenly among people, competitive pressure, here called adverse selection, will force insurers to make as fine a differentiation among insured risks — and hence in the premiums — as is possible, considering initial measurement and subsequent monitoring costs. The idea of insurance is frustrated where the insured can affect the size of the insured risk after its measurement by the insurer. The problem is known as moral hazard. To counteract it the insurer, short of refusing to insure altogether, can raise his premiums, monitor the behavior of the insured and agree only to partial insurance, leaving the insured with part of the burden of uncertainty. Moral hazard pervades trades in risk, and many rules of law could be analyzed as means of reducing it.

Risk sharing is the second form of trade in risk that was studied. In contrast to insurance, the person who agrees to share part of some risk does so in consideration of an uncertain gain or payment. The key problem in risk sharing is the temptation for those who take part in it to "free ride" on the efforts of the others. This might be seen as a form of moral hazard. As in the case of insurance, it calls for monitoring, and the cost of monitoring sets limits to the viability of the risk-sharing institution itself. The choice of the optimal level of monitoring requires an information tradeoff of the kind discussed in Chapter 5.

Risk sharing appears to occur mostly in business ventures, presumably because insurance is not viable here. Partnerships are the obvious example of it. Apart from talents and knowledge, the partners also share risk. It is frequently desirable for risk sharing to be limited; silent partners and common shares in companies reflect this idea. Shares have the additional feature of being conceived for the purpose of trade so as to make it easier for investors to diversify their holdings. It was shown that uncertainty about a share's earning potential would be reflected in a higher required yield for investors, whereas the expectation of a change in the earning potential would lead to a (windfall) gain or loss in the share price. Creditors, too, are — willy-nilly — made to share the risk of their debtor's business since, in case of bankruptcy, they cannot expect to be fully reimbursed. They, too, engage in monitoring of the debtor's activity, and it was argued that the cost of monitoring could explain such institutions as the nullity of transactions on the eve of bankruptcy (actio Pauliana) and secured credit.

Differences in ability to cope with risk explain a variety of legal rules. Impossibility or force majeure doctrines and warranties were discussed. The argument also provided a justification for lawyers' intuitive sense that accident law cannot have the unique function of minimizing the cost of accidents and their prevention. How accidents are borne is an equally relevant question, which Calabresi has been the first to raise in the economic analysis of law. In general, if people differ in their ability to cope with risk and would pay to have risk removed from them, the way in which risk is spread among people enters into the calculation of what is a Pareto optimum for society as a whole.

Arrow has made a very interesting observation about where these considerations may lead us:

> It may be useful to remark here that a good part of the
> preference for redistribution expressed in governmental
> taxation and expenditure policies and private charity can be
> reinterpreted as desire for insurance. It is noteworthy that
> virtually nowhere is there a system of subsidies that has as
> its aim simply an equalization of income. The subsidies or
> other governmental help go to those who are disadvantaged
> in life by events the incidence of which is popularly regarded
> as unpredictable: the blind, dependent children, the medically
> indigent. Thus, optimality, in a context which includes risk-
> bearing, includes much that appears to be motivated by
> distributional value judgments when looked at in a narrower
> context.[29]

CHAPTER 9

An Application:

Reflections on Consumer Protection Law

The costliness of information in all the facets analyzed in Part II makes explicable many rules of law that in a mainstream economic analysis would remain unexplained. In this chapter we look at one area, consumer protection law, where this would seem to be particularly true. Information problems of one kind or another appear to be at the root of the consumer's predicament. Economic analysis is capable here of clarifying the rather unsatisfactory theoretical foundation that lawyers advance for consumer protection. The analysis will draw mostly on literature and law on consumer protection in Quebec. The issues to be discussed should nonetheless be familiar to readers in other jurisdictions.

The Plight of the Consumer

Popular outcry of the kind that has given rise to consumer protection legislation is a relatively recent phenomenon. It is usually attributed to growing industrial concentration and increased sophistication of marketing methods known since the Second World War. These developments are believed to have eroded "the principle of the equality of parties to a contract [which] no longer reflects the true relation of strength between business enterprises and consumers."[1]

Inadequate Information

The disequilibrium is thought to have two dimensions. The consumer is considered to be inadequately informed for the choices he has to make and, in part as a result of it, open to exploitation. The consumer's difficulty in informing himself is seen as follows: "[I]n this consumer society . . . individuals can no longer judge for themselves all the increasingly sophisticated features of the products presented to them."[2] This is true in particular for the dangers of those products or services. The same source implies that this leads to fraud, abusive clauses and the degradation of the quality of products, to which the only effective remedy in many instances is thought to be consumer protection law.[3] But even this remedy gives cause for worry since "the law is absolutely not known" among consumers.[4] Worse still, with a little knowledge consumers believe themselves protected where they are not and are thus even more vulnerable to deceit. For instance, sales by itinerant vendors in Quebec can be cancelled within five days; most consumers believe that this holds for *all* sales.[5]

Exploitation

Exploitation occurs where firms are seen "unilaterally to dictate their will to consumers":[6]

> [The consumer] cannot in the vast majority of cases negotiate
> the price or the conditions of purchase of goods and services,
> and he is all the more vulnerable as these are frequently
> essential goods and services under the control of powerful
> firms, frequently monopolies.[7]

The object of scorn in these cases is the standard form contract, which is drafted by the stronger party and, of course, to its own advantage. And thus one is faced with

[d]wellings sold without warranty, waiver of liability clauses in all areas, excessive penalty clauses, warranties that are costlier to exercise than the purchase itself, assessment of the value of the performance left to the discretion of one of the parties, etc.[8]

The consumer stands to be exploited in a different way as well, namely, by fly-by-night operators. In modern form, these are "small firms that hope to plunder the entire region in a few weeks, disappear immediately afterwards, and emerge elsewhere under a new name."[9]

Postulation of Consumer Rights

In the presence of the difficulties just outlined, consumer advocates feel that law is necessary, as one author puts it, "to reestablish . . . a balance between the forces of consumers and business firms in the commercial market."[10] The law should seek to guarantee to the consumer a set of fundamental rights. One source formulates this set as follows. To alleviate the consumer's information problem, he sees the need for a *right to be informed*, a *right to be protected against misleading advertising*, and what might be termed a *right to be free from intruding information*, by which is meant subliminal advertising as well as messages addressed to particularly vulnerable audiences, such as children and welfare recipients.[11] Exploitation should be countered, in the author's view, by a *right to standard contracts negotiated or approved by the Consumer Protecton Office and to be adopted by all sellers in a branch* and a *right to revision of contracts on the ground of "lésion."*[12] Whatever the merits of this list — other authors might have put the accent elsewhere — we should like to make one addition, namely, the *right to effective recourse* against violations of consumer law. An empirical study by Masse and Marois makes it abundantly clear that the enforcement of rights cannot be taken for granted; consumers and the agencies to which they go for help vary greatly in their ability to obtain what is due to them.[13]

An Economic Analysis of the Consumer's Plight

The implementaton of the rights postulated for consumers requires, even on summary analysis, several derogations from the ordinary rules of the market. In line with our analysis in Chapter 2, we would expect to find uncommon forms of market failure, which could justify the uncommon measures proposed to give substance to the "consumer rights." This question will be studied in this and the next section.

The Rules of the Market

In general, competitive markets work to the benefit of consumers in that prices are kept at their lowest level, the variety of commodities and their characteristics correspond to what people prefer, and there is pressure on suppliers to innovate.[14] Even with respect to the tricky item that information is, competition will ensure, as we argued earlier, that satisfactory quantities of it are available, and its truthfulness can in many cases be guaranteed by such institutions as brand names or the reputation (goodwill) of firms.

These benefits of competitive markets, in standard microeconomic theory, stem from free exchange among consenting parties. The agreement of both parties ensures that the exchange constitutes a Pareto gain. In some instances market forces alone cannot ensure that no transactions that are not Pareto gains take place. In these cases the law steps in to complement the market. Some transactions are considered flawed from the very beginning. Contracts concluded by minors can in most cases be annulled on behalf of them. Contracts concluded mistakenly can be voided on the ground of error. Of course, the law ensures here that mere disappointed hopes will not vitiate the contract, as purchasers would surely abuse the power to rid themselves of their buy on this ground. Where error is provoked by the seller, the purchaser can annul the contract for reason of fraud and has recourse in damages against the vendor. This complements market pressures toward honesty, which, as we saw in Chapter 7, are not perfect and do not exclude fly-by-night operations.

Once the contract is validly formed, the law provides means to ensure its execution. This enables parties to agree to obligations that are to be performed far in the future without requiring costly safeguards to ensure such performance. In case of nonperformance, recourses in damages or — in some cases — specific performance are open to the party against whom the breach has been committed. Recourse for latent defects too can be seen as a means of extending contracts into the future; the vendor warrants for a certain time the absence of defects that are not visible at the time of sale. Warranties are specified by law in the absence of contrary agreement by the parties. But even where the vendor stipulates that he is not obliged to any warranty, he is liable for his own acts. A different rule would create moral hazard of some sort.[15]

These are, in outline, the rules of the market. Lawyers summarize them in the principles of freedom of contract and consensualism: One can agree, without formality, to whatever one likes, but, once committed, must abide by one's obligation.[16] These principles are in very important respects set aside by consumer protection law. What appears to work for contracting parties in general does not where consumers are involved. The difference between the two groups perhaps explains why courts have not been able to extend traditional principles of law to suit the alleged needs of the consumer. Such a policy risks, in the words of Baudouin:

> to state general principles that could be applied in situations
> that do not warrant such an extension of the existing law.
> One might, in the long term perhaps, see consumers
> everywhere and hence protect against their will, and even
> over their outspoken objection, people who have neither need
> nor desire for it and perhaps paralyze as well the
> development of certain sectors of business.[17]

The Consumer's Predicament in the Market

What distinguishes the consumer from other market participants?

The Consumer — a Small-Scale Participant.   Perhaps a lawyer's definition can give a clue here: "The consumer is the non-professional purchase of consumption goods for his personal use."[18] The consumer, one might paraphrase, is a small-time decisionmaker whose interests in any one purchase are too small to warrant a great deal of information processing. Bounded rationality should be particularly obvious in his decision making, and much of the information he needs for his purchases he will seek to acquire from other market participants, with the problems that implies. Furthermore, as consumers act generally on a small scale and for their own use, one should expect them to be averse to risk, in particular sensitive to hazards that endanger life or limb. Finally, one would expect that the scale at which consumers operate will not justify in many cases even minimal expenses necessary to enforce their rights.[19]

Informational Disadvantages. In themselves, these characteristics are not novel; it is hard to believe that consumers have not always lived under such constraints. What has changed, however, is the environment in which consumers exercise their choices. Increased wealth makes it possible for consumers to buy more commodities in any period than before. Hence, they would use more information than before, even though, of course, with increased wealth one can also more easily afford to make the wrong choice for want of information.

The greater diversity of available products and their increased technicity should accentuate the consumer's need for information. In particular, one would expect to see a need for information about the dangers of products. With increasing wealth the value of human life and limb are implicitly but constantly reevaluated upwards.[20]

Industrial concentration, whether pursued because of the economies of scale in production or because of the better risk-bearing capacity of larger units, affects consumers as well. Economies of scale in the physical production of goods are followed by similar economies in the informaton processing required to bring the product to the consumer. Advertising has already been discussed; standard contracts are information assets that reduce transaction costs; research on safety and other features of products shows substantial economies of scale in most instances. Manufacturers have a clear and increasing comparative advantage over individual consumers in producing such information. They have a comparative advantage as well with respect to risk bearing, as we noted in Chapter 8. With the large numbers involved in mass production, manufacturers can act as if they were risk neutral, in contrast with their customers, who act as individuals.

Powerlessness. Economies of scale are possible only if manufacturers can offer relatively uniform products with respect to physical qualities as well as the terms and conditions surrounding their sale. One would expect the manufacturer, in deciding what to include in his product, to add features only if he thought that consumers would be willing to pay for them, i.e., if the increased cost would be offset by increased benefits. If consumers were fully informed, competition would lead to products corresponding exactly to consumer preferences. But this is no longer so where consumers focus on only a few features and tend to misestimate small probabilities.[21]

Let us take a feature that is not in the public eye because it is not one of those on which comparison shoppers focus their attention or because its addition to the product is not perceived as an advantage by these shoppers because of the small probabilities involved. Examples of such "irrelevant" features might be the safety devices in cars that we now consider necessary, but which were thought superfluous in the 1950s. Presumably, people regarded car accidents at the time as hazards associated with driving, preventable only, if at all, by driving skill. Focus at the time was on size and power. An example of a feature ignored because of misperceived probabilities might be a repossession clause in a condition sales contract or a giving-in-payment clause in a hypothec in Quebec; in both cases a defaulting debtor is deprived of all rights in the object of the security, which can be very harsh in cases where a substantial portion of the debt has been paid. Such clauses might well be ignored because most consumers consider themselves unlikely to go into default.

Why do sellers not offer safer products in the first example, more clement terms for default in the second? The reason is that this would add to their cost and yet not make a *perceived* difference, for which consumers would be willing to pay, in their product. Indeed, manufacturers can afford to disappoint some consumers since, as long as the public eye does not focus on these features and, hence, they are not on the comparison shoppers' list, no competitor will attract customers by offering a better deal on these items.[22] Disappointed consumers under these circumstances have nowhere to turn, even in a perfectly competitive market. It is quite conceivable that most consumers are in the disappointed minority with respect to some features, even as they are satisfied with the product in most other regards. This result may explain the observation that firms "unilaterally dictate their terms" to consumers, even though they heed pressure from consumers *as a group* in a competitive market.

The paradox set out here holds equally well for information. Sellers will not produce information that is costly to them, unless it is in the public eye.[23] They will not, for instance, undertake research on the dangers of drugs, cars or toys, unless the safety of these products has become an issue. Nor will they produce information if doing so entails the risk of losing sales. Tobacco manufacturers will not stress the carcinogenic qualities of their cigarettes, even if theirs are better in this respect than those of the competitors. Nor will a car manufacturer publicize that his cars will run three years before rust spots appear on them as opposed to the two years for his competitors' products. To call attention to such negative features is damaging to all manufacturers alike.

How far can manufacturers stretch their disdain for the minority — in other words, when will features be brought into the public eye? From the manufacturer's point of view, the tipping point is where the dissatisfied minority has grown sufficiently — that is, where the demand for the new feature is high enough — that by changing his product or its "packaging" and advertising the new feature, he can attract new clients and increase his total revenues. What causes shifts in the demand for some feature? Standard microeconomic theory stresses income, the relative price of substitutes and complements, and changing tastes.[24] This last factor should be particularly interesting in the context of bounded rationality. Shifts in public concern could be triggered by dramatic accidents (recall the availability heuristic), newspaper reports in some cases, actions by organized groups and so on.[25] Hence, if such shifts are considered beneficial to the economy, the availability of information that is not in the hands of sellers as well as the presence of organized consumer groups in the market would be desirable.

The Problems of Grouping Consumer Interests. Implicit in the foregoing discussion is the suggestion that if consumers could band together, many of the problems discussed would not arise. Why are consumer groups so sparse? Trebilcock attributes it to the free-rider problem.[26] Those who would undertake action on behalf of consumers usually do not have a high enough personal stake to compensate them for the cost of their efforts; nor can they "appropriate" the positive results they achieve in order to extract payment for their use by other consumers. Olson argues that, because of this paradox, organizations providing collective benefits, which cannot be appropriated, will supply some noncollective good — such as a magazine or reductions on some goods or services — as well to entice their members.[27] Others believe that tax deductibility of contributions to interest groups will counter the free-rider problem.[28] In spite of these measures, the problem is likely to persist sufficiently for interest-group promotors to ask for public subsidies. Public subsidization, however, raises other problems: Which constituency does the group represent and for what action? In the absence of signals by the represented consumers themselves in the form of payments, it is difficult to judge whether action by a consumer-interest group will in fact bring a Pareto gain for the group they claim to represent. All in all, grouping of consumer interests is likely to remain problematic.

Summary. The essence of the consumer's plight in the modern market is the substantial and growing difference in scale between his operations and those of the producers and sellers with whom he deals. This means that the consumer is at a disadvantage in all the uses of information discussed in Part II. Moreover, his stake in a wrong done to him is usually not large enough to warrant a recourse in law. The difference in scale may also explain why consumers may have a feeling of powerlessness where they deal with large-scale producers. While uniformity of products may itself make it impossible to please everyone at once — who could afford a car hand-built to suit his personal taste? — in other instances a more subtle mechanism is a work. Sellers will not add features that are costly to them but whose benefit is not perceived by the majority of clients, even though it is by some and even though the majority might choose differently if it were better informed. Bounded rationality plays havoc with the principles that people know what is best for them and that the market will provide it.

Imperfections and Proposed Remedies in the Consumer Market

We must now return to the alleged abuse of consumers as it emerged from statements quoted at the beginning of this chapter. The question here is whether those phenomena constitute market failure and whether proposed remedies could improve matters.[29]

Monopoly

Where monopoly exists, there is inequality of bargaining power of a kind in which one party might "unilaterally dictate" the terms of an agreement to the other. Short of foregoing the product altogether, the "weaker" party has no choice but to accept. Monopoly is indeed one of the traditional forms of market failure. It raises problems for all market participants, not for the species "consumer" only. Be that as it may, it should be stressed that monopoly is much rarer than the loose use of the term by some consumerists might suggest. It would be deceiving to speak of monopoly in all situations where a serious disproportion exists between the interests of the parties to an exchange.[30] We shall not deal further with this problem nor with the special form in which it presents itself in regulated monopolies.[31]

Fly-by-Night Operators

This group abuses consumer confidence by misrepresenting experience features, by taking payment without delivering promised goods and so on, while making it effectively impossible for consumers to discipline them through market forces or by law. One might think that consumers could avoid falling into this trap by dealing only with established firms, for the value of their reputation makes such practices unprofitable. But this ignores that competition is fostered when consumers seek out newcomers to the market, who innovate in products, accessory services, or prices. How should consumers distinguish these newcomers from the crooks who look for a quick profit? Hence one should not expect market forces to discipline the crooks. Dissolution of the contracts for reason of fraud is ineffective as well, since the vendor has disappeared or is bankrupt or otherwise without assets. The civil recourse against "judgment-proof" defendants is useless. Traditionally, the law seeks to discourage these fraudulent practices by making them criminal offences. Experience shows, however — as economic analysis would predict[32] — that this remedy is relatively ineffective because of the difficulty of proving these cases.

It is quite conceivable that the speed of communication and transportation as well as the ease with which one can set up and liquidate corporate vehicles facilitate the operation of the fly-by-night. In any event, consumers may become his victims where they cannot, within their normal information constraints, distinguish him from honest traders. Clearly, the autonomous market forces leave us with an imperfection. The remedies proposed here are mainly mandatory permits for sellers in the fly-by-night category, mandatory security to guarantee performance of the seller's obligations, and the obligation to put in a trust account monies paid in advance by consumers.[33]

Permits may be suspended or withdrawn by the issuing authority where the solvability or honesty of the holder is in doubt. Since the permit is necessary for the trader to do business, it represents a capital asset that opens the way for a stream of future benefits and is similar in this respect to reputation, discussed in Chapter 7. As a guarantee it will be effective if consumers insist on seeing the permit and if violations are in fact brought to the attention of the issuing authority and lead to suspension or nonissuance of permits. To what extent both these conditions will be satisfied is an empirical question. For the first condition knowledge of the law on the consumer's part would seem to be an important factor. For the second the budget of the policing authority as well as the discretion left to it by the courts in lawsuits, which are sure to arise, would seem to be the most relevant considerations. It should be noted that the permit system, along with the possible benefits just mentioned, certainly creates costs for all the sellers who are subject to it: costs of formalities to be performed, dues, waiting and so on. Whether on balance the benefits of the permit system over the autonomous market outweigh the costs of its implementation is a question that cannot be answered in the abstract. It is clear, however, that the costs of the permit system are spread over a large group, whereas the costs of dishonesty in the autonomous market fall on a few consumers who are the victims of it. For risk-averse consumers, this may be an important consideration, as we argued in Chapter 8.

Mandatory security or surety is a direct cost to the seller. If he gives security on capital, it restricts his freedom to dispose of it; if he contracts with an insurance company to set up a suretyship, he owes premiums. Consumers, who will pay for these costs in the end, have the guarantee that they can effectively exercise a recourse against the vendor and perhaps, where an insurance company is involved, that the monitoring undertaken by that company will eliminate some dishonest or insolvent traders. Mandatory security has the further effect of making a guarantee or an insurance premium against dishonesty part of the normal business costs of the sellers concerned.

The obligation to deposit advance payments made by consumers into a *trust account* is an additional guarantee for the consumer that, in case of trouble, he can get his money back. It would also seem to facilitate the task of officers who investigate commercial fraud; misappropriation of funds is more easily established than other fraudulent manoeuvres. As with permits and mandatory security, this device increases transaction costs.

All in all, it is not possible for us to determine in the abstract whether the various devices proposed create a net social benefit, in particular whether the reduction in dishonesty they achieve outweighs the direct costs of the measures — increased prices as well as the cost of the enforcing authority — and the indirect ones in the form of the disincentive effect they may have on innovation in marketing. As a sure benefit of these measures for risk-averse consumers, one should count the fact that they tend to spread the cost associated with dishonesty rather than leave it on the heads of a few victims, as the autonomous market would.

Lack of Information for Consumers

Our analysis in Chapter 7 shows that the consumer's inability to extract for himself the information he wants for his purchases need not impair the functioning of a competitive market. Information will be made available as a product in the market. Indeed, some kinds of information are overabundantly available and, in fact, forced on the consumer. Most people would presumably not be willing to pay for all the information they absorb through television and newspapers. Moreover, if a seller would rather not divulge some information that consumers desire, competitors who have a better product will attract clients by revealing the information.

Yet all is not perfect in the information market. Apart from the problem of trustworthiness of information provided by sellers, to be discussed below, we saw earlier in this chapter that they have an interest in not revealing information that is a net cost to them, even if it is in fact of interest to consumers. Moreover, even where information is made available, the consumer may still find it less than helpful in comparing products. These two problems are met by measures meant to ensure disclosure and uniformity of information.

The Obligation to Disclose. In ordinary civil law there is no general obligation to disclose information to one's contracting partner.[34] Only in special cases does the law attach consequences to nondisclosure. Where a party has started to reveal relevant facts, he must reveal all of them, not only those favorable to his cause, and he must declare them truthfully. Failure to do so constitutes fraud, with the consequences discussed earlier. In the contract of sale, the purchaser who discovers a latent defect in the object can return it to the vendor and claim the purchase price or keep it and recover part of the price corresponding to the estimated reduction in value resulting from the defect. Where the vendor specializes in the type of object sold or is its manufacturer, the purchaser has a further action in damages against him. These recourses are not open for *apparent* defects, and one must conclude that in revealing the defect, the vendor shields himself from recourses. A third area of law in which nondisclosure of information has legal consequences is insurance; withholding relevant facts of which one is aware voids the insurance contract.

These rules seem to be roughly compatible with Kronman's theory about disclosure.[35] The theory says that where a party incurs costs to acquire information in order to make profitable transactions with it, the law will not oblige him to divulge it. If, however, he acquires the information casually — that is, in the course of other activities — he must divulge it. To oblige people to divulge information in the first case would discourage them from generating it and thus dry up a socially useful source of exploration and innovation. In the examples given above, the vendor of a commodity such as a house has information on its defects as a result of living in it, specializing in the trade, or constructing it. The insured has acquired information relevant to the insurer in a casual way. Finally, one who starts to reveal some information must be presumed to have given up the possibility of making a profit from not revealing it at all or, to put it differently, he has agreed to supply his partner with the information.

One might object that manufacturers are liable for the damages suffered as a result of latent defects, even if they show that they could not have known them by taking reasonable precautions — that is, by incurring costs to detect them. But the issue is different here. The reason for such a rule could be that the manufacturer is considered better able than his customers to develop the relevant information or, if he prefers it, to bear the risk of unknown defects.

Consumer protection law extensively codifies the obligation to disclose information on the price, terms and accessory services for various commodities, such as credit, repairs of cars and electrical equipment, used cars, and fitness, training or educational services. It also regulates the contents of labels on food and drugs, ticketing in stores, information to be provided by itinerant salesmen, and so forth. In several instances these moves can be seen as attempts to standardize information, the substance of which would be provided anyway, but in a form less transparent to the consumer. This question will be discussed below. In most cases, however, the information to be disclosed might otherwise not be explicitly transmitted to the consumer, for reasons discussed in the second section. Thus, a document of warranty must state, among other things, whether it can be transferred or not, who undertakes it, and who can act, for example, repair, on behalf of the warrantor.[36] If the contractual warranty is valid only if maintenance is done by an authorized dealer, any other serviceman, before undertaking work for the consumer, must warn him in writing that it will not be covered by the manufacturer's warranty.[37] A used car offered for sale must have on it a label that states, among other things, whether it has served as a taxi or police vehicle or in some other demanding use, and what repairs the dealer has made to it.[38]

Clearly, the information required here is available to the seller without additional cost, so that there is no reason to protect it on account of Kronman's theory.[39] If it is not revealed otherwise, the explanation must lie in the perversity discussed in the second section or in the fact that consumers truly attach no importance to it and useless transaction costs are avoided by leaving it out. Which of the hypotheses is accurate must be settled by field work; if, after introduction of the new rules, one saw an increase in the price variance for the items on which consumers are now better informed, the first hypothesis would be more plausible. The better items should fetch higher prices, the poorer ones lower prices than before. In the absence of information allowing them to discriminate quality categories, consumers would pay the average price for all items and assume the uncertainty with regard to their true quality. This uncertainty itself is a cost to risk-averse consumers and tends to reduce the price they are willing to pay for the item in question. Disclosure rules remove part of this uncertainty from consumers, and this should perhaps be reflected in a rise of the average price of the items in question. But notice that the increased transaction costs will raise prices as well. Hence the observation of a price rise does not in itself authorize the conclusion, which some would like to draw, that consumer law is ineffective and merely drives prices up. All in all, disclosure rules can quite conceivably entail social gains that outweigh the increased transaction costs they impose on traders.

Standardization of Information.   Uniform information is an advantage to consumers, in that it facilitates comparison shopping. A variety of rules — unit pricing, egg and meat grading, standard content requirements on food lables or used cars, standard terms in contracts, and so on — are issued to this end. In many cases the market itself will arrive at uniformity. Where it does not, uniform presentation of information that is to be disclosed anyway should bring social gains at little increase in transaction costs.

Misleading Information

In Chapter 7 the incentives for the seller to provide biased information were analyzed. The limit is set by the cost of the consumer's next-best source of information. Our analysis made it clear that social gains could be made if one could break the perverse dilemma in which the honest trader loses clients to those who distort information. The law may attempt to do this, but the result of such efforts is that as consumers believe that they can safely rely on information by the seller, the occasional decepton that escapes detection is highly profitable, much more so than without the rules against misleading information. Rules against this form of decepton bring a social gain if the reduction in the cost of dishonesty to the public is greater than the cost of enforcing the rules. It requires little argument to see that the profitability of misleading information as well as the cost of detecting and proving it in court varies among different forms of deception. Bait-and-switch selling — in which a spectacular bargain is offered, but the vendor has only a few items in stock, which are quickly sold out — is more easily established than the misleading character of an "illustrated advertisement [implying] that womens' two piece swim suits cost $7.95 when investigation showed [that the firm] charged $7.95 for each piece."[40] Moreover, even where there are conceivable gains from issuing and enforcing rules against deceptive information, budget constraints on the enforcing authority may be such that optimal enforcement is not achieved, indeed that there is not even a net social gain from its activity.[41]

Legislation applicable in Quebec contains a variety of rules against misleading advertising. Federal law prohibits such practices as making false representations to the public, misuse of tests and testimonials by known personalities, double ticketing (where the price charged is more than the lowest indicated on any ticket), "bait-and-switch selling," sale above the advertised price and so on.[42] The new Quebec *Consumer Protecton Act* covers much of the same ground.[43] We know of no empirical study attempting to assess the effect of these rules and to compare it — in some fashion — with the cost of their implementation.

A different type of disincentive for sellers to distort information is provided in this last act as well. It stipulates that the commodity that is sold must conform to its description in the contract or in an advertisement, that warranties promised in advertising, even if not reproduced in the written contract, will be upheld against the vendor, and that statements by the representative of the vendor must be honored by the latter.[44] Arguably, these stipulations duplicate ordinary civil law. Whatever may be of that, they put part of the initiative to enforce honesty in information by sellers in the hands of the primarily interested party: the consumer. How effective this is, given the consumer's difficulty in exercising legal recourses, is an open question.

Standard Form Contracts

Standard form contracts appear to epitomize, in the eyes of consumer advocates, the plight of the consumer. Their terms are seen as "unilaterally dictated" rather than agreed, and they seem to reflect the market power of one of the parties over the other: take it or leave it. Such observations are thought to justify interventions to restore a balance between the parties; courts might strike down clauses as against "l'ordre public économique,"[45] and the legislator might prohibit some clauses, prescribe others.

Standard Contracts as Transaction Costs Reducing Assets. While there may be reason for uneasiness with standard form contracts, the criticism sketched above appears to us, in its generality, to be unjustified. First and foremost, standard contracts are used to facilitate the exchange of goods and services. They are devices that reduce transaction costs. If each contract for a relatively standardized good or service had to be negotiated separately, the cost of doing business would escalate enormously and, as a result, many goods and services would be priced out of existence.[46] Standard form contracts are capital information goods, allowing their drafters to realize economies of scale. In a competitive market, these should normally benefit the consumer.

Standard Contracts and Market Power. The use of standard contracts cannot be taken as evidence of abuse of market power by a monopoly or a cartel of producers. Indeed, standard forms are used in a wide variety of industries, most of which are at least workably competitive. Dry-cleaners, hotels, parking lots, insurance companies, landlords of residential premises, real estate agents and many others use standard forms in dealing with their customers. The fact that contracts are offered here on a take-it-or-leave-it basis is evidence, as Trebilcock reminds us, "not of market power but of a recognition that neither producer — nor consumer — interests in aggregate are served by incurring the costs involved in negotiating separately every transaction."[47]

Nor is it surprising that, in situations where standard contracts are appropriate, their creation should be undertaken by the party who presumably can do this most cheaply, in practice the vendor. This does not mean that the contract would not generally reflect consumer preferences. Long-term relationships and the disciplining force of consumers' option to change suppliers should normally provide the latter with the incentive to cater to consumer preferences with regard to terms, as much as to price and other readily inspected features.

How Is the Consumer Exploited? The argument so far amounts to the proposition that contracting through standard forms conforms to the voluntary exchange assumed in the neoclassical model, provided only that account is taken of the (information) cost of producing individualized — rather than mass — transactions. But this is not the only role of information in the piece. In our discussion of the "powerlessness" of the consumer earlier in this chapter, we noted that in many circumstances it would be irrational for the consumer to investigate all aspects of a commodity he wishes to acquire. In very classical terms, the search effort required would not be worth its cost in terms of reduced chances of disappointment.

Consumers will therefore focus on only a few features of the product, such as its price, outward appearance and major conditions of sale. On these features, which, we said, are in the public eye, competition will heed consumer preference. On all other terms (and features of the product), the market will lead to "harsh-term-low-price" policies;[48] producers prepared to offer more lenient terms for a higher price will be outbid by competitors, as consumers are unable to perceive the additional benefit that they get in exchange for the higher price. Moreover, as long as such features stayed out of public view for the majority of consumers, producers would have an interest in ignoring small groups of them who would seek a change of terms. Even if dissatisfied, these consumers would have nowhere to turn, as no competitor would find it profitable to change his terms.

We argued earlier that this phenomenon would present itself with respect to substantive features as well as information that could be provided by the seller. One would expect it to be more severe, as Trebilcock observes, "in markets involving expensive and complex goods and services which consumers purchase infrequently and of which they have little 'experience' information."[49] Terms of contracts should, in general, be costlier to search than most physical features of commodities and hence more subject to the perversity.[50] It may take the form of stiff penalty clauses (forfeiture of the object of a security in case of default in repaying a loan), extensive waiver-of-liability clauses, declaration of default of the debtor unilaterally by the credit grantor, and so on.

Interventions I: Prohibition or Prescription of Clauses.   Consumer protection law contains several dispositions prohibiting such (draconian) clauses[51] or prescribing others,[52] such as mandatory warranty or even entire contracts.[53] Trebilcock, commenting on Goldberg's article recommending such interventions,[54] sees several difficulties with them. First, he asks how one is to decide whether in aggregate consumers are better off as a result of legislation that prohibits harsh terms, but leads to higher prices. If true consumer preferences can never be revealed because of information difficulties, how can one compare the merits of the new milder terms/higher price contract with the previous harsher terms/lower price package?[55] If one is to look for a benchmark in the revealed preferences of other consumers in the market, he argues, difficulties of perception are apparently not so great that the market could not correct itself; hence, in his view, it is better left alone. But this is not entirely to the point.

While it may be true that consumer preferences on the terms that are not in public view would normally not be revealed, they may well be where it is made cheaper to search and compare those terms and where public attention is focused on them. The first possibility is plausible, in our view, on the evidence with unit pricing, admittedly a not altogether similar kind of information. On this account one would expect emphasis on clearly stated, intelligible, and conspicuous clauses and on simplified and uniform categories of warranties, waivers, and so on.[56] Admittedly, the industry itself could formulate rules to this effect, but this raises problems of cartelization, which creates a substantial risk of harm to consumers and is forbidden for that reason.

The legislature can also attempt to focus attention on clauses thought to be harmful, but misperceived by consumers. It can do this by funding independent studies and consumer-interest groups. Moreover, it is quite conceivable that the threat of legislation itself, with the debate that often surrounds it, may focus attention on "harsh terms." For instance, hypothec contracts in Quebec used to contain as a standard clause the provision that the loan cannot be paid in advance of the term without a substantial penalty. In 1979 there was discussion of legislation prohibiting such clauses and allowing consumers to reimburse at all times, with some provisos.[57] Within six months or so, the market responded by offering various packages in which the option to reimburse was granted for a slightly higher interest rate (¼ percent, for instance). One could argue that the market would have arrived at this result autonomously. But that contention is unproven and, even if one granted it, the adjustment is likely to have been quicker this way. Whether the time gained is worth the cost of the public debate is a question on which we shall not speculate here.

This leaves us with the question of determining under which circumstances one might think consumers better off from legislation prohibiting certain clauses and proscribing others. Repossession clauses with the possibility for the credit grantor to declare default of the debtor unilaterally will surely, as we saw in Chapter 1, lower the cost of credit through the incentives they give the debtor not to default and through the possibility they offer the creditor to recover more than his actual cost. The creditor is, as it were, insured against default by the debtor. But notice that in insurance the law forbids an insured amount above the actual damages, a rule that can be analyzed as a means to avoid moral hazard by the insured. Restrictions on creditors' repossession should be seen in the same way.[58]

A second class of rules imposes substantive obligations, such as warranties, on vendors and restricts their right to free themselves of these obligations by contract. In the third section of Chapter 8, we discussed the reasons for mandatory warranties. Manufacturers of mass-produced goods generally have an advantage over consumers or their insurers in preventing accidents through better design and perhaps as well in risk bearing with respect to the accidents that do occur. Because of the risk of moral hazard by customers who use the product and because of the problems of misperception by this group, manufacturers are unlikely to assume this extensive warranty autonomously.[59] Given mandatory warranty, the prohibition to exclude it contractually follows naturally. It is clear that the warranty comes at a price and that the market will express its cost in price or other terms.[60]

Interventions II: Agencies Negotiating on Behalf of the Consumers. A second approach to the problems raised by standard form contracts is to provide a mechanism whereby agents negotiate them on behalf of consumers. Masse proposes such agency powers for the Consumer Protection Office.[61] While the proposal overcomes the constraints of bounded rationality facing individual consumers, the question of representativity becomes acute. An agency without an explicit and regularly renewed mandate must now act for a group of individuals with diverse interests on a variety of issues.

Conclusion. All in all, it seems to us quite conceivable that various interventions in the field of standard form contracts would, with further evidence from observation, be judged beneficial in the sense that the improvement in market performance could be said to outweigh the costs. This would be so for rules imposing uniformity, for studies of standard forms that might bring disadvantageous, but misperceived, clauses into public view, as well as for some specific prohibitions and prescriptions with respect to penalty clauses, waivers of liability, and warranties. Whether standard contracts negotiated for consumers by the Consumer Protection Office will be equally beneficial seems to us less certain.

The Quality of Goods and Services

The Alleged Degradation of Quality. Along with fraud and abusive clauses, degradation of the quality of goods and services was seen by sources quoted at the beginning of this chapter as an important aspect of the consumer's plight in modern society.[62] In the abstract this complaint is hard to place. Quality, after all, should be seen in relation to price. What then should we read in this remark? Surely not that for a given price the quality one can expect goes down over time; with inflation this is a totally uninteresting observation. Nor could it mean that the quality of products available in earlier days is no longer attained. It seems difficult to believe that this would be true for those who are willing to pay the price. Of course, the price differential between first and lower quality may not be the same as of old. Where this is true — not for all products, we should think — it may indicate nothing more shocking than different technology.

Perhaps the alleged degradation of quality means that, in the least expensive and, one must presume, lowest grades, products have a lower quality than before. And this may well be true. But as the overall access to commodities has expanded, it is most likely that the lowest grades of products can be bought by groups of the population who previously could not afford those commodities at all. One may regret that no better quality of product can be offered for the price this group can pay. But short of changing the distribution of wealth in society, with its attendant difficulties, one will have to accept this limitation of our productive capacity.

One last interpretation fits better into the discussion in this chapter. It is that in modern society, producers, for reasons discussed in the second section, are better able than their predecessors to offer poor-quality-low-price products. This fear leads us back to discussions in the three previous subsections. One might reply by referring to remedies discussed there.

Dangerous Products. Consumer protection legislation contains a variety of rules with regard to the safety of products offered to the public. There are norms for food, drugs and dangerous products generally.[63] Electrical equipment is to be certified,[64] and cars must have a variety of safety features and withstand certain tests meant to measure their solidity and safety for occupants.[65] The structure of buildings is subject to norms.[66]

There can be no question that the hazards these norms seek to prevent are quite damaging to the victims, even though they materialize in only a tiny fraction of the objects involved or in very unlikely circumstances. These hazards are of a kind likely to be misperceived by consumers. These are presumably major reasons for the regulation of safety, which consists mainly of preventive measures. One may not market products without permission and, if unsuspected dangers emerge, public authority can summarily order the withdrawal of the products concerned from the market.

Opponents of such measures argue that they unnecessarily retard innovation, that they prevent people from trading on their taste for risk, and that they entail further social waste because the norms can be only imperfectly applied by the regulating authority.[67] Some of the opponents would argue that the market can take care of itself, provided that it opens the way for negligence actions against manufacturers. Against this view, one must recall the difficulties for consumers to exercise legal recourses because of their small stakes and because damages awarded by the courts ordinarily undercompensate them, as we saw in Chapter 3. Furthermore, in cases resulting from injuries inflicted by dangerous products, negligence as well as causality are frequently very difficult to prove in court.[68] All of this would lead to the result that the manufacturer of the hazardous product is made to feel less than the actual social cost of the accidents he causes and hence has less than optimal incentives to introduce accident-preventing modifications in his products.

Strict liability eases the evidentiary problem, but leaves us with the two other constraints. It also saddles the manufacturer with the burden of the accidents that cannot be prevented, presumably on the grounds discussed earlier for imposing mandatory warranties on him. Strict liability for manufacturers is proposed in Quebec's new Civil Code.[69] Should this prove to be insufficiently effective, Cornell et al. propose "lowering standards of proof, raising compensation limits under workmen's compensation, or imposing taxes on product- and work-related accidents."[70] Complementary to this, they recommend that public authority disseminate information that "can be obtained and understood so easily that people will use it."[71]

Why, then, use standards at all? Cornell et al. feel that they are appropriate "when decisions are numerous and information complex" and "if the nature of a hazard is uncertain."[72] In these cases public authority can acquire and process information with economies of scale not open to private-market participants. Where this argument does not lie — that is, in cases where the industry is sizable and has its own research facilities — strengthening of the liability system and of facilities for consumers to sue should provide the appropriate incentives for safety in products.

Enforcement of Rights and Sanctions

The Creation of Evidence. Since a major disincentive for consumers to sue sellers is their problem of proving the case, consumer protection legislation imposes practices for accumulating evidence ahead of litigation and facilitates the consumer's tasks during trial. Several contracts must be witnessed by a document under the *Consumer Protection Act*[73] and, for repair services, a written estimate before the actual work is undertaken is mandatory.[74] During trial the consumer is allowed to introduce witnesses, even to contradict the terms of a written agreement.[75]

Reducing Procedural Costs. The institution of the class action before the regular courts as well as the possibility for consumers to sue manufacturers before small-claims courts should foster the effective functioning of market forces and the courts system that complements them. The problems surrounding these institutions were discussed in Chapter 3. Contingent fees have been proposed as a means of removing from the consumer the cost associated with the rejection of his claim against a vendor.[76] It would lead us too far afield to discuss the potentially offsetting disadvantages of this institution.[77]

Sanctions. It has been observed that the traditional sanctions of the civil law are not sufficiently effective in consumer transactions.[78] Voiding a contract is not always the best way of helping the consumer; maintaining it, but at a more advantageous price to him, is usually more to the point. This sanction is known as the *revision* of the contract by the court and lies in cases of *lésion*. Under ordinary civil law this sanction exists only for minors and interdicted persons.[79] The *Consumer Protection Act* allows it in all cases

> where the disproportion between the respective performances of the parties is so considerable as to amount to the exploitation of the consumer or where the obligation of the consumer is excessive, abusive or unconscionable.[80]

The difficulties with this rule are determining when it applies and how it should be applied. In a competitive market it is easy enough to decide that a consumer has been exploited where, for instance, for a second-hand car he has paid a price for which elsewhere he would have had a new car of the same make. But such cases could be handled with a suitably interpreted notion of *dol* (fraud) or error, when one takes into consideration the conditions in which the contract has been formed and the ability of each party to avoid mistakes. In more complex agreements, nonequivalence is not so readily determined, as Trebilcock's analysis of the contract between a young (and initially unknown) songwriter and an established music-publishing company shows.[81] In discussing the issue of substantive unfairness, he argues that substantial nonequivalence of the obligations of the contracting parties could arise only where there is abnormal market power or aberrations in the process of contract formation.[82] Under the latter heading one finds a discussion of "unfair surprise," which is extended to cover situations in which the consumer is at a serious informational disadvantage — that is, those we analyzed in previous subsections. The question of whether there was exploitation now parallels the economic issue of whether consumers would have chosen differently, had they been fully aware of *all* the aspects of the transaction. This is not an easy question to answer.

Once it has been decided that the contract is flawed by *lésion*, the judge must undertake to revise the contract and reduce the consumer's obligations. Presumably he would seek to approximate the competitive market value of what the consumer has received and adjust his obligations accordingly. This evaluation is necessarily imprecise, but perhaps not more so than where the judge assesses damages in a tort action.

The second innovative sanction in the *Consumer Protection Act* is *punitive* or *exemplary damages*.[83] The act is silent about the criteria to be used in determining when they should be awarded and what the amount should be. Several arguments are possible. First, one might see here a response to the problem that judicially awarded damages never fully compensate the victim of a wrong, in particular where the loss is nonmaterial and hence difficult to evaluate. Opening the possibility for such compensation should strengthen the consumer's incentive to sue sellers at whose hands he has suffered. This would tend to make sellers aware of the full social costs of their activity.

A second interpretation is that this kind of damage award has a penal function and would be appropriate where the seller would not normally be used for his wrongdoings because the stakes for individual consumers were too small or because the loss they suffered was difficult to detect. In this interpretation the amount of damages should be the loss incurred by any one individual multiplied by the number of individuals who may have suffered such a loss, but have not taken legal action. It should be added that while in this interpretation, too, the seller is made to realize the full social cost of his activity, the normal way of aggregating a multitude of similar claims is the class action.

Conclusion

The literature on consumer protection leaves one with the impression that in the modern market the consumer is the underdog, the weaker party, misinformed about the choices open to him and exploited by other market participants. In this chapter we have examined how such intuitive impressions could be explained by an economic analysis. In essence the consumer's problem is his comparatively small stake in the choices he makes in the market. They limit the amount of information processing he can rationally afford to undertake for his choices, they make him a comparatively poor risk bearer, and they restrict his desire to enforce his rights in the courts. Exploitation can be thought to take place where a stronger party imposes his will on a weaker one. If a monopoly exists, such a relation is readily explicable. But even in a competitive setting, such a phenomenon may appear because consumers can take account of only a few aspects involved in their choices. On these, competition will follow consumer preferences. On the ignored features, competition will lead to harsh-policy-low-price or perhaps poor-quality-low-price products or services, even though consumers might desire otherwise if they were fully appraised of the consequences of their choice.

These theoretical considerations set the stage for a discussion of alleged problems in the consumer market and the remedies proposed for them. Monopoly is a form of market failure, but not particular to the consumer market and therefore not further analyzed here. Fly-by-night operators are apt to be a problem in the consumer market. Permits, mandatory surety, and obligatory trust accounts for advance payments by customers are likely to be effective remedies. Whether their benefits outweigh the costs in terms of administrative expenses and delayed innovation cannot be determined in the abstract.

Lack of information may well be a problem, as circumstances can be thought of in which sellers have an interest in not disclosing information that is privately costly to them. The obligation to disclose is apt to bring us nearer to a situation in which all information is produced for which, fully informed, consumers would be willing to pay. Uniformization of information facilitates comparison shopping and should foster competition in the market at virtually negligible cost.

Misleading information is surely a deficiency in the information market. It remains to be seen how effective rules against it are, as increased consumer reliance on information in the market makes it all the more profitable for a seller to cheat occasionally. Moreover, rules of this kind may be difficult to enforce, as the question of what is "misleading" raises tricky evidentiary problems.

Standard form contracts are the object of scorn in much of the consumer literature. Yet it should be obvious that they are devices for reducing transaction costs and are not in themselves evidence of excessive market power. It is conceivably because of misperception problems for consumers — the limited focus discussed earlier as well as the difficulty in assessing small probabilities — that, within limits, onerous clauses can be put past unwary consumers. Against that possibility, two remedies are proposed. The first is to prescribe or to prohibit certain clauses, the other to have public agencies negotiate on behalf of the consumer. With respect to the first option, it may be asked how one can be sure that consumers fare better as a result of such an intervention if their true preferences can never be fully revealed. We argued that the preferences may be revealed if information is made cheaper or if public attention is focused on the items in question. Public authority can contribute to this process and thereby improve the functioning of the information market. But, assuming that this is not feasible, one could still, for particular clauses, construct an argument that they are likely to bring about a misallocation of resources. Blanket repossession clauses at the discretion of the credit grantor fall in this category for the same reasons that in insurance contracts we do not allow overinsurance — namely, because of moral hazard — and that in criminal law we do not allow boiling in oil as a sanction, even though it would surely have a disincentive effect. Overdeterrence leads to other perversities. A second kind of clause that the legislator proscribes is waivers, in particular with respect to warranties. Mandatory warranties could be justified by the better accident-prevention and risk-bearing potential of manufacturers, even though there is a risk of abuse (moral hazard) of the product by the consumer. An altogether different way of dealing with the problem of standard contracts is to authorize a public agency to negotiate them on behalf of consumers. While this may overcome the misperception problem, it raises the more serious issue of the representativity of the agency.

A further problem identified in the consumer literature is the alleged deteriorating quality of goods and services. We found it difficult to understand precisely what is meant here. If it is not a restatement of problems discussed above, the more plausible interpretation seems to be that the least expensive products in a modern market do not have the quality of those available in earlier days. But this may simply reflect the possibility that some groups of the population can now afford products that were previously entirely out of their reach. It is perhaps regrettable that better quality cannot be offered at their prices, but that reflects the current limits of our productive capacity and knowledge. Short of modifying the distribution of wealth — a different issue — this is inescapable.

The hazards of products are another aspect of the quality of goods and services. It is usually felt necessary to control the problem by setting quality norms, enforced by a public authority that has the power to ban hazardous products summarily. The question has been raised whether the market and liability rules would not be equally effective while entailing lower costs in terms of administration and delayed innovation. The answer lies perhaps in the imperfections of the legal recourses as they can be exercised by consumers: small stakes, less than full compensation, substantial difficulty in proving causality, and — where applicable — negligence. Removing such handicaps for the consumer might well be the most effective response to product hazards. Only in cases of great complexity and high uncertainty would preventive powers and standard setting be preferable.

The last type of possible imperfection we discussed concerns the enforcement of rights. Various measures are aimed at accumulating evidence for the consumer's case and facilitating his task in court. Whether they are worth their additional administrative cost cannot be determined in the abstract. The same conclusion applies to procedural innovations, such as small-claims court, class actions, and, for Quebec at least, contingent fees. With regard to new sanctions, we mentioned revision of contracts and exemplary damage awards. The problem with the first is to determine precisely how far one intends to curtail the principle *pacta sunt servanda*. This leads one into an investigation of circumstances in which the consumer can be thought not to have adequately realized the implications of a transaction, as opposed to simply regretting it or discovering a better deal after the fact. Surely, this is no trivial question. Exemplary damages could be appropriate where the loss to the consumer is difficult to evaluate; they bring us closer to full compensation, an idea whose importance was mentioned earlier. They could also be used in cases where only one consumer sues, while many have suffered the same loss as he or she has. Exemplary damages could then make the producer realize the full social cost of his activities. But in this function, punitive damages would overlap with the institution of the class action.

It may be interesting to return to the consumer rights discussed at the beginning of the chapter. Let us leave aside here the third of the three information rights — that is, the right to be free from intruding information. It raises issues not discussed in this text. The right to be informed is to a very great extent guaranteed by market forces and, where this is so, the consumer is better served by a right to workable competition. Even where we could identify incentives for sellers not to reveal information, it is not clear that in all these cases the consumer would be well served with more information. Hence, while there are circumstances in which the consumer truly wants information against the seller's will and might be helped by an obligation for the seller to disclose, we would think that these represent a limited range of cases and scarcely warrant the postulation of a fundamental right.

The right to be protected against misleading information, too, is largely guaranteed by the market itself. To be sure, within limits there is scope for deception, and it is quite conceivable that rules against dishonesty and their enforcement by public authority entail benefits that could be judged to outweigh their social cost. But it is almost certain that an all-out war against dishonesty — as a fundamental right would require — would not be cost effective in this sense.

Information about consumer law may not be sufficiently available ·in the market because of free-rider problems in its provision. The legal profession, which is the normal source of such information, appears not yet to have found ways in which its services can effectively be made available at the small scale of most consumer transactions. In part, this is due to a lack of innovation that could be attributed to such things as excessive control of prices and of advertising. Be that as it may, public subsidy of legal information to the consumer could conceivably improve the functioning of the market. Presumably, over time such information would become available through other means that the market would invent.

A right to standard contracts negotiated by the Consumer Protection Office may well be a mixed blessing only, as we argued in the text. We would not see scope here for a "right."

The right to revision may sometimes provide useful incentives to sellers, but is problematic because of the difficulties in deciding precisely how far it should go. We predict that the courts will express reservation with respect to this remedy, which is announced as generally applicable to consumer transactions in Article 272 of the *Consumer Protection Act* of Quebec.

Finally, we would argue that the right to effective recourse is not in itself guaranteed by market forces and, fully extended with due regard for the consumer's particular handicaps, will only serve to foster market forces. All in all, while information raises problems for consumers, rights to it are not, in our view, the most effective ways to cope with those problems. Competitive markets and effective legal recourse would seem more fundamental. Only peripherally will rules for disclosure and honesty in information improve the consumer's lot.

CHAPTER 10

General Conclusion

The argument set forth in these pages can be summarized as follows. What is known as the economic analysis of law provides a descriptive theory of why legal rules are what they are. The theory states that legal rules reflect a concern for the optimal allocation of society's scarce resources. While the theory has considerable initial plausibility and covers a wide variety of phenomena, there are many areas where it appears not to be able to account for observed legal rules, at least not in the form in which it is practiced by most of its current admirers. Unexplained areas of this kind would be the inroads that strict liability makes into the fault system and consumer law into private law generally.

The thesis advanced here is that the scope of the theory can be usefully enlarged by removing from it a simplification that is increasingly being dropped in economics proper, namely, the assumption that information is costless and abundantly available. In fact, information must frequently be acquired by means of scarce resources that have alternative uses. Its absence is usually a source of disutility.

Introducing the costliness of information into economic thinking, and hence into the economic analysis of law, is no minor undertaking because information occurs in various roles in virtually all aspects of the economic model. Moreover, while it resembles ordinary economic commodities in that its production requires scarce resources, it differs from them in that it is usually not readily amenable to market exchange; the use of information cannot be controlled as easily as that of physical commodities.

If the economic theory of law is correct, one would expect that in the presence of information costs, the law will be found to choose among conceivable rules and institutions those that tend to minimize such costs. To elaborate this thesis, it is useful to make an inventory and an analysis of the points at which the information problem manifests itself in the economic model. They can be divided into two large classes, namely, activities aimed at acquiring information, termed "search" here, and those designed to reduce the impact of a lack of information, termed "risk-bearing." For convenience, search activities can be further analyzed as information processing by individuals and information acquisition in markets.

It would appear that information constraints do indeed account for phenomena that in earlier economic writings on law remained puzzling. Information constraints on human information processing explain why consumers would have difficulty in evaluating small hazards in commodities they buy and perhaps also why legal reasoning appears to involve the pursuit of values under the constraints of legal standards or directives, rather than simply the application of rules. Search in markets might explain rules with respect to advertising, product standardization, and disclosure of information. Risk bearing, too, promises interesting insights. The phenomenon known as moral hazard explains, for instance, why one cannot insure an object for more than its actual value and why insurance contracts can be voided on the ground of misrepresentation by the insured. Partnership and bankruptcy can be analyzed as forms of risk sharing in commercial ventures where, for reasons of moral hazard, insurance is not viable. Consumer law, as a distinct field of law, has as one of its pillars the informational disadvantages that beset consumers in a modern economy.

On the whole we believe that our examination of the incidence of information cost would support the thesis that it forms a useful refinement for economic analyses of law. It is hoped that the ideas drawn from the literature and surveyed here can serve as patterns or models that help to recognize information contraints in new situations to be analyzed. If the economic theory of the law is to gain support, new situations will have to be analyzed and precise empirical tests will have to be set up. The support for a theory stems as much from the breadth of the phenomena for which it can account as from the instances in which it is empirically shown to explain what its rival or rivals cannot. The analysis in this text shows, in our view, that the economic approach in a world of costly information holds considerable promise of providing a convincing theory of law.

Notes

The following abbreviations are used in the references:

Am. Econ. Rev.	American Economic Review
Ann. Rev. Psych.	Annual Review of Psychology
Behav. Sc.	Behavioral Science
Bell J. Econ.	Bell Journal of Economics
(and Mgmt. Sc.)	(and Management Science)
Brit. J. Law & Soc.	British Journal of Law and Society
Can. Bus. L.J.	Canadian Business Law Journal / Revue canadienne du droit de commerce
Can. J. Econ.	Canadian Journal of Economics / Revue canadienne d'économique
Cogn. Psych.	Cognitive Psychology
Econ. Inq.	Economic Inquiry
Int. Rev. Law Econ.	International Review of Law and Economics
J. Econ. Iss.	Journal of Economic Issues
J. Econ. Lit.	Journal of Economic Literature
J. Econ. Th.	Journal of Economic Theory
J. Law Econ.	Journal of Law and Economics
J. Leg. Stud.	Journal of Legal Studies
J. Math. Psych.	Journal of Mathematical Psychology

J. Pol. Econ.	Journal of Political Economy
J. Pub. Econ.	Journal of Public Economics
Law Lib. J.	Law Library Journal
Law Quart. Rev.	Law Quarterly Review
Law & Soc. Rev.	Law & Society Review
Minn. L. Rev.	Minnesota Law Review
Nat. Res. J.	Natural Resources Journal
Northw. U.L. Rev.	Northwestern University Law Review
Osgoode Hall L.J.	Osgoode Hall Law Journal
Psych. Bull.	Psychological Bulletin
Psych. Rev.	Psychological Review
P.U.F.	Presses universitaires de France
P.U.Q.	Presses de l'Université du Québec
P.U.M.	Presses de l'Université de Montréal
Quart. J. Econ.	Quarterly Journal of Economics
Rev. d'écon. pol.	Revue d'économie politique
Rev. Econ. Stud.	Review of Economic Studies
Rev. Soc. Econ.	Review of Social Economy
R.S.C.	Revised Statutes of Canada
South. Calif. L. Rev.	Southern California Law Review
S.Q.	Statutes of Quebec
U.	University
U. Chic. L. Rev.	University of Chicago Law Review
U. Ill. Press	University of Illinois Press
U. Miami L. Rev.	University of Miami Law Review
U. Mich. Press	University of Michigan Press
U. Penn. L. Rev.	University of Pennsylvania Law Review
U. of T. L.J.	University of Toronto Law Journal
(. .) L.J.	(. .) Law Journal
(. .) L. Rev.	(. .) Law Review
(. .) U.P.	(. .) University Press

Chapter 1

1. R.A. Posner, "The Economic Approach to Law," *Texas L. Rev.* 53 (1975):757–782, p. 759. In a similar vein see his "Some Uses and Abuses of Economics in Law," *U. Chic. L. Rev.* 46 (1979):281–306, and "The Present Situation in Legal Scholarship," *Yale L.J.* 90 (1981):1113–1130.

2. R.H. Coase, "The Problem of Social Cost," *J. Law Econ.* 3 (1960):1–44; G. Calabresi, "Some Thoughts on Risk-Distribution and the Law of Torts," *Yale L.J.* 70 (1961):499–553.

3. E.J. Furubotn and S. Pejovich, eds., *The Economics of Property Rights*, (Cambridge, Mass.: Ballinger, 1974); B.A. Ackerman, ed., *Economic Foundations of Property Law* (Boston: Little, Brown, 1975); H.G. Manne, ed., *The Economics of Legal Relationships* (St. Paul, Minn.: West, 1975); A.T. Kronman and R.A. Posner,

The Economics of Contract Law (Boston: Little, Brown, 1979); P. Burrows and C.J. Veljanovski, eds., *The Economic Approach to Law* (Woburn, Mass.: Butterworth 1981); H.D. Assman, C.R. Kirchner, and E. Schanze, *Ökonomische Analyse des Rechts* (Kronberg/Ts., Germany: Athenäum Verlag, 1978).

4. G. Calabresi, *The Costs of Accidents* (New Haven, Conn.: Yale U.P., 1970); G. Tullock, *The Logic of the Law* (New York: Basic Books, 1972); R.A. Posner, *Economic Analysis of Law* 2nd ed. (Boston: Little, Brown, 1977); B.A. Ackerman, *Private Property and the Constitution* (New Haven, Conn.: Yale U.P., 1976); G. Calabresi and P. Bobbitt, *Tragic Choices — The Conflicts Society Confronts in the Allocation of Tragically Scarce Resources* (New York: Norton, 1978); A. Jacquemin and G. Schrans, *Le droit économique*, 2nd ed. (Paris: P.U.F. (Que sais-je 1383), 1974); A.A. Schmid, *Property, Power, and Public Choice: An Inquiry into Law and Economics* (New York: Praeger, 1978); W.Z. Hirsch, *Law and Economics: An Introductory Analysis* (New York: Academic Press, 1979); J.L. Migué, *L'économiste et la chose publique*, (Montreal: P.U.Q. 1979); J.M. Oliver, *Law and Economics* (London: Allen and Unwin, 1979); W.J. Samuels and A.A. Schmid, *Law and Economics — An Institutional Perspective* (Boston, Mass.: Nijhoff, 1981); G. Tullock, *Trials on Trial — The Pure Theory of Legal Procedure* (New York: Columbia U.P., 1980); R.A. Posner, *The Economics of Justice* (Cambridge, Mass.: Harvard U.P., 1981); of related interest are S.S. Nagel and M.G. Neef, *Decision Theory and the Legal Process* (Lexington, Mass.: Lexington Books, 1979); S. Pejovich, *Fundamentals of Economics — A Property Rights Approach* (Dallas, Texas: Fisher Institute, 1979); D.C. North and R.L. Miller, *The Economics of Public Issues*, 2nd ed. (New York: Harper & Row, 1973).

See also: W.J. Samuels, "Legal-Economic Policy: A Bibliographical Survey," *Law Lib. J.* 58 (1965):230–252, and "Law and Economics: A Bibliographical Survey 1965–1973," *Law Lib. J.* 66 (1973):96–110; M.J. Trebilcock, J.R.S. Prichard, and J. McDonald, "Selected Bibliography: Economic Analysis of Commercial Law," in J.S. Ziegel, ed., *Proceedings of the Seventh Annual Workshop on Commercial and Consumer Law* (Toronto: Canada Law Book, 1979), 153–164.

The *Journal of Law and Economics*, the *Journal of Legal Studies*, and the *International Review of Law and Economics* are devoted exclusively to the field of interest here.

5. Posner, "Economic Approach to Law," op. cit. (nt. 1), p. 764.

6. Ibid., pp. 758–759.

7. See nt. 2.

8. See, e.g., T.L. Becker, ed., *The Impact of Supreme Court Decisions* (New York: Oxford U.P. 1969); see also various studies reprinted in L.M. Friedman and S. Macaulay, eds., *Law and Behavioral Sciences*, 2nd ed. (Indianapolis, Ind.: Bobbs-Merrill, 1977.

9. See, for instance, G.A. Schubert, *The Judicial Mind Revisited* (New York: Oxford U.P., 1973); S. Goldman and T.P. Jahnige, *The Federal Courts as a Political System* (New York: Harper & Row, 1971). For a similarly oriented study in the area of criminal law, see J. Hogarth, *Sentencing as a Human Process* (Toronto: University of Toronto Press, 1969).

10. Admittedly this is a rather sweeping statement, borrowed from Posner, "Economic Approach to Law," op. cit. (nt. 1). Yet I find it hard, reading through the

texts mentioned in the two previous footnotes and others in the same field, or in criminology for that matter, to reach a substantially different conclusion. Even a sociologist is ready to admit such a thesis; see K.D. Opp, "The Emergence and Effects of Social Norms. A Confrontation of Some Hypotheses of Sociology and Economics," *Kyklos* 32 (1979):775–801.

In the second edition of *Economic Analysis of Law*, op. cit., p. 21, Posner writes:

> Whatever its deficiencies, the economic theory of law appears to be the most promising positive theory of law extant. While anthropologists, sociologists, psychologists, political scientists, and other social scientists besides economists also make positive analyses of the legal system, their work is thus far insufficiently rich in theoretical and empirical content to afford serious competition to the economists. (The reader is challenged to adduce evidence contradicting this presumptuous, sweeping, and perhaps uninformed judgment.)

11. References to empirical work will be found throughout this text. They make readily apparent the variety of human behavior to which the approach is applicable. In a recent article Posner has applied himself to the question of the philosophical status of the economic theory of law, which he sees as distinct from utilitarianism and from what he terms "Kantianism." R.A. Posner, "Utilitarianism, Economics, and Legal Theory," *J. Leg. Stud.* 8 (1979):103–140, and in his *Economics of Justice*, op. cit. nt. 4.

On why economists have been tempted to move into other social sciences, see R.H. Coase, "Economics and Contiguous Disciplines," *J. Leg. Stud.* 7 (1978):201–210; G.W. Nutter, "On Economism," *J. Law Econ.* 22 (1979):263–268; R. Brenner, "Economics — An Imperialist Science," *J. Leg. Stud.* 9 (1980):179–188.

12. G.S. Becker, *The Economic Approach to Human Behavior* (Chicago: U. Chicago Press, 1976), p. 8.

13. Ibid., p. 5.

14. Ibid.

15. Ibid.

16. Ibid.; and G.J. Stigler and G.S. Becker, "De Gustibus Non Est Disputandum," *Am. Econ. Rev.* 67 (1977):76–90.

17. Becker, *Economic Approach*, op. cit. (nt. 12), p. 7.

18. Ibid.

19. A.D. De Groot, *Methodology — Foundations of Inference and Research in the Behavioral Sciences* (The Hague: Mouton (1969) pp. 26–27. Also, differently, the "Kuhnian" theory: T.S. Kuhn, *The Structure of Scientific Revolutions*, 2nd. ed. (Chicago: U. Chic. Press, 1970); also his "Objectivity, Value Judgment, and Theory Choice," reprinted in T.S. Kuhn, *The Essential Tension* (Chicago: U. Chicago Press, 1977); I. Lakatos and A. Musgrave, eds., *Criticism and the Growth of Knowledge*, (Cambridge: Cambridge U.P., 1970); S. Toulmin, *Human Understanding* (Princeton, N.J., Princeton U.P., 1972).

A very interesting study, which examines Becker's approach in the light of the compromise that must be struck between the predictive power of a theory and its descriptive or explanatory relevance, is R.B. McKenzie, "On the Methodological Boundaries of Economic Analysis," *J. Econ. Iss.* 12 (1978):627–645.

20. C. Masse and M. Marois, *La règle du jeu — enquête auprès des organismes de consommation et des consommateurs plaignants*, Groupe de recherche en jurimétrie, Faculté de droit, Université de Montréal, 1976, p. 1 (my translation); see also E.P. Belobaba, "Unfair Trade Practices Legislation: Symbolism and Substance in Consumer Protection," *Osgoode Hall L.J.* 15 (1977):1–62, p. 60: "No society should tolerate marketplace abuses, particularly where the most vulnerable victim is often the low-income consumer whose experience with the unscrupulous businessman reinforces his increasing sense of helplessness, frustration, and outrage."

21. D. Caplovitz, *The Poor Pay More: Consumer Practices of Low-Income Families* (New York: Free Press, 1963); also D. Cayne and M. J. Trebilcock, "Market Considerations in the Formulation of Consumer Protection Policy," *U. of T.L.J.* 23 (1973):396–430.

22. Cayne and Trebilcock, "Market Considerations," op. cit. (nt. 21), p. 400 (emphasis added).

23. In the literature on the economics of insurance, this is known as *adverse selection*. See Chapter 8 on risk bearing.

24. Further on the subject of specialization of this kind in underdeveloped countries: G. Akerlof, "The Market for 'Lemons': Qualitative Uncertainty and the Market Mechanism," *Quart. J. Econ.* 89 (1970):488–500, esp. pp. 497–499.

25. See Cayne and Trebilcock, "Market Considerations," op. cit. (nt. 21), p. 416.

26. In an earlier study (C. Masse, E. Mackaay, and J. Hérard, *Vivre ou Exister — Etude de l'efficacité sociale des programmes juridiques d'aide aux débiteurs surendettés*, Groupe de recherche en jurimétrie, Faculté de droit, Université de Montréal, 1974, p. 107) we found that

> "Tout nous incite à croire que les inscrits à la loi Lacombe qui se situent au-dessous du seuil de pauvreté, et il s'agit là de la majorité, *se sont endettés pour se procurer le minimum vital* représenté par le seuil de pauvreté" (emphasis added).

27. Cayne and Trebilcock, "Market Considerations," op. cit. (nt. 21), p. 415. See also S.M. Crafton, "An Empirical Test of the Effect of Usury Laws," *J. Law Econ.* 23 (1980):135–145; J. Ordover and A. Weiss, "Information and the Law: Evaluating Legal Restrictions on Competitive Contracts," *Am. Econ. Rev.* 71 (1981):399–404.

28. Cayne and Trebilcock, "Market Considerations," op. cit. (nt. 21), p. 416.

29. Ibid., p. 418.

30. Ibid.

31. Ibid., p. 419.

32. Ibid.

33. It has been argued that the rental market is imperfect because of the cost of moving; once a tenant lives in a building, his landlord has what one might call a "local monopoly." If the tenant moves to another building, he has moving costs, whereas if he stays in the same one, he does not. Hence, the present landlord is thought to be able to extract a higher rent in consideration of the moving costs avoided. Of course, where long-term leases exist, moving costs can be written off over long periods, and the argument should not carry all that much weight. Even in inflationary times one could think of long-term leases with inflation-escalator

clauses. Hence this "local monopoly" would not appear to justify rent control. And even if it was felt to be a serious factor, one might think that a policy of subsidization of moving costs would undo the local monopoly and thereby foster competition.

34. Report in the *Financial Post* of 4 February 1978, p. 4.

35. Cayne and Trebilcock, "Market Considerations," op. cit. (nt. 21), pp. 419, 420.

36. Ibid., p. 422; see also *Rent Control — A Popular Paradox* (Vancouver: The Fraser Institute, 1975), pp. 145–160; S.N.S. Cheung, "Rent Control and Housing Reconstruction: The Postwar Experience of Prewar Premises in Hong Kong," *J. Law Econ.* 22 (1979):27–53; G. Matthews, *La théorie économique et le contrôle des loyers*, INRS-Urbanisation, Montréal, 1978; a report in the *Toronto Star* of 3 September 1977 mentions that some New York landlords are willing to pay to see their buildings set afire (p. B4).

37. Cayne and Trebilcock, "Market Considerations," op. cit. (nt. 21), p. 422.

38. This statement should not be read to imply that it is not desirable to help consumers or the poor. I think it is, but that is not a statement that can be derived from economic theory, as will be argued in Chapter 2. There are some who disagree with it; see Posner, *Economic Analysis of Law*, op. cit. (nt. 4), p. 344ff.

While the statement in the text requires some interpretation as well (when, after all, is a legislative policy a success, given a stated intent?), it would seem that most observers could agree with it. It should be noted that most real programs of the kind discussed in the second section are more complex and sometimes more subtle than may have been suggested. We state, without further argument, that these refinements would not affect the essence of the analysis.

Chapter 2

1. H.H. Liebhafsky, "Price Theory as Jurisprudence: Law and Economics, Chicago Style," in W.J. Samuels, ed., *The Chicago School of Political Economy*, (East Lansing, Mich.: Association for Evolutionary Economics and Michigan State University, 1976), pp. 237–257.

2. See, e.g., P.A. Samuelson, *Foundations of Economic Analysis* (New York: Atheneum, 1967); J. de V. Graaff, *Theoretical Welfare Economics* (London: Cambridge U.P., 1975); D.M. Winch, *Anaytical Welfare Economics* (New York: Penguin, 1971).

3. It should be stressed that this concept is important to economists outside the mainstream tradition as well. On this subject see, for instance, E.J. Mishan, "How Valid are Economic Evaluations of Allocative Changes," *J. Econ. Iss.* 14 (1980):143–161.

4. See, for instance, H. Van den Doel, *Democracy and Welfare Economics* (Cambridge: Cambridge U.P., 1979) pp. 6, 7.

5. R. Boudon, *Effets pervers et ordre social* (Paris: P.U.F. 1977) p. 12 (my translation).

6. Ibid., p. 58 (my translation). On p. 187 Boudon writes:

Dans certains de ces aspects la sociologie contemporaine apparaît souvent comme une sociologie sans sujet: l'*homo sociologicus* y est décrit soit comme programmé par les "structures sociales", soit comme déterminé par ses origines sociales et sa position sociale.

Dans le texte qui suit j'ai essayé de montrer que ce paradigme déterministe est à la fois inutile et coûteux. En refusant à l'agent social la faculté de choix, de décision, de création, d'innovation, le sociologue tombe dans la tentation permanente de la sociologie, le sociologisme. Il est alors frappé d'une sorte de cécité. A partir du moment où le déterminisme est partout, quelle différence y a-t-il entre la poussée de fièvre qui m'impose le lit, la sanction pénale qui me dissuade de réaliser certains désirs, la faiblesse de mes ressources qui m'impose de m'écarter de certains objets de consommation?

7. K.J. Arrow, *Social Choice and Individual Values*, 2nd ed. (New Haven, Conn., Yale U.P., 1963).

8. The developers will, of course, be prepared to offer at most a sum just less than their prospective net gains, where a normal return on capital is part of the costs.

9. See the discussion on expropriation in the next chapter. In practice, solutions are adopted whereby losers are compensated at "fair market value," which usually ignores highly individual aspects of the loss. The compensation procedure is for this reason said to exhibit "monetary bias."

10. In practice, some compensation might take place through taxes and redistributive measures.

11. It is important to stress that a Pareto optimum need not be attained through decentralized markets. It is possible to reach a Pareto optimum in a centrally planned economy in which consumers make their preferences known to the planning agency and in which the planning agency decides on the allocation of resources. This observation means that in discussing a Pareto optimum one must (implicitly) refer to the social institutions through which it is to be realized. On this question, see J.H. Dales, "Beyond the Marketplace," *Can. J. Econ.* 8 (1975):483–503.

12. Graaff, *Theoretical Welfare Economics*, op. cit. (nt. 2), pp. 142–155.

13. Posner's formulation. Posner, *Economic Analysis of Law*, op. cit. (ch. 1, nt. 4), p. 9.

14. Graaff, *Theoretical Welfare Economics*, op. cit. (nt. 2).

15. See, for instance, K.J. Arrow, "Limited Knowledge and Economic Analysis," *Am. Econ. Rev.* 64 (1974):1–10, in particular p. 4; C. de Ribet-Petersen, "L'information: propagation et création structurelles au sein de la firme et sur le marché," in F. Bloch-Lainé et F. Perroux, *L'entreprise et l'économie du XXe siècle*, Vol. 2 (Paris: P.U.F., 1968) pp. 489–511; F. Perroux, *Pouvoir et économie* (Paris: Bordas, 1973); J. Attali, *La parole et l'outil* (Paris: P.U.F., 1975); also K.J. Arrow, "The Future and the Present in Economic Life," *Econ. Inq.* 16 (1978):157–169.

16. Cf. E.J. Mishan, *Cost-Benefit Analysis*, 2nd ed. (New York: Praeger, 1976), p. xi:

And one can, indeed, lay down simple and sufficient conditions under which the uncompromising pursuit of profits acts always to serve the public interest. These conditions can be boiled down to two: that all effects relevant to the welfare of all individuals be properly priced on the market, and that perfect competition prevail in all economic activities.

17. See M. Preston, *Public Goods and the Public Sector* (London: Macmillan, 1972), p. 12ff; also A. Wolfelsberger, *Les biens collectifs* (Paris: P.U.F., 1975); for a very different perspective see E. Ullmann-Margalit, *The Emergence of Norms* (Oxford: Clarendon Press, 1977), pp. 49–53.

18. The problem is therefore that we do not know exactly how much of a public good it would be optimal to produce. If people are not made to pay according to what they consume, they will misstate their preferences. A mechanism recently proposed in the economic literature is thought to be able to overcome this predicament. The mechanism is generally referred to as the "demand-revealing process." See T.N. Tideman and G. Tullock, "A New and Superior Process for Making Social Choices," *J. Pol. Econ.* 84 (1976):1145–1159; T.N. Tideman, ed., Special Supplement to Spring 1977 issue of *Public Choice* 29–2 (1977):1–43. It would take us too far afield to discuss the proposal in detail. Essentially, it consists in asking people to vote not by agreeing or disagreeing with the options proposed, but rather by attaching to each of them the price one would be willing to pay for that option to be adopted. The prices for the options are then summed over all voters, and the highest priced option is chosen. But this is not the end of the process. For each voter it is now determined whether without his price the winning option would still have won. If not, i.e., if his contribution is essential, he is *made to pay the minimal amount necessary, over and above the sum of the prices indicated by the other voters, to make the winning option the highest priced one.* This procedure is repeated for all voters who attach a positive amount to the winning option. The proceeds from this "Clarke tax" are distributed equally over all voters or otherwise disposed of, but *not* given to the "losers" to avoid overstating of losses. It can be shown that voters are thus motivated not to misstate their preferences, that they acquire goods at their marginal social cost, and that Arrow's voting paradox is avoided.

A good summary of these ideas in French will be found in H. Lepage, *Demain le capitalisme* (Paris: Librairie générale française (coll. pluriel) 1978) pp. 268–272. For a critique see W.H. Riker, "Is A New and Superior Process Really Superior?" *J. Pol. Econ.* 87 (1979):875–890.

19. The transaction-cost problem appears to be very general indeed and is the object of much research. To the extent that transaction costs stem from scarcity or cost of information, the considerations of Part II should be relevant. Mishan (*Cost-Benefit Analysis*, op. cit. (nt. 16), p. 155) gives a list of factors that contribute to transaction costs. In his recent *Introduction to Normative Economics* (New York: Oxford U.P., 1981), he defines transaction costs (p. 403) as "all costs incurred in negotiating terms or in discovering, correcting, maintaining, or defending any change in economic organisation, particularly a change toward an optimal position."

20. Graaff, *Theoretical Welfare Economics*, op. cit. (nt. 2), p. 143. For some kinds of uncertainty, markets exist; see further Part II, Chapter 8 on risk bearing.

21. External effects may also be favorable (positive externalities or external economies). Examples are street lights, education, the pleasurable smell of one's neighbor's freshly cut lawn. (This last example is from Mishan, *Cost-Benefit Analysis*, op. cit. (nt. 16), p. 111.)

22. Coase, "Problem of Social Cost," op. cit. (ch. 1, nt. 2).

23. C.L. Schultze, *The Public Use of Private Interest* (Washington, D.C.: Brookings, 1977), p. 42; see further the discussion of the Coase theorem in Chapter 3. A very perceptive recent article on the subject is C.J. Dahlman, "The Problem of Externality," *J. Law Econ.* 22 (1979):141–162.

24. These factors, especially significant transaction costs, may also account other kinds of market imperfection discussed in the literature. Mishan mentions the *speed* of adjustment in a competitive economy [E.J. Mishan, "The Folklore of the Market: An Inquiry into the Economic Doctrines of the Chicago School," in Samuels, *The Chicago School,* op. cit. (nt. 1), p. 102].

25. R.G. Lipsey, and K. Lancaster, "The General Theory of Second Best," *Rev. Econ. Stud.* 24 (1956–57):11–32.

26. O.A. Davis, and A. Whinston, "Piecemeal Policy in the Theory of Second Best," *Rev. Econ. Stud.* 34 (1967):323–331, and "Welfare Economics and the Theory of Second Best," *Rev. Econ. Stud.* 32 (1965):1–14.

27. E.J. Mishan, *The Costs of Economic Growth* (Harmondsworth, U.K.: Penguin, 1975), p. 80.

28. Davis and Whinston, "Piecemeal Policy," op. cit. (nt. 26), pp. 324, 330.

29. Mishan argues that such natural units would be difficult to circumscribe. And if one had guidelines to do it, they would be "far too complex to be of any practical use" [Mishan, *Costs of Economic Growth*, op. cit. (nt. 27), p. 77].

30. Samuelson, *Foundations*, op. cit. (nt. 2), p. 203.

31. D.G. Hartle, "Another Perspective on Competition Policy," unpublished paper, workshop on Competition Policy, University of Toronto, 16 March 1978, p. 2.

32. P. Hennipman, *Welvaartstheorie en economische politiek* (Alphen aan den Rijn, Netherlands: Samson, 1977), pp. 42–45.

33. Doubts have also been expressed about the realism of some of the assumptions on which the neoclassical model rests. As this discussion would lead us too far afield, a short note on some of the main reservations will suffice.

A first observation is about the postulate of consumer sovereignty. It is argued that consumer preferences are not independently given (exogenous variables) but can, to some extent, be infuenced by other economic actors. Advertising is believed to constitute such an influence, at least in the writings of Galbraith and in Mishan's *The Cost of Economic Growth*, op. cit. (nt. 27), to name just these authors. Against this view and arguing that advertising is merely informative are, for instance, L. Benham and A. Benham, "Regulating Through the Professions: A Perspective on Information Control," *J. Law Econ.* 18 (1975):421–447; L. Benham and A. Benham, "The Effect of Advertising on the Price of Eyeglasses," *J. Law and Econ.* 15 (1972):337–352; P. Nelson, "Information and Consumer Behavior," *J. Pol. Econ.* 78 (1970):311–329; P. Nelson, "Advertising as Information," *J. Pol. Econ.* 82 (1974):729–754; L.G. Telster, "Advertising and Competition," *J. Pol. Econ.* 72 (1964):537–562. Comanor and Wilson, in their *Advertising and Market Power* (Cambridge, Mass.: Harvard U.P., 1974) argue that advertising does affect tastes and show that intensive use of it is associated with entry barriers to the industries concerned and with significant monopoly profits.

Manipulation of consumer tastes may come about in another way as well, namely, in the decision by firms about what research to undertake. To an extent these decisions may be driven by consumer preferences, but where they are autonomously made, "consumers may feel some alienation if their 'needs' have been induced by unknown forces" [Heertje, *Economics and Technical Change* (New York: Wiley, 1977), p. 247].

A second reservation concerns the postulates of independence of consumer preferences. Duesenberry, in *Income, Saving and the Theory of Consumer Behavior* (Cambridge, Mass.: Harvard U.P., 1949), advances what is known as the *relative income hypothesis:* The satisfaction that income procures for consumers depends not only on its absolute level, but also (and perhaps more) on its magnitude in relation to that of their peer groups. An absolute gain that is less than that of one's neighbors would count as a loss. The Pareto criterion could be redefined accordingly, but this creates substantial complications for the neoclassical model.

A third reservation about the neoclassical model is its static character. It does not, in this view, allow adequately for what appears to be the major source of social gains, namely, invention and innovation. It cannot adequately state how much research is optimal and whether deviations from competitive markets should be tolerated in order to foster invention. For a thorough discussion of these problems, see Heertje, *Economics and Technical Change*, p. 208ff. Mishan discusses the implications of taking the *variety* of goods to choose from as a maximand beside efficiency [E.J. Mishan, "The Effect of Externalities on Individual Choice," *Int. Rev. Law Econ.* 1 (1981):97–109].

34. And, of course, for given social institutions, as we argued in nt. 11.

35. A.G. Papandreou, *Paternalistic Capitalism* (Toronto: Copp Clark, 1972), p. 19 (N.B. he dissociates himself from that position).

36. Mishan, "Folklore of the Market," op. cit. (nt. 24), p. 103.

37. A.M. Polinsky, "Economic Analysis of Law as a Potentially Defective Product: A Buyer's Guide to Posner's Economic Analysis of Law," *Harvard L. Rev.* 87 (1974):1655–1681, p. 1680.

38. A.M. Okun, *Equality and Efficiency — The Big Tradeoff* (Washington, D.C.: Brookings 1975), p. 92. Lindblom contests the thesis that redistribution will necessarily reduce incentives. See his *Markets and Hierarchies — The World's Political-Economic Systems* (New York: Basic Books, 1977), pp. 43, 44. Also V. Goldberg, "On Positive Theories of Redistribution," *J. Econ. Iss.* 9 (1977):119–132.

39. Okun, *Equality and Efficiency*, op. cit. (nt. 38), p. 19ff.

40. Ibid., p. 20.

41. Robbins, as quoted by Hennipman, *Welvaartstheorie*, op. cit. (nt. 32) p. 52, ref. 137.

42. Generally on the subject see Hennipman, *Welvaartstheorie*, op. cit. (nt. 32); also A. Heertje, *Echte economie — Misverstanden over en misstanden in de economie* (Arbeiderspers, 1977), ch. 1; compare also the following quotation from L. Silk, *The Economists* (New York: Basic Books, 1976), p. 232, who perceives renewed interest in

> . . . the critical questions of justice and equality, and how these questions relate to such other economic objectives as efficiency, growth, welfare, and freedom. If economists would presume to minister to the ills of society, as they do, they cannot simply select those goals or values that conveniently fit in the traditional concepts and models and data of their discipline.

43. Graaff, *Theoretical Welfare Economics*, op. cit. (nt. 2), pp. 170–171.

44. Ibid., p. 168; see also Mishan "How Valid?" op. cit. (nt. 3).

45. Ibid., p. 170.

46. Hennipman, *Welvaartstheorie*, op. cit. (nt. 32), p. 51.
47. Heertje, *Echte economie*, op. cit. (nt. 42), p. 19 (my translation).
48. Hennipman, *Welvaartstheorie*, op. cit. (nt. 32), p. 65.
49. Ibid. (my translation).
50. Becker, *Economic Approach*, op. cit. (ch. 1, nt. 12), p. 4.
51. This question has been clarified greatly by McKenzie's recent article ["Methodological Boundaries," op. cit. (ch. 1, nt. 19)]. If our aim is to explain or to describe choices among scarce resources, we may well adopt a purely subjective position and admit any good for which we observe, after the fact, that individuals express a demand. Yet if we wish to make predictions, as the Chicagoans following Friedman stipulate we should in order to do scientifically meaningful work, we shall have to presume *ex ante* that people have certain preferences. In predictive science, one must, in other words, limit the degree of subjectivity of people's preferences. The more precise one's predictions are to be, the more one will have to specify the cost and benefits that compose people's utility functions. But in doing so, one loses the descriptive power of the theory. McKenzie illustrates this argument by pointing to Becker's and Skinner's work (pp. 638–639). Becker's theory of the family certainly leads to nontrivial and testable hypotheses. Yet one can reasonably object to it that it does not account for the 'raw emotion' within the family. Skinner presents perhaps the most deterministic theory of human behavior. Whatever its predictive merits, this theory entails a total denial of subjectivity of choice. People are represented as choosing automatons.
52. Hennipman, *Welvaartstheorie*, op. cit. (nt. 32), p. 140.
53. Arrow, "Limited Knowledge," op. cit. (nt. 15), p. 1.
54. Ibid., p. 2.
55. Posner *Economic Analysis of Law*, op. cit. (ch. 1, nt. 4), p. 17; similarly Hennipman, *Welvaartstheorie*, op. cit. (nt. 32), p. 72.
56. This extension is not itself without problems. McKenzie ["Methodological Boundaries," op. cit. (ch. 1, nt. 19), p. 635] sees the viability of an 'economics of information' hampered by an infinite regress. This comes about as follows. At the outset, each individual faces an optimization problem. In order to solve it, he needs, among other things, to be informed about his own values. But the process of informing oneself requires resources and one must now determine the optimal amount of resources for this purpose. McKenzie writes:

If we use resources in an economic way to determine what we value, then how do we go about using our resources to determine in an economic way how we go about using our resources to determine what we value, and so on, *ad infinitum*? At some point, the individual must assert in some noncalculating way how he will use resources to establish what he wants: He must, in effect, take a stab in the dark, which cannot be explained in any more satisfactory way than to say that it is done.

Chapter 3

1. Posner, *Economic Analysis of Law*, op. cit. (ch. 1, nt. 4), pp. 122–124; R.A. Posner, "A Theory of Negligence," *J. Leg. Stud.* 1 (1972):29ff; G. Calabresi and J.T. Hirschoff, "Toward a Test for Strict Liability in Torts," *Yale L.J.* 81 (1972):1055–1085, esp. pp. 1057, 1059; also Calabresi, *Costs of Accidents*, op. cit. (ch. 1. nt. 4), p. 276.

2. W.Y. Oi, "The Economics of Product Safety," *Bell J. Econ. and Mgmt. Sc.* 4 (1973):3–28; V. Goldberg, "The Economics of Product Safety and Imperfect Information," *Bell J. Econ. and Mgmt. Sc.* 5 (1974):683–688; W.Y. Oi, "Reply to Professor Goldberg," *Bell J. Econ. and Mgmt. Sc.* 5 (1974):689–696. See further R.S. Higgins, "Products Liability Insurance, Moral Hazard, and Contributory Negligence," *J. Leg. Stud.* 10 (1981):111–130.

3. S. Peltzman, "The Effects of Automobile Safety Legislation," *J. Pol. Econ.* 83 (1975):677–725; L.S. Robertson, "A Critical Analysis of Peltzman's 'The Effects of Automobile Safety Legislation,' " *J. Econ. Iss.* 11 (1977):587–600, Peltzman's reply in the same journal, pp. 672–678, and a rejoinder on pp. 679–683. Peltzman's study has been the object of a public debate at the University of Miami's Law and Economics Center; see *Auto Safety Regulation: The Cure or the Problem*, H.G. Manne and R.L. Miller, eds., (Glen Ridge, N.J.: Thomas Horton and Daughters, 1976). Peltzman's observations have *not* been found to apply to Sweden and other Scandinavian countries. See B. Lindgren and C. Stuart, "The Effects of Traffic Safety Regulation in Sweden," *J. Pol. Econ.* 88 (1980):412–427. Peltzman's methods have recently been questioned in an article by R.J. Arnould and H. Grabowski, "Auto Safety Regulation: An Analysis of Market Failure," *Bell J. Econ.* 12 (1981):27–48.

4. For instance, Hann's critical review of Ehrlich's work, which purported to show that capital punishment actually deters. R.G. Hann, *Deterrence and the Death Penalty: A Critical Review of the Research of Isaac Ehrlich*, Report Submitted to the Solicitor General of Canada, 1976. Ehrlich's position can be found in the following articles: I. Ehrlich and J.C. Gibbons, "On the Measurement of the Deterrent Effect of Capital Punishment and the Theory of Deterrence," *J. Leg. Stud.* 6 (1977):35–50; I. Ehrlich, "The Deterrent Effect of Capital Punishment: A Question of Life and Death," *Am. Econ. Rev.* 65 (1975):397ff.; I. Ehrlich, "Participation in Illegitimate Activities: A Theoretical and Empirical Investigation," *J. Pol. Econ.* 81 (1973):521–565; I. Ehrlich, "Capital Punishment and Deterrence: Some Further Thoughts and Additional Evidence," *J. Pol. Econ.* 85 (1977):741–788; I. Ehrlich and R. Mark, "Fear of Deterrence: A Critical Evaluation of the 'Report of the Panel on Research on Deterrent and Incapacitative Effects,' " *J. Leg. Stud.* 6 (1977):293–316.

5. The group includes Posner, Landes, Ehrlich, Becker, Cheung, Tullock, Manne and Demsetz. For significant publications from this group, see Manne, *Economics of Legal Relationships*, op. cit. (ch. 1, nt. 3) and other references to these authors in nts. 3 and 4 of ch. 1.

6. Polinsky, whose review of Posner's book is devoted mostly to a discussion of its economic premises, states ["Economic Analysis," op. cit. (ch. 2, nt. 37), p. 1657]:

Posner argues his case in an adversary spirit, and although he
initially concedes that his analysis has limitations, he virtually
ignores them and their implications thereafter.

7. See, for instance, P. Burrows, *The Economic Theory of Pollution Control* (Cambridge, Mass.: MIT Press 1980); R. Dorfman and N.S. Dorfman, eds., *Economics of the Environment* (New York: Norton, 1977); D.N. Dewees, C.K. Everson, and W.A. Sims, *Economic Analysis of Environmental Policies* (Toronto: U. Toronto P., 1975); A.V. Kneese and C.L. Schultze, *Pollution, Prices, and Public Policy* (Washington, D.C.: Brookings, 1975). See also I. Burton et al., *The Environment as a*

Hazard (New York: Oxford U.P., 1978); P. Slovic, "Judgment, Choice and Societal Risk Taking," in R.R. Hammond, ed., *Judgment and Decision in Public Policy Formation* (Boulder, Colo.: Westview Press, 1978), pp. 98–111; V. Goldberg, "The Economics of Product Safety and Imperfect Information," *Bell J. Econ. and Mgmt. Sc.* 5 (1974):683–688.

8. More on this subject in Part II. See also my "Can Consumer Protection Be 'Efficient' — Economic Analysis of Law in a World Where Information Is Not Costless," in J.S. Ziegel, ed., *Proceedings of the Seventh Annual Workshop on Commercial and Consumer Law, Toronto, October 21–22, 1977*, (Toronto: Canada Law Book, 1979), pp. 121–136.

9. Goldberg, "Economics of Product Safety," op. cit. (nt. 2); also "Regulation and Administered Contracts," *Bell J. Econ. and Mgmt. Sc.* 7 (1976):426–448. See also J.H. Dales, "Beyond the Marketplace," *Can. J. Econ.* 8 (1975):483–503.

10. B.A. Ackerman, "Regulating Slum Housing Markets on Behalf of the Poor: Of Housing Codes, Housing Subsidies and Income Redistribution Policy," *Yale L.J.* 80 (1971):1093–1197.

11. Calabresi, *Costs of Accidents*, op. cit. (ch. 1, nt. 4).

12. Posner, *Economic Analysis of Law*, op. cit. (ch. 1, nt. 4), p. 179.

13. Ibid., p. 22ff. and 185ff.

14. Ibid., pp. 187–188. In his recent book, *The Economics of Justice* (Cambridge, Mass.: Harvard U.P., 1981), p. 115, Posner puts this thesis more cautiously, stating that wealth maximization "seems to have played an *important role* in the growth of the common law, which is not surprising when the limitations of common law as a means of redistributing, as distinct from creating, wealth are taken into account. Wealth maximization is *not*, however, *the only conception of the good or the just* that has influenced law . . ." (emphasis added).

The first part of this book is devoted to answering the criticism leveled against wealth maximization both as an ethical principle and as a description of the aim of the common law. Much of the criticism has appeared in a special issue of the *Hofstra Law Review* 8 (1980):485–770 and 811–972 under the title *Symposium on Efficiency as a Legal Concern*. A more direct defence by Posner appeared in the same review, Vol. 9 (1981), pp. 775–794 under the title: "A Reply to some Recent Criticism of the Efficiency Theory of the Common Law."

Other important articles questioning the foundations of economic analysis of law are: R.M. Dworkin, "Is Wealth a Value?" *J. Leg. Stud.* 9 (1980):191–226; A.T. Kronman, "Wealth Maximization as a Normative Principle," *J. Leg. Stud.* 9 (1980):227–242; A. Leff, "Unspeakable Ethics, Unnatural Law," *Duke L.J.* (1979):1229–1249; C.G. Veljanovski, "The Economic Approach to Law — A Critical Introduction," *Brit. J. Law & Soc.* 7 (1980):158–193; C.G. Veljanovski, "Wealth Maximization, Law and Ethics — On the Limits of Economic Efficiency," *Int. Rev. Law Econ.* 1 (1981):5–28; E. Weinreb, "Utilitarianism, Economics, and Legal Theory," *U. of T.L.J.* 30 (1980):307–332.

15. Posner, *Economic Analysis of Law*, op. cit. (ch. 1, nt. 4), p. 189. Other inferences may be made as well. One is that where historical research reveals a change in the law, one should look for changes in technology, relative scarcity of resources, or other "economic factors" to explain it. Interesting studies in this perspective are M.S. Arnold, "Accident, Mistake, and Rules of Liability in the Fourteenth Century Law of Torts," *U. Penn. L. Rev.* 128 (1979):361–378; J. Baechler, *Les origines du capitalisme* (Paris: Gallimard, 1971); D.C. North and R.P.

Thomas, *The Rise of the Western World* (Cambridge: Cambridge U.P., 1973); R.A. Posner, "A Theory of Primitive Society," *J. Law Econ.* 23 (1980):1–53, reproduced with modifications as Chapters 6 and 7 in *The Economics of Justice,* op. cit. (nt. 14).

   16. Posner, *Economic Analysis of Law,* op. cit. (ch. 1, nt. 4), pp. 404–405. On p. 404 Posner writes: "Although the correlation is far from perfect, judge-made rules tend to be efficiency promoting while those made by legislatures tend to be efficiency reducing." Compare this with the following statements taken from a comment by Becker on a new theory of regulation by Peltzman (*J. Law Econ.* 19 (1976):245–248, p. 248:

> Peltzman's approach and my elaboration imply that usually the most efficient methods are used for any *given* redistribution of resources, . . . Economists are no more able to discover better ways to redistribute than they are able to discover ways to produce the products of business. . . . That is to say, the methods used to accomplish any given end tend to be the most efficient available, in the public as well as the market sector, and the efficiency of methods should not be confused with the attractiveness of the ends themselves, . . .

   17. G. Hardin, "The Tragedy of the Commons," in G. Hardin, *Exploring New Ethics for Survival — The Voyage of the Spaceship Beagle* (New York: Penguin Books, 1973) pp. 250–264; H.S. Gordon, "The Economic Theory of a Common Property Resource: The Fishery," in H. Manne, ed., *Economics of Legal Relationships,* op. cit. (ch. 1, nt. 3) pp. 413–436; for a more general treatment of the so-called prisoner's dilemma as a source of legislation, see E. Ullmann-Margalit, *Emergence of Norms,* op. cit. (ch. 2, nt. 17), pp. 18–73, and A. Schotter, *The Economic Theory of Social Institutions* (Cambridge: Cambridge U.P., 1981), p. 22ff.
   18. Hardin, "Tragedy of the Commons," op. cit. (nt. 17), p. 254.
   19. Gordon, "Economic Theory," op. cit. (nt. 17), pp. 424–425.
   20. J.M. Buchanan and G. Tullock, *The Calculus of Consent* (Ann Arbor: U. Mich. P., 1974), esp. ch. 15, 18, 19.
   21. See H. Demsetz, "Information and Efficiency: Another Viewpoint," in D.M. Lamberton, ed., *Economics of Information and Knowledge* (Harmondsworth, U.K.: Penguin, 1971), pp. 160–186, p. 170ff. See further Chapter 8 on risk bearing.
   22. Consider such issues as whether one can sell a kidney or when a person is legally dead and his organs available for transplants and so on. An interesting article on these problems in Quebec law is F. Héleine, "Le dogme de l'intangibilité du corps humain et ses atteintes normalisées dans le droit des obligations du Québec contemporain," *Revue du Barreau du Québec* 36 (1976):2–115.
   23. S. Pejovich, "Towards an Economic Theory of the Creation and Specification of Property Rights," in Manne, *Economics of Legal Relationships,* op. cit. (ch. 1, nt. 3), pp. 37–52, p. 40. See also the review article by de Alessi, *The Economics of Property Rights: A Review of the Evidence,* Univ. of Miami, Law and Economics Center, Working Paper No. 78–2, 1978.
   24. An interesting article about how property rights might be distributed among people is Umbeck's "Might Makes Right: A Theory of the Foundation and Initial Distribution of Property Rights," *Econ. Inq.* 19 (1981):38–59.

25. See also Lepage, *Demain le capitalisme,* op. cit. (ch. 2, nt. 18), pp. 93–115.

26. H. Demsetz, "Toward a Theory of Property Rights," in Manne, *Economics of Legal Relationships,* op. cit. (ch. 1, nt. 3), pp. 23–36; Fredlund has looked at the implications of Demsetz's thesis among certain animal groups: "Wolves, Chimps and Demsetz," *Econ. Inq.* 14 (1976):279–290; a further study of Indians in this vein is J. Baden, R. Strone, and W. Thurman, "Myths, Admonitions and Rationality: The American Indian as a Resource Manager," *Econ. Inq.* 19 (1981):132–143; see also D.E. Ault and G.L. Rutman, "The Development of Individual Rights to Property in Tribal Africa," *J. Law Econ.* 22 (1979):163–182.

27. But in all other respects the neoclassical world: perfect competition, no transaction costs and so on. More on this in the next section.

28. Think of pollution of all sorts, congestion. See references at nt. 7.

29. D.G. Hartle, *A Theory of the Expenditure Budgetary Process* (Toronto: University of Toronto Press (for Ontario Economic Council), 1976, pp. 8, 9.

30. O.A. Davis and M.I. Kamien, "Externalities, Information and Alternative Collective Action," in Joint Economic Committee, U.S. Congress, *The Analysis and Evaluation of Public Expenditures: The PPB System,* in Dorfman and Dorfman, *Economics of the Environment,* op. cit. (nt. 7), p. 120ff.

31. Schultze, *Public Use,* op. cit. (ch. 2, nt. 23), p. 81.

32. Posner, *Economic Analysis of Law,* op. cit. (ch. 1, nt. 4), p. 37.

33. See Ibid., pp. 47–48, and W.F. Baxter and L.R. Altree, "Legal Aspects of Airport Noise," *J. Law Econ.* 15 (1972):1ff., cited there.

34. G. Calabresi and A.D. Melamed, "Property Rules, Liability Rules, and Inalienability: One View of the Cathedral," in Ackerman, *Economic Foundations of Property Law,* op. cit. (ch. 1, nt. 3), p. 39.

35. Okun, *Equality and Efficiency,* op. cit. (ch. 2, nt. 38), p. 20.

36. Becker, *Economic Approach,* op. cit. (ch. 1, nt. 12), p. 211.

37. Coase, "Social Cost," op. cit. (ch. 1, nt. 2).

38. To avoid confusion, it should be added immediately that the theorem does *not* state that "internalization" has no effect on the distribution of wealth, as we shall see below.

39. Note that *all* farmers are subject to this rule.

40. Coase explicitly pointed this out. Coase, "Social Cost," op. cit. (ch. 1, nt. 2), section II.

41. For instance, the Symposium on the Coase theorem in the *Natural Resources Journal* 13 (1973):557–716 and 14 (1974):1–86, most notably the articles by Mishan and Samuels in the Symposium; H. Demsetz, "When Does the Rule of Liability Matter?" in Manne, *Economics of Legal Relationships,* op. cit. (ch. 1, nt. 3), pp. 168–183; H. Demsetz, "Some Aspects of Property Rights," repr. in Manne, *Economics of Legal Relationships,* op. cit., pp. 184–193; H. Demsetz, "Wealth Distribution and the Ownership of Rights," *J. Leg. Stud.* 1 (1972):223ff., V.A. Aivazian, and J.L. Callen, "The Coase Theorem and the Empty Core," *J. Law Econ.* 24 (1981):175–181 with Coase's Reply, pp. 183–187; G. Calabresi, "The Decision for Accidents: An Approach to Nonfault Allocation of Costs," *Harvard L. Rev.* 78 (1965):713–745; G. Calabresi, "Transaction Costs, Resource Allocation and Liability Rules — A Comment," in Manne, *Economics of Legal Relationships,* op. cit. 204–211; V. Goldberg, "Commons, Clark and the Emerging Post-Coasian Law and Economics," *J. Econ. Iss.* 10 (1976):877–893; W.G. Nutter, "The Coase Theorem on Social Cost: A Footnote," *J. Law Econ.* 11 (1968):503–507; R. Turvey, "On

Divergences Between Social and Private Cost," *Economica* 30 (1963):309–313; E.J. Mishan, "The Postwar Literature on Externalities: An Interpretative Essay," in Manne, *Economics of Legal Relationships*, op. cit. (ch. 1, nt. 3), 392–411.

42. H. Demsetz, "When does the Rule of Liability Matter?" *J. Leg. Stud.* 1 (1971):13ff. See also the articles by Samuels and Mishan in *Natural Resources Journal* (nt. 41).

43. Chapter 2, third section. Note that since rights affect wealth and wealth affects demand, a shift in the allocation of rights may well result in different demand patterns and hence in a different Pareto optimum.

44. Mishan, "The Postwar Literature" op. cit. (nt. 41), p. 397; also *Cost-Benefit Analysis*, op. cit. (ch. 2, nt. 16), p. 139ff.; *Costs of Economic Growth*, op. cit. (ch. 2, nt. 27), p. 93.

45. The size of the difference between the $5,000 one would pay and the $15,000 one would insist on receiving is not implausibly high. Knetsch and Weinrib, in a recent study, mention examples in which a ratio of one to four was encountered. Their own experiment in a Vancouver cafeteria shows smaller, but still significant, differences in the same direction. Moreover, these differences were observed with respect to amounts — all less than $6, which may be considered trivial in relation to the total wealth of those who participated in the experiment. If further experiments confirm these results, one would have to conclude that the asymmetry discussed in the text holds for all transactions; this would substantially reduce the relevance of the Coase theorem (J.L. Knetsch and E. Weinrib, *Legal Rules, Efficiency and Alternative Measures of Economic Loss*, University of Toronto, Law and Economics Workshop Series, No. WS II–7, 1979). See also I.M. Gordon and J.L. Knetsch, "Consumer's Surplus Measures and the Evaluation of Resources," *Land Economics* 55 (1979):1–10.

46. Mishan, "Postwar Literature," op. cit. (nt. 41), p. 399.

47. Mishan, *Cost-Benefit Analysis*, op. cit. (ch. 2, nt. 16), p. 155. See also Chapter 2, note 19. In a recent article, Dahlman defines transaction costs as including "search and information costs, bargaining and decision costs, policing and enforcement costs" ["The Problem of Externality," *J. Law. Econ.* 22 (1979):141–162, p. 148].

On the problems that transaction costs raise for the analysis, see also P.H. Greenwood and C.A. Ingene, "Uncertain Externalities, Liability Rules and Resource Allocation," *Am. Econ. Rev.* 68 (1978):300–310.

48. In the United States such arrangements, known as "contingent fees," are admissible in any law suit. It has been observed that in class actions such an arrangement makes the lawyer unduly interested in settling the case out of court. This is no doubt the reason for rules providing for judicial supervision of the amount of the lawyer's fee in case of a settlement.

49. Demsetz, "Some Aspects," op. cit. (nt. 41), p. 187.

50. Calabresi and Melamed, "Property Rules," op. cit. (nt. 34). See also A.M. Polinsky, "On the Choice between Property Rules and Liability Rules," *Econ. Inq.* 18 (1980):233–246; A.M. Polinsky, "Resolving Nuisance Disputes: The Simple Economics of Injunctive and Damage Remedies," *Stanford L. Rev.* 32 (1980):1075–1112.

51. Posner, *Economic Analysis of Law*, op. cit. (ch. 1, nt. 4), p. 180.

52. Consider, for instance, that product liability, to be discussed in a later section, was fully jurisprudentially developed.

53. In the Quebec Civil Code, general civil delictual responsibility is covered in articles 1053 to 1056. By contrast, property rights occupy most of the second book, and the general theory of obligations and special contracts take up the better part of the third book.

54. This tradeoff is discussed in more detail in Part II, ch. 5. See also my "Les notions floues en droit ou l'économie de l'imprécision," *Langages* 12 (1979):33–50.

55. Posner, *Economic Analysis of Law*, op. cit. (ch. 1, nt. 4), pp. 45–46.

56. Ibid., p. 46.

57. On the choice between prior and posterior evaluation of damages see Demsetz, "Some Aspects," op. cit. (nt. 41), p. 187; also D. Wittman, "Prior Regulation versus Post Liability: The Choice Between Input and Output Monitoring," *J. Leg. Stud.* 6 (1977):193–211.

58. Posner, *Economic Analysis of Law*, op. cit. (ch. 1, nt. 4), pp. 45, 51, 97, 180.

59. This is Calabresi's formulation. "Transaction Costs" op. cit., (nt. 41), p. 209.

60. Ibid.

61. Posner, *Economic Analysis of Law*, op. cit. (ch. 1, nt. 4), pp. 65, 69. See also generally on the subject of an economic analysis of contract law: R.L. Birmingham, "Breach of Contract, Damage Measures, and Economic Efficiency," *Rutgers L. Rev.* 24 (1970):273–292; W. Bishop, "Negligent Misrepresentation Through an Economist's Eyes," *Law Quart. Rev.* 96 (1980):360–379; Cayne and Trebilcock, *op. cit.* (ch. 1, nt. 21); S. Cheung, "The Structure of a Contract and the Theory of a Non-Exclusive Resource," *J. Law Econ.* 13 (1970):49ff.; R. Epstein, "Unconscionability: A Critical Appraisal," *J. Law Econ.* 18 (1975):293–315; M. Fontaine, "Le droit des obligations et l'économie," *Reflets et perspectives de la vie économique* 14 (1975):47–61; C.J. Goetz and R.E. Scott, "Measuring Seller's Damages: The Lost-Profits Puzzle," *Stanford L. Rev.* 31 (1979):323–373; C.J. Goetz and R.E. Scott, "Enforcing Promises: An Examination of the Basis of Contract," *Yale L.J.* 89 (1980):1261–1322; D. Harris, A.I. Ogus, and J. Phillips, "Contract Remedies and the Consumer Surplus," *Law Quart. Rev.* 95 (1979):581–610; T. Jackson, " 'Anticipatory Repudiation' and the Temporal Element of Contract Law: An Economic Inquiry into Contract Damages in Cases of Prospective Nonperformance," *Stanford L. Rev.* 31 (1978):69–119; P. Joskow, "Commercial Impossibility, the Uranium Market and the Westinghouse Case," *J. Leg. Stud.* 6 (1977):119–176; B. Klein, and K.B. Leffler, "The Role of Market Forces in Assuring Contractual Performance," *J. Pol. Econ.* 89 (1981):615–641; A.T. Kronman, "Mistake, Disclosure, Information, and the Law of Contracts," *J. Leg. Stud.* 7 (1978):1–34; A.T. Kronman, "Contract Law and Distributive Justice," *Yale L.J.* 89 (1980):472–511; J.T. Landa, "A Theory of the Ethically Homogeneous Middleman Group: An Institutional Alternative to Contract Law," *J. Leg. Stud.* 10 (1981):349–362; T.J. Muris, "Opportunistic Behavior and the Law of Contracts," *Minn. L. Rev.* 65 (1981):521–590; J.M. Perloff, "Breach of Contract and the Foreseeability Doctrine of *Hadley* v. *Baxendale*," *J. Leg. Stud.* 10 (1981):39–63; J.M. Perloff, "The Effects of Breaches of Forward Contracts Due to Unanticipated Price Changes," *J. Leg. Stud.* 10 (1981):221–235; R.A. Posner, and A.M. Rosenfield, "Impossibility and Related Doctrines in Contract Law: An Economic Analysis," *J. Leg. Stud.* 6 (1977):83–118; R.A. Posner, "Gratuitous Promises in Economics and Law," *J. Leg. Stud.* 6 (1977):411–426; G.L. Priest, "Nonconform-

ing Goods under the Uniform Commercial Code: An Economic Approach," *Harvard L. Rev.* 91 (1978):960–1001; S. Shavell, "Damage Measures for Breach of Contract," *Bell J. Econ.* 11 (1980):466–490; R.E. Speidel, "Excusable Non-performance in Sales Contracts: Some Thoughts on Risk Management," *South Calif. L. Rev.* 32 (1980):241–280; R.E. Speidel, "Court-Imposed Price Adjustments under Long-Term Supply Contracts," *Northw. U.L. Rev.* 76 (1981):369–422; M.J. Trebilcock, "The Doctrine of Inequality of Bargaining Power: Post-Benthamite Economics in the House of Lords," *U. of T. L.J.* 26 (1976):359–385; J. Umbeck, "A Theory of Contract Choice and the California Gold Rush," *J. Law. Econ.* 20 (1977):421–437; H.R. Weinberg, "Sales Law, Economics, and the Negotiability of Goods," *J. Leg. Stud.* 9 (1980):569–592; the Reader by Kronman and Posner, op. cit. (ch. 1, nt. 3).

For a view outside of the mainstream position, see, for instance, V. Goldberg, "Competitive Bidding and the Production of Precontract Information," *Bell J. Econ.* 8 (1977):250–261.

62. Posner, *Economic Analysis of Law,* op. cit. (ch. 1, nt. 4), p. 70.

63. Ibid., p. 90.

64. Penalty clauses are means to ensure that the debtor will find it preferable to perform the contract rather than breach and pay the stipulated penalty, normally well beyond the actual damages suffered. It is not hard to see that the question of permissibility of penalty clauses in this function is related to the problem of whether courts should issue injunctions to ensure specific performance by debtors. The common law is reluctant with regard to both these solutions and sees monetary compensation as the rule in cases of breach of contract. According to Kronman, it will allow specific performance in cases where the subject matter of the contract is "unique." The economic rationale for such a rule is, in Kronman's view, that in such cases the appropriate damages are considerably more difficult to determine than for goods with ready substitutes in the market and that the search effort by the creditor to locate the debtor, which for "unique" products is likely to be substantially higher than for current ones, is entirely wasted, as no similar goods can be located with the same information. Both arguments involve the costliness of information that "market actors" as well as judges must face, a topic further discussed in Part II. See Kronman, Specific Performance, *U.Chic. L. Rev.* 45 (1978):351–382; C.J. Goetz and R.E. Scott, "Liquidated Damages, Penalties and the Just Compensation Principle: Some Notes on an Enforcement Model and a Theory of Efficient Breach," *Columbia L. Rev.* 77 (1977):554–594; P.H. Rubin, "Unenforceable Contracts: Penalty Clauses and Specific Performance," *J. Leg. Stud.* 10 (1981):237–247; A. Schwartz, "The Case for Specific Performance," *Yale L.J.* 89 (1979):271–306. Compare also the discussion of absolute rights versus entitlements to damages only in the fourth section of this chapter.

It is interesting to note that the civil law considers specific performance as the normal solution to breach of contract. Restrictions on the monetary value stipulated in penalty clauses are much less stringent than in the common law, and in various European jurisdictions (but not in Quebec) courts will readily issue *astreintes,* which might be considered as judicially created penalty clauses. How this rather substantial difference between common law and civil law should have arisen would be the subject of an interesting historical study. It might well have something to do with the types of contract (commercial exchange of movables versus land transactions?) that were prevalent in England and France, respectively, in the formative eras of the two systems. Whatever may be of that, Goetz and Scott conclude their article by stating that restrictions on the use of penalty clauses create losses from an economic point of view, as they prevent people from expressing their idiosyncratic losses as well as those that are uncertain and difficult to prove according to rules of evidence. These restrictions should, in their view, be lifted. It will be interesting to see whether the similarity between the underlying economic systems will lead, as economic analysis of law would predict, the two legal families to converge on this point. In this regard it should be noted that the French Civil Code, since 1975, empowers the courts to reduce or increase penalties, "which are manifestly excessive or derisory" (Articles 1152 and 1231 C.N.) This power cannot be contractually excluded. It can be exercised in cases of total as well as partial breach of contract. Belgian courts have, without an explicit code provision, undertaken to annul such clauses as against public order or as tainted by an unlawful cause. See A. Weil et F. Terré, *Droit civil — Les obligations*, 3rd ed., (Paris: Dalloz, 1980) nos 461 and 462 (p. 532ff.). The New Dutch Civil Code (6.1.9.18 Nw. B.W.) also gives the courts powers similar to those of the French Civil Code.

65. Kronman, "Mistake, Disclosure," op. cit. (nt. 61).

66. Ibid., p. 26.

67. Posner, *Economic Analysis of Law*, op. cit. (ch. 1, nt. 4), p. 134ff.

68. Posner and Rosenfield, "Impossibility," op. cit. (nt. 61).

69. 126 Mont. 514, 254 P. 2d 1076 (1963) as cited by Posner and Rosenfield, p. 101.

70. Ibid. Also in Kronman and Posner, *Economics of Contract Law*, op. cit. (ch. 1, nt. 3), pp. 125–126.

71. Posner, *Economic Analysis of Law*, op. cit. (ch. 1, nt. 4), p. 88. See also nt. 64.

72. Ibid., p. 94.

73. Masse and Marois, "Règle du jeu," op. cit. (ch. 1, nt. 20).

74. Posner, *Economic Analysis of Law*, op. cit. (ch. 1, nt. 4), pp. 84–88; Epstein "Unconscionability," op. cit. (nt. 61); Trebilcock, "Inequality of Bargaining Power," op. cit. (nt. 61).

75. Posner, *Economic Analysis of Law*, op. cit. (nt. 61), pp. 85–6; see also Kronman, "Mistake, Disclosure," op. cit. (nt. 61).

76. Recall the examples given in the second section of Chapter 1.

77. Epstein, "Unconscionability," op. cit. (nt. 61), p. 315.

78. For instance, A.M. Linden writes on p. 1 of Wright and Linden, *The Law of Torts — Cases, Notes and Materials*, 5th ed. (Toronto: Butterworths, 1970): "The purpose of the law of torts is to adjust these losses and to afford compensation for injuries sustained by one person as the result of the conduct of another." But in the preface he notes explicitly that the two main functions of tort law are compensation and deterrence (p. ix).

J-L. Baudouin, in his *La responsabilité civile délictuelle* (Montreal: P.U.M., 1973) writes: "La responsabilité civile entraîne l'obligation de rétablir l'équilibre économique rompu et de réparer le dommage causé à la victime" (p. 4).

79. Posner, *Economic Analysis of Law*, op. cit. (ch. 1, nt. 4), p. 143. Generally on the economic analysis of tort law; see also J.P. Brown, "Toward an Economic Theory of Liability," *J. Leg. Stud.* 2 (1973):323–349; J.R. Chelius, "Liability for Industrial Accidents: A Comparison of Negligence and Strict Liability Systems," *J. Leg. Stud.* 5 (1976):293–309; R. Cooter, L. Kornhauser, and D. Lane, "Liability Rules, Limited Information, and the Role of Precedent," *Bell J. Econ.* 10

(1979):366–373; H. Demsetz, (nt. 41); "Rule of Liability" op. cit. P.A. Diamond, "Single Activity Accidents," *J. Leg. Stud.* 3 (1974):107–164; P.A. Diamond, "Accident Law and Resource Allocation," *Bell J. Econ. and Mgmt. Sc.* 5 (1974):366–405; P.A. Diamond and J. Mirrlees, "On the Assignment of Liability: The Uniform Case," *Bell J. Econ.* 6 (1975):487–516: D. Epple, "Product Safety: Liability Rules, Market Structure and Imperfect Information," *Am. Econ. Rev.* 68 (1978):80–95; R.A. Epstein, "A Theory of Strict Liability," *J. Leg. Stud.* 2 (1973):151–204; R.A. Epstein, "Defenses and Subsequent Pleas in a System of Strict Liability," *J. Leg. Stud.* 3 (1974):164–215; R.A. Epstein, "Intentional Harms," *J. Leg. Stud.* 4 (1974):391–442; J. Green, "On the Optimal Structure of Liability Laws," *Bell J. Econ.* 7 (1976):553–574; R.S. Higgins, "Producers' Liability and Producer Related Accidents," *J. Leg. Stud.* 7 (1978):299–321; R.S. Higgins, "Products Liability Insurance, Moral Hazard and Contributory Negligence," *J. Leg. Stud.* 10 (1981):111–130; W.M. Landes and R.A. Posner, "Joint and Multiple Tortfeasors: An Economic Analysis," *J. Leg. Stud.* 9 (1980):517–555, R.N. McKean, "Products Liability: Trends and Implications," *U. Chic. L. Rev.* 38 (1970):3–63; R.N. McKean, "Products Liability: Implications of Some Changing Property Rights," *Quart. J. Econ.* 84 (1970):611–626; H. Manne, ed., Edited Transcript of the AALS-AEA Conference on Products Liability, in Manne, *Economics of Legal Relationships,* op. cit. (ch. 1, nt. 3), pp. 273–295; J.A. Ordover, "Costly Litigation in the Model of Single Activity Accidents," *J. Leg. Stud.* 7 (1978):243–261; A.M. Polinsky, "Resolving Nuisance Disputes," op. cit. (nt. 50); R.A. Posner, "A Theory of Negligence," *J. Leg. Stud.* 1 (1972):29ff.; A.M. Polinsky, "Strict Liability: A Comment," *J. Leg. Stud.* 2 (1973):205ff.; A.M. Polinsky, "The Concept of Corrective Justice in Recent Theories of Tort Law," *J. Leg. Stud.* 10 (1981):187–206; S.A. Rea, "Lump-Sum versus Periodic Damage Awards," *J. Leg. Stud.* 10 (1981):131–154; M.J. Rizzo, "Law amid Flux: The Economics of Negligence and Strict Liability in Tort," *J. Leg. Stud.* 9 (1980):291–318; M. J. Rizzo and F.S. Arnold, "Causal Apportionment in the Law of Torts: An Economic Theory," *Columbia L. Rev.* 80 (1980):1399–1429; W.H. Rodgers, "Negligence Reconsidered: The Role of Rationality in Tort Theory," *South. Calif. L. Rev.* 54 (1981):1–34; S. Shavell, "Strict Liability versus Negligence," *J. Leg. Stud.* 9 (1980):1–25; S. Shavell, "An Analysis of Causation and the Scope of Liability in the Law of Torts," *J. Leg. Stud.* 9 (1980):463–516; G. Tullock, "Negligence Again," *Int. Rev. Law Econ.* 1 (1981):51–62; D. Wittman, "First Come, First Served: An Economic Analysis of 'Coming to the Nuisance,' " *J. Leg. Stud.* 9 (1980):557–568; D. Wittman, "Optimal Pricing of Sequential Inputs: Last Clear Chance, Mitigation of Damages, and Related Doctrines," *J. Leg. Stud.* 10 (1981):65–91.

See further historical studies: P.S. Atiyah, "Liability for Railway Nuisance in the English Common Law: A Historical Footnote," *J. Law Econ.* 23 (1980):191–196; J.L. Croyle, "Industrial Accident Policy of the Early Twentieth Century," *J. Leg. Stud.* 7 (1978):279–297; E. Mackaay, "Veranderingen in het stelsel van vergoeding en verhaal van schade — Economische kanttekeningen," *Nederlands Juristenblad* 55 (1980):813–825; E. Mackaay, "Le droit relatif aux accidents — une interprétation économique," *Revue juridique Thémis* (forthcoming).

Obliquely related to the topic is W.M. Landes and R. A. Posner, "Salvors, Finders, Good Samaritans, and Other Rescuers: An Economic Study of Law and Altruism," *J. Leg. Stud.* 7 (1978):83–128. One of the questions asked there is what would happen to the incentives to rescue if one instituted liability for failure to rescue as opposed to no legal consequence at all.

80. Posner, *Economic Analysis of Law*, op. cit. (ch. 1, nt. 4) p. 122. See my article, "Les notions floues," op. cit. (nt. 54), p. 45.

81. Posner, *Economic Analysis of Law*, op. cit. (ch. 1, nt. 4), p. 124.

82. Ibid.

83. These situations are studied in game theory. On this vast subject see, apart from Ullmann-Margalit, *Emergence of Norms*, op. cit., (ch. 2, nt. 17); T.C. Schelling, *Strategy of Conflict* (London: Oxford U.P., 1963); A. Rapoport, *Two-Person Game Theory — The Essential Ideas* (Ann Arbor: U. Mich. P., 1970).

84. Posner, *Economic Analysis of Law*, op. cit. (ch. 1, nt. 4), p. 135.

85. See, for instance, R. Zarnett, "Tort Liability for Defective Automobile Design," *Osgoode Hall L.J.* 13 (1975):483–500 (in a Symposium on No-Fault Automobile Insurance) who approvingly quotes the conclusion by the Nader group that "damage suits have created some pressure for the safer design of motor vehicles" (p. 497).

86. This holds equally for prescribed safety features and similar regulatory measures. See the Oi-Goldberg exchange, op. cit. (nt. 2).

87. Posner, *Economic Analysis of Law*, op. cit. (ch. 1, nt. 4), pp. 137–142.

88. See Epstein, "Intentional Harms", op. cit. (nt. 79).

89. Posner, *Economic Analysis of law*, op. cit. (ch. 1, nt. 4), p. 143.

90. It is easily seen that this argument can be generalized to other ways in which the courts do not make the manufacturer — or other person or group causing injuries to third parties — pay the entire cost of the damages he inflicts. Thus, if courts refuse to award damages for pain and suffering on the ground that it is too difficult to evaluate them precisely, one would expect less prevention than would have occured in a — hypothetical — market in which manufacturers would have to buy the right to inflict pain and suffering on victims.

91. Posner, *Economic Analysis of Law*, op. cit. (ch. 1, nt. 4), p. 49. See also on G. Tullock, *Trials on Trial — The Pure Theory of Legal Procedure* (New York: Columbia U.P., 1980).

92. W.M. Landes and R.A. Posner, "Legal Precedent: A Theoretical and Empirical Analysis," *J. Law Econ.* 19 (1976):249–307, p. 271ff., and the same, "Adjudication as a Private Good," *J. Leg. Stud.* 8 (1979):235–284, p. 239. See also A.M. Polinsky, "Private versus Public Enforcement of Fines," *J. Leg. Stud.* 9 (1980):105–127.

93. For instance, how can adequate notice be given to all members of the "class"? Should all members of the class be bound by the decision or should they have the option of "opting out"? How does one make sure that, where the decision is in favor of the class, the sums to be paid by defendant are adequately distributed among the class members? A different kind of problem is that the lawyer representing the class is not as well supervised as one who works for a private client. He might well prefer to settle the case out of court rather than assume the uncertainty and the cost of a trial. Hence one will have to supervise his fees in the case of a settlement. Notice that settlements may well frustrate in part the purpose of the class action.

See further on the subject of class actions: R. Bernstein, "Judicial Economy and Class Action" *J. Leg. Stud.* 7 (1978):349–370; S. Chester, "Class Action to Protect the Environment: A Real Weapon or Another Lawyer's Word Game?" in J. Swaigen, ed., *Environmental Rights in Canada* (Toronto: Butterworths, 1981), pp. 60–150; K.W. Dam, "Class Actions: Efficiency, Compensation, Deterrence, and Conflict of Interest," *J. Leg. Stud.* 4 (1975):47–73; D.N. Dewees, J.R.S. Prichard, and M.J. Trebilcock, "An Economic Analysis of Cost and Fee Rules for Class Actions," *J. Leg. Stud.* 10 (1981):155–185; J.R.S. Prichard, "Private Enforcement and Class Actions," in J.R.S. Prichard, W. Stanbury, and T. Wilson eds., *Canadian Competition Policy — Essays in Law and Economics* (Toronto: Butterworths, 1979) pp. 217–251.

94. To illustrate this by a small numerical example, let us represent the errors of the first kind by X, those of the second kind by Y, X and Y being expressed as percentages. Suppose that, *for given administrative cost*, we can trade off X for Y subject to the function

$$XY = .01$$

For $Y = 10\%$ we have $X = 10\%$, for $Y = 5\%$, $X = 20\%$. If W_Y and W_X designate the relative weights attached to each kind of error, we must minimize the function

$$F = X.W_X + Y.W_Y$$

Substituting for Y the earlier function, we have

$$F = X.W_X + (1/100X).W_Y$$

This function reaches a minimum when its first derivative is equal to zero, i.e.,

$$f' = W_X - (1/100 \ X^2).W_y = 0$$

This can be simplified to

$$X^2 = (1/100) \ W_y/W_X$$

hence

$$X = .1 \ \sqrt{W_Y/W_X} \qquad\qquad Y = .1 \ \sqrt{Y_X/W_Y}$$

For $W_X = W_Y$, one has $X = Y = .1$. For $W_X = 9W_Y$ (where X represents the conviction of an innocent person) one has $X = 3.33\%$ and $Y = 30\%$.

Another important aspect of procedure is its adversarial or "inquisitorial" character. Anglo-Saxon courts are thought to operate adversarially, whereas other countries, in particular those in Western Europe, are said to have "inquisitorial" courts. Such a difference between countries with interlinked economics and having reached a similar stage of economic development requires explanation in an economic analysis of law. G. Tullock, in "The Efficient Organization of Trials," *Kyklos* 28 (1975):745–762 and in Ch. 6 ("Technology: The Anglo-Saxons vs. The Rest of the World") of *Trials on Trial*, op. cit. (nt. 91) denounces adversarial procedure as a fact-finding method. His position has elicited various comments in *Kyklos* 30 (1977):507–519. Experimental studies on the quality of fact finding under either system do not come squarely on Tullock's side. (It must be noted that these studies do not take explicit account of the costs of either system.) See J. Thibaut and L. Walker, *Procedural Justice — A Psychological Analysis* (Hillsdale, N.J.: Lawrence Erlbaum Ass., 1975) and S. La Tour et al., "Procedure: Transnational Perspectives and Preferences," *Yale L.J.* 86 (1976):258–292. Thibaut and Walker's study has been criticized on methodological grounds: R.M. Hayden and J.K. Anderson, "On the Evaluation of Procedural Systems in Laboratory Experiments: A critique of Thibaut and Walker," *Law and Human Behavior* 3 (1979):21–38.

On the problems before small claims courts, see K. Economides, "Small Claims and Procedural Justice," *Brit. J. Law & Soc.* 7 (1980):111–121.

95. See Landes and Posner, "Adjudication", op. cit. (nt. 92); Posner, *Economic Analysis of Law,* (1977), op. cit. (ch. 1, nt. 4), p. 434.

96. Landes and Posner, "Adjudication", op. cit. (nt. 92), p. 247. In this article, Landes and Posner argue that arbitrators, because of their dependence on parties for future business, would have an incentive to issue rulings that are relatively acceptable to both parties. Hence their rulings would tend to be imprecise and case specific. Where parties have a long-range interest in the solution of a particular recurring problem, they would look for a mode of dispute resolution that could set precedents and follow them in the future. Such an institution would have to be independent from the parties, as the courts in fact are. Hence one might expect that the drive for the courts to have a monopoly of dispute resolution in the final resort would coincide with the growing of business enterprises with long-range, recurring interests. A thesis for historians to verify.

97. S. Macaulay, "Elegant Models, Empirical Pictures, and the Complexities of Contract," *Law & Soc. Rev.* 11 (1977):507–528, pp. 513–514. See similarly: R.B. Ferguson, "The Adjudication of Commercial Disputes and the Legal System in Modern England," *Brit. J. Law & Soc.* 7 (1980):141–157.

98. H. Rubin, "Why is the Common Law Efficient?" *J. Leg. Stud.* 6 (1977):51–63; G.L. Priest, "The Common Law Process and the Selection of Efficient Rules," *J. Leg. Stud.* 6 (1977):65–82; J.C. Goodman, "An Economic Theory of the Evolution of the Common Law," *J. Leg. Stud.* 7 (1978):393–406; the March 1979 issue of the *Journal of Legal Studies* (Vol. 8, No. 2) in which appears Landes and Posner's article cited in nt. 92; R. Cooter, and L. Kornhauser, "Can Litigation Improve the Law Without the Help of Judges?" *J. Leg. Stud.* 9 (1980):139–163; Mackaay, "Un modello formale di sviluppo giurisprudenziale," *Informatica e Diritto* 5 (1979):199–225; W.M. Landes and R.A. Posner, "Legal Change, Judicial Behavior and the Diversity Jurisdiction," *J. Leg. Stud.* 9 (1980):367–386; G. Priest, "Selective Characteristics of Litigation," *J. Leg. Stud.* 9 (1980):399–421; M.J. Rizzo, "Can There Be a Principle of Explanation in Common Law Decisions: A Comment on Priest," *J. Leg. Stud.* 9 (1980):423–427; R.P. Terrebonne, "A Strictly Evolutionary Model of Common Law," *J. Leg. Stud.* 10 (1981):397–407; A. Hollander and E. Mackaay, "Are Judges Economists at Heart?" in C. Ciampi, ed., *Artificial Intelligence and Legal Information Systems,* (Amsterdam: North-Holland, 1982), pp. 129–150.

The variety of the models offered here is very likely to be only a temporary state of affairs. It is certainly not to the credit of this type of explanation of the common law. In defending the economic analysis of law against Dworkin's attack, Posner states the problem quite correctly, in our view (*Economics of Justice,* op. cit. (ch. 1, nt. 4), p. 115):

> There are also the evolutionary models of the common law that
> Dworkin mentions. No doubt it is an embarrassment to the
> supporters of the economic theory of the common law that there are

so many explanations of why the common law is efficient. But the empirical regularity found by the economic theorists is not so arbitrary and improbable that it should be disregarded until we have a generally accepted theory tying this regularity to the motivations or the biology of judges, litigants, or legislators.

99. Michelman criticizes Posner for this view. See his "Norms and Normativity in the Economic Analysis of Law," *Minn. L. Rev.* 62 (1978):1015–1048, p. 1041.

100. All references given in nt. 98, except the Landes-Posner article.

101. Landes and Posner, "Adjudication, op. cit. (nt. 92).

102. See the March 1979 issue of the *Journal of Legal Studies* and Michelman's article cited in nt. 99.

103. S. Peltzman, "An Evaluation of Consumer Protection Legislation: The 1962 Drug Amendments," *J. Pol. Econ.* 81 (1973):1049–1091.

104. M. Friedman, *Capitalism and Freedom* (Chicago: U. Chic. P., 1962), pp. 137–160.

105. See, for instance, K.J. Galbraith, *American Capitalism* (Harmondsworth, U.K.: Penguin, 1963); J. K. Galbraith, *The Affluent Society* (New York: New American Library 1958); *The New Industrial State* (New York: New American Library, 1967); *Economics and the Public Purpose* (New York: New American Library 1973); also Mishan, *Costs of Economic Growth*, op. cit. (ch. 2, nt. 27), p. 149; Hennipman, *Welvaartstheorie*, op. cit. (ch. 2, nt. 32), p. 142.

106. See ref. at nts. 2 and 3; generally on this subject N.W. Cornell, R.G. Noll, and B. Weingast, "Safety Regulation," in H. Owen and C.L. Schultze, eds., *Setting National Priorities — The Next Ten Years* (Washington, D.C.: Brookings, 1976), pp. 457–504.

107. Demsetz, "Toward a Theory," op. cit. (nt. 26), pp. 24–25.

108. This is Posner's term: *Economic Analysis of Law*, op. cit., (ch. 1, nt. 4), p. 179ff.

Chapter 4

1. Goldberg, "Economics of Product Safety," op. cit.; "Regulation and Administered Contracts," op. cit.; "Competitive Bidding," op. cit. (ch. 3, nts. 2, 9, 61). The question of the cost of information in the economic theory of law has also been stressed recently by Diamond and by Posner. See P.A. Diamond and E. Maskin, "An Equilibrium Analysis of Search and Breach of Contract, I: Steady States," *Bell J. Econ.* 10 (1979):282–316. Posner, *Economics of Justice*, op. cit. (ch. 1, nt. 4), pp. 8, 9.

2. V. Goldberg, "On Positive Theories of Redistribution," *J. Econ. Iss.* 11 (1977):119–132; "Institutional Change and the Quasi-Invisible Hand," *J. Law Econ.* 17 (1974):461–492; "Remarks on the State of the Orthodoxy," *J. Econ. Iss.* 9 (1975):237–241; "Commons, Clark and the Emerging Post-Coasian Law and Economics," *J. Econ. Iss.* 10 (1976):877–893; "Public Choice — Property Rights," *J. Econ. Iss.* 8 (1974):555–579; "Toward an Expanded Economic Theory of Contract," *J. Econ. Iss.* 10 (1976):45–61; also his remarks in *J. Leg. Stud.* 8 (1979) pp. 371, 372;

"Relational Exchange," *American Behavioral Scientist* 23 (1980):337–352; "The Law and Economics of Vertical Restrictions: A Relational Perspective," *Texas L. Rev.* 58 (1979):91–129.

Goldberg and Samuels defend the so-called (neo-)institutional approach. Without denying that the neoclassical model has some relevance, the proponents of this approach maintain that it fails to answer the critical questions: those of the distribution of power and the study of the institutions in which it is embodied. Others following this approach: Veljanovski, "Economic Approach," op. cit. (ch. 3, nt. 14), p. 187ff.; O.E. Williamson, *Markets and Hierarchies* (New York: Free Press, 1975); O.E. Williamson, "Transaction-Cost Economics: The Governance of Contractual Relations," *J. Law. Econ.* 22 (1979):233–261. This group frequently cites the legal analysis of I.R. MacNeil, who has recently entered the law and economics debate himself. See, for instance, his "Power, Contract, and the Economic Model," *J. Econ. Iss.* 14 (1980):909–923; *The New Social Contract — An Inquiry into Modern Contractual Relations* (New Haven, Conn.: Yale U.P., 1980); "Economic Analysis of Contractual Relations: Its Shortfalls and the Need for a 'Rich classificatory Apparatus,' " *Northw. U.L. Rev.* 75 (1980–1981):1018–1063; "The Many Futures of Contracts," *South. Calif. L. Rev.* 47 (1974):691–816.

Blaug takes a rather critical view of the institutionalists. He writes on p. 126 of his *The Methodology of Economics — or How Economists Explain* (Cambridge U.P., 1980):

There may be such a thing as a school of institutionalism, but it clearly has no unique methodology denied to orthodox economists.

A much better description of the working methodology of institutionalists is *storytelling* . . . . Storytelling makes use of the method that historians call *colligation*, the bundling together of facts, low-level generalizations, high level theories, and value judgements in a coherent narrative, held together by a glue of an implicit set of beliefs and attitudes that the author shares with his readers. In able hands, it can be extremely persuasive and yet it is never easy to explain afterwards why it has persuaded. . . .
However, because storytelling lacks rigor, lacks a definite logical structure, it is all too easy to verify and virtually impossible to falsify. It is or can be persuasive precisely because it never runs the risk of being wrong.

3. Ackerman, *Economic Foundations*, op. cit. (ch. 1, nt. 3); "Regulating Slum Housing Markets on Behalf of the Poor: Of Housing Codes, Housing Subsidies and Income Redistribution Policy," *Yale L.J.* 80 (1971):1092–1197; with J. Sawyer, "The Uncertain Search for Environmental Policy: Scientific Factfinding and Rational Decisionmaking along the Delaware River," *U. Penn. L. Rev.* 120 (1972):419–502; with S. Rose-Ackerman, J.W. Sawyer, and D.W. Henderson, *The Uncertain Search for Environmental Quality* (New York: Free Press, 1974); *Private Property*, op. cit. (ch. 1, nt. 4)

4. F.I. Michelman, "Pollution as a Tort: A Non-Accidental Perspective on Calabresi's Costs," *Yale L.J.* 80 (1971):647–686; "Property, Utility and Fairness: Comments on the Ethical Foundations of Just Compensation Law," *Harvard L.*

Rev. 80 (1968):1165–1258. See also his "Norm and Normativity in the Economic Theory of Law," *Minn. L. Rev.* 62 (1978):1015–1048; "A Comment on Some Uses and Abuses of Economics in Law," *U. Chic. L. Rev.* 46 (1979):307–315; "Constitutions, Statutes, and the Theory of Efficient Adjudication," *J. Leg. Stud.* 9 (1980):431–461; with D. Kennedy, "Are Property and Contract Efficient?" *Hofstra L. Rev.* 8 (1980):711–770. Kennedy has recently published "Cost-Benefit Analysis of Entitlement Problems: A Critique," *Stanford L. Rev.* 33 (1981):387–445.

5. W.J. Samuels, "Legal-Economic Policy," op. cit. (ch. 1, nt. 4); "Interrelations between Legal and Economic Processes," *J. Law Econ.* 14 (1971):435–450; "In Defense of a Positive Approach to Government as an Economic Variable," *J. Law Econ.* 15 (1972):453–459; "The Economy as a System of Power and Its Legal Bases: The Legal Economics of Robert Lee Hale," *U. Miami L. Rev.* 27 (1973):261–371; "John Henry Beale's Lectures on Jurisprudence, 1909," *U. Miami L. Rev.* 29 (1975):260–280; "Commentary: An Economic Perspective on the Compensation Problem," *Wayne L. Rev.* 21 (1974):113–134. Outside the law and economics area, but also of interest here are "The Chicago School of Political Economy: A Constructive Critique," in W.J. Samuels, ed., *The Chicago School of Political Economy* (East Lansing, Mich.: Ass'n of Evolutionary Economics and Michigan State University, 1976), pp. 1–18 and "Chicago Doctrine as Explanation and Justification," in same, pp. 363–396, and "Further Limits to Chicago School Doctrine," in same, pp. 397–457; "Information Systems, Preferences, and the Economy in the JEI," *J. Econ. Iss.* 12 (1978):23–41; "Economics as a Science and Its Relationship to Policy: The Example of Free Trade," *J. Econ. Iss.* 14 (1980):163–185. See also "The Coase Theorem and the Study of Law and Economics," *Nat. Res. J.* 14 (1974):1–33, in which he writes on p. 32:

> The present "economic" approach is dominated by a narrow (Chicago-Austrian) approach to a narrow aspect or problem (allocation). There is more to both economics and law than can be accommodated by such an approach, particularly when it more resembles an economic theology than science.

6. E.J. Mishan, "The Economics of Disamenity," in *Symposium on the Coase Theorem,* op. cit. (ch. 3, nt. 4) pp. 55–86; "Folklore of the Market," op. cit. (ch. 2, nt. 24); *Costs of Economic Growth,* op. cit.; (ch. 2, nt. 27); *The Economic Growth Debate — An Assessment* (London: Allen and Unwin, 1977); "How Valid," op. cit.; (ch. 2, nt. 3); "The Effects of Externalities on Individual Choice," *Int. Rev. Law Econ.* 1 (1981):97–109.

7. See, for instance, C.E. Baker, "The Ideology of the Economic Analysis of Law," *Philosophy and Public Affairs* 5 (1975):3–48; "Starting Points in the Economic Analysis of Law," *Hofstra L. Rev.* 8 (1980):939–972; "Neutrality, Process, and Rationality as Flawed Bases for Interpreting Equal Protection," *Texas L. Rev.* 58 (1980):1029–1096; Dworkin, "Is Wealth a Value?" op. cit. (ch. 3, nt. 14), and "Why Efficiency?" *Hofstra L. Rev.* 8 (1980):563–590. Also C. Fried, *Right and Wrong* (Cambridge, Mass.: Harvard U.P., 1978), esp. pp. 81–107, and his *Contract as Promise — A Theory of Contractual Obligation,* (Cambridge, Mass.: Harvard U.P., 1981); Leff, "Unspeakable Ethics," op. cit. (ch. 3, nt. 14); remarks by Markovits published in the *Journal of Legal Studies* 8 (1979):370, 371, 379; Weinreb, "Utilitarianism," op. cit. (ch. 3, nt. 14).

8. Calabresi, "Some Thoughts," op. cit. (ch. 1, nt. 2).

9. Calabresi, *Costs of Accidents*, op. cit. (ch. 1, nt. 4); a very good summary of the theory of this book can be found in Michelman, "Pollution," op. cit. (nt. 4). See also I. England, "The System Builders: A Critical Appraisal of Modern Tort Theory," *J. Leg. Stud.* 9 (1980):27–69, pp. 33–51.

10. G. Calabresi and J.T. Hirschoff, "Toward a Test for Strict Liability," *Yale L.J.* 81 (1972):1055–1085; G. Calabresi, "Optimal Deterrence and Accidents — To Fleming James, Il miglior Fabbro," *Yale L.J.* 84 (1975):656–671; see also the older "The Decision for Accidents: An Approach to Nonfault Allocation of Costs," *Harvard L. Rev.* 78 (1965):713–745; "Views and Overviews," *Illinois Law Forum* (1967):600–611; "Does the Fault System Optimally Control Primary Accident Costs?" *Law and Contemporary Problems* 33 (1968):429–463; "Torts — The Law of a Mixed Society," *Texas L. Rev.* 56 (1978):519–534.

11. G. Calabresi, "Concerning Cause and the Law of Torts: An Essay for Harry Kalven," *U. of Chic. L. Rev.* 43 (1976):69–108.

12. G. Calabresi and K.C. Bass, "Right Approach, Wrong Implications: A Critique of McKean on Products Liability," *U. Chic. L. Rev.* 38 (1970):74–91.

13. G. Calabresi, "The Problem of Malpractice — Trying to Round out the Circle," *U. of T. L.J.* 27 (1977):131–141.

14. Calabresi, "Transaction Costs" op. cit. (ch. 3, nt. 41); Calabresi and Melamed, "Property Rights", op. cit., (ch. 3, nt. 34)

15. Calabresi and Bobbitt, *Tragic Choices*, op. cit. (ch. 1, nt. 4). Similar on more philosophical questions: G. Calabresi, "Access to Justice and Substantive Law Reform: Legal Aid for the Lower Middle Class," in M. Cappelletti and B. Garth, *Access to Justice* Vol. III (Alphen aan den Rijn, Netherlands and Milan, Italy: Sijthoff-Guiffrè, 1979), pp. 169–190; G. Calabresi, "About Law and Economics: A Letter to Ronald Dworkin," *Hofstra L. Rev.* 8 (1980):553–562.

16. Calabresi, *Costs of Accidents*, op. cit. (ch. 1, nt. 4), p. 24.

17. Michelman, "Pollution as a Tort," op. cit., (nt. 4), p. 652; Calabresi, *Costs of Accidents*, op. cit. (ch. 1, nt. 4), p. 301ff.

18. Calabresi, *Costs of Accidents*, op. cit., (ch. 1, nt. 4), p. 26.

19. Ibid., p. 27.

20. Ibid., p. 29.

21. R.A. Posner, "Book Review of Calabresi's Costs of Accidents," *U. Chic. L. Rev.* 37 (1970):636–648.

22. Ibid., p. 638. While it is true that justice is only referred to as a constraint on schemes one could imagine in pursuit of the goal of reducing accident costs, it is questionable whether Posner reads Calabresi's intention correctly. Calabresi's recent book suggests rather that he did not mean to neglect such "nonefficiency" values, as we shall argue in what follows.

23. Calabresi, *Costs of Accidents* op. cit. (ch. 1, nt. 4), pp. 56, 206, 220.

24. Posner, "Book Review," op. cit. (nt. 21), pp. 639, 640, 646.

25. Ibid., p. 644.

26. Ibid. (emphasis added).

27. Ibid., p. 638.

28. Ibid.

29. Posner's discussion might suggest that Calabresi's secondary costs are a confusion in an economic perspective. This view appears to be mistaken. In a recent paper Shavell submits that those costs might correspond to what economists would

term the "disutility due to risk bearing" [S. Shavell, "Accidents, Liability, and Insurance," Harvard Institute of Economic Research, Discussion Paper No. 685 (1979), p. ii].

30. Calabresi and Bobbitt, Tragic Choices, op. cit. (ch. 1, nt. 4), p. 24ff.

31. Ibid., p. 49.

32. Ibid., p. 40 (emphasis added).

33. Ibid., p. 78.

34. Ibid., p. 54.

35. In his article on the malpractice problem, Calabresi writes "Old subterfuges, once exposed, can almost never regain credibility," ("Problem of Malpractice," op. cit. (nt. 13), p. 140).

36. Posner, Economic Analysis of Law, op. cit. (ch. 1, nt. 4), p. 10.

37. Ibid. p. 143 (emphasis added).

38. Ibid., p. 429 (emphasis added).

39. H.L.A. Hart, "American Jurisprudence Through English Eyes: The Nightmare and the Noble Dream," Georgia L. Rev. 11 (1977):969–990, pp. 988–89. Posner has responded in a recent article ("Utilitarianism," op. cit. (ch. 1, nt. 11), arguing that one should not, as is often done, confuse a utilitarian conception of law with the economic theory of law as he and others have developed it. Wealth maximization, which Posner considers fundamental to his analysis of law, can not be equated with happiness maximization as utilitarians would presumably propose it. Posner writes, for instance, "The fact that the term 'thief' is used pejoratively even in societies where theft, being punished very severely, is unlikely to be resorted to except in cases where the utility to the thief exceeds the victim's disutility is a datum about our ethical beliefs that utilitarianism cannot account for, and wealth maximization can" (p. 123). Posner also submits that "the economic approach is less hospitable than the utilitarian to redistribution" (p. 130). He further argues that in a society where envy is widespread, a utilitarian would see reason for public intervention leading to redistribution of wealth, as this would increase overall happiness. Economic theory, by contrast, would not see in this phenomenon itself a ground for intervention, as it does not constitute a market failure (p. 132). (It should be recalled, however, that in the definition of a Pareto optimum, envy — i.e., interdependence of utility functions of individuals — is presumed to be absent.)

40. Calabresi, "Optimal Deterrence" op. cit. (nt. 10), p. 657.

41. Ibid.

42. Calabresi, Costs of Accidents, op. cit. (ch. 1, nt. 4), p. 109ff.

43. Ibid., p. 56; see also pp. 91, 96, 148.

44. Ibid., p. 56. Further on this subject: G.T. Schwartz, "Contributory and Comparative Negligence: A Reappraisal," Yale L.J. 87 (1978):696–727.

45. Calabresi, "Optimal Deterrence" op. cit. (nt. 10), p. 668.

46. Calabresi, Costs of Accidents, op. cit. (ch. 1, nt. 4), p. 58.

47. Ibid., p. 59.

48. See the analysis of credit ceilings in Chapter 1.

49. Calabresi, Costs of Accidents, op. cit. (ch. 1, nt. 4), p. 146.

50. Ibid., pp. 145, 148.

51. Ibid., p. 136ff.

52. Ibid., p. 139ff.

53. Ibid., p. 141.

54. Further on this subject, see Calabresi, *"Concerning Cause,"* op. cit. (nt. 11).

55. Calabresi, *Costs of Accidents,* op. cit. (ch. 1, nt. 4), pp. 143–144.

56. Ibid., p. 147.

57. Ibid., p. 148.

58. Ibid., p. 150.

59. Ibid., p. 152ff.

60. Calabresi and Hirschoff, "Toward a Test," op. cit. (nt. 10); Calabresi, "Optimal Deterrence," op. cit. (nt. 10); Calabresi and Melamed, "Property Rules," op. cit. (ch. 3, nt. 34).

61. Calabresi and Hirschoff, "Toward a Test," op. cit. (nt. 10), p. 1060; Calabresi, "Optimal Deterrence," op. cit. (nt. 10), p. 666.

62. Calabresi and Hirschoff, "Toward a Test," op. cit. (nt. 10), p. 1061. By "reverse Hand test" they mean a regime in which one starts with the proposition that the injurer is liable and allows him to shift the burden by showing that the victim has been negligent.

63. See Calabresi, *Costs of Accidents,* op. cit. (ch. 1, nt. 4), p. 245; also J.R. Chelius, "Liability for Industrial Accidents: A Comparison of Negligence and Strict Liability Systems," *J. Leg. Stud.* 5 (1976):293–309.

64. But see Part II, Chapter 9.

65. Calabresi and Melamed, "Property Rules," op. cit (ch. 3, nt. 34), p. 35.

66. Calabresi, *Costs of Accidents,* op. cit. (ch. 1, nt. 4), p. 255.

67. Ibid., pp. 256–257.

68. Ibid., p. 255.

69. Ibid., p. 108.

70. Ibid., p. 126.

71. Ibid., p. 108.

72. Ibid., p. 123; the tradeoff with respect to the precision of statutory language is similar to that discussed in ch. 3, fourth section; see ref. at ch. 3, nt. 54.

73. Calabresi, *Costs of Accidents,* op. cit. (ch. 1, nt. 4), p. 124.

74. Tullock likes to illustrate this by supposing that the penalty for even minor offences would be to boil the victim in oil. Presumably a variety of quite legitimate activities would stop, along with those that were meant to be eliminated. Notice also that since it is now hard to distinguish between these minor offences and the very serious ones in the penalties meted out, there is less reason for those (hardened criminals) who are willing to run the risk of being boiled in oil to stop at minor infractions. On the advantages and disadvantages of precision in legal language see my article, "Les notions floues," op. cit. (ch. 3, nt. 54).

75. Calabresi and Bobbitt, *Tragic Choices,* op. cit. (ch. 1, nt. 4), p. 48.

76. Ibid., p. 122.

77. On this subject, see, e.g., R.S. Summers, "Evaluating and Improving Legal Processes — A Plea for Process Values," *Cornell L. Rev.* 60 (1974):1–52; see also D. Kennedy, "Legal Formality," *J. Leg. Stud.* 2 (1973):251–298; and N. Luhmann, *Legitimation durch Verfahren,* 2nd ed. (Darmstadt, Germany: Luchterhand, 1975).

Chapter 5

1. C. Cherry, *On Human Communication* 2nd ed. (Cambridge, Mass.: MIT Press, 1966), p. 244.

2. Ibid., p. 170.

3. This is not true for so-called risk preferers, defined as those who value an uncertain gain higher than its mathematically expected value. Not to be confused with this is the observation that in some circumstances one may wish to have information withheld because others might be expected to use it and, in some cases, draw the wrong conclusions from it or simply cause disutility to the persons concerned. This appears to be the core of the privacy problem. See Posner, *Economics of Justice*, op. cit. (ch. 1, nt. 4), Part III.

A similar consideration seems to be at the root of society's use of *subterfuges*, as Calabresi and Bobbitt call them [*Tragic Choices*, op cit. (ch. 1, nt. 4), p. 78] (see Chapter 3).

4. F. Knight, *Risk, Uncertainty and Profit* (Chicago: U. Chic. Press, 1971). On p. 313 one reads: "Change of some kind is prerequisite to the existence of uncertainty; in an absolutely unchanging world the future would be accurately foreknown, since it would be exactly like the past". On the same page he points to the paradox ". . . that the existence of a problem of knowledge depends on the future being different from the past, while the possibility of the solution of the problem depends on the future being like the past."

5. This distinction is made at p. 19ff. of the cited text. Stigler, in his introduction to this edition, states that "modern analysis no longer views the two classes as different in kind" (p. xiv).

6. See Chapter 3. Cf. Dahlman, "Problem of Externality," op. cit. (ch. 2, nt. 23).

7. This tradeoff was explicitly stated in G.J. Stigler's early article, "The Economics of Information," *J. Pol. Econ.* 69 (1961):213–225. See also K.J. Arrow, "The Future and the Present in Economic Life," *Econ. Inq.* 16 (1978):157–169, pp. 163–166.

8. Let S be the total cost of search as a function of the amount of search i; let U be the total cost of uncertainty, also a function of i; let R be the reduction in the total cost of uncertainty as a function of i. We must first show that Max $(R - S)$ = Min $(U + S)$. This can be proved as follows. Let L be the total cost (loss) due to uncertainty if no search is undertaken. It follows from the definitions that $R = L - U$. Substituted in the formula to be maximized, this becomes Max $(L - U - S)$. But since L is independent of the amount of search i, one may rewrite this as L + Max $(- U - S)$, which in turn may be rewritten as L − Min $(U + S)$. The term to be optimized is now the same as in the second formula. Q.E.D.

That Max $(R - S)$ is equivalent to setting marginal revenue equal to marginal cost is easily seen if one reads R as the revenue function and S as the cost function for a product that is information. The equivalence in this form is shown in standard microeconomic texts.

9. These diagrams also appear in R. Bartlett, *Economic Foundations of Political Power* (New York: Free Press, 1973), p. 30.

10. It is interesting to illustrate this point by assuming particular functions. Let the uncertainty cost be defined by the function

$$U = \frac{K}{i^p},$$

where K is a scalar, $p > 1$, and i the amount of search. Let the search cost similarly be given by the function

$$S = L. \, i^q,$$

where L is a scalar and $q > 1$. The function to be minimized is

$$M = U + S = K. \, i^{-p} + L. \, i^q.$$

It can be shown that M is minimal for

$$i^* = (p.K/q.L)^{1/(p+q)}.$$

It is obvious that exhaustive searching (where i would be infinite) is generally not the optimal solution. We shall not develop here the formulas for the optimal values for M^*, U^* and S^*.

Now let changes take place in the two functions such that

$$U_N = a. \, U$$

($a > 1$ reflects an increase in the cost of uncertainty).

$$S_N = b. \, S$$

($b < 1$ reflects a decrease in the cost of search). Per definition we have

$$M_N = U_N + S_N = a. \, U + b. \, S .$$

We should like to determine the *direction of change* in the optimal values of different variables as a function of a and b. It can be shown that

$$\frac{i_N^*}{i^*} = (a/b)^{1/(p+q)} \tag{1}$$

and that

$$\frac{M_N^*}{M^*} = \frac{U_N^*}{U^*} = \frac{S_N^*}{S^*} = (a^q .b^p)^{1/(p+q)} \tag{2}$$

Since we are interested only in determining whether these formulas are larger or smaller than unity as a function of values of a and b, and since $0 < 1/(p+q) < \frac{1}{2}$, we ignore the exponent $1/(p+q)$ for present purposes. Hence we have

for (1) $(a/b) \lessgtr ?$ 1   (1A)

for (1) $(a^q.b^p) \lessgtr ?$ 1   (2A)

These formulas allow one to arrive at the following — intuitively obvious — results:

1. The optimal amount of search reacts *positively* to increases in the benefits (a), but negatively to increases in the cost (b) (in both cases less than proportionally if the exponent, which is smaller than one-half, is taken into account).

2. The minimum cost attributable to the costliness of information (M) reacts positively to both these changes.

3. If search becomes cheaper ($b<1$), the amount of it undertaken (i) will go up, but the total cost due to information (M) will go down.

4. If, however, the uncertainty costs go down ($a<1$), both these values decline. Hence a reduction in the cost of uncertainty (or in what is at stake in the decision) does not have the same effects as an increase in search efficiency.

11. A. Downs, *An Economic Theory of Democracy* (New York: Harper & Row, 1957), pp. 207, 219.

12. Simon, in a recent article, writes on this subject: "The global optimization problem is to find the least-cost or best return decision, *net* of computational costs. We formulate this problem in terms of a tradeoff between the marginal computational cost and the marginal improvement in the substantive decision it is expected to produce . . . ." [H.A. Simon, "On How to Decide What to Do," *Bell J. Econ.* 9 (1978):494–507, p. 495].

13. A.T. Kronman, "Specific Performance," in Kronman and Posner, *Economics of Contract Law,* op. cit. (ch. 1, nt. 3), p. 187.

14. McKenzie, "Methodological Boundaries," op. cit. (ch. 1, nt. 19), pp. 634–635. See also ch. 2, nt. 56.

15. J.G. March, "Bounded Rationality, Ambiguity, and the Engineering of Choice," *Bell J. Econ.* 9 (1978):587–608, p. 595.

16. Ibid.

17. Knight, *Risk,* op. cit. (nt. 4), p. 261.

18. K.E. Boulding, "The Economics of Knowledge and the Knowledge of Economics," in D.M. Lamberton, ed., *Economics of Information and Knowledge,* (Harmondsworth, U.K.: Penguin, 1971), p. 23.

19. This is not true in cases in which one can expect to make gains from having information before others or before it is publicly available. Kronman discusses such situations in his "Mistake, Disclosure, Information, and the Law of Contracts," *J. Leg. Stud.* 7 (1978):1–34. On p. 9 and ff. he discusses the *Laidlaw* v. *Organ* case (15 U.S. (2 Wheat.) 178), in which a purchaser, having privileged knowledge of the impending lift of a blockade, concluded a highly profitable transaction that the other party subsequently sought to have annulled for nondisclosure of the information.

20. The phenomenon of "natural monopolies" has been used as a justification for regulation of the industry concerned. Whether natural monopolies in fact exist and whether they warrant regulatory intervention are hotly debated questions. See for instance M.J. Trebilcock, L. Waverman, and J.R.S. Prichard, "Markets for Regulation — Implications for Performance Standards and Institutional Design," in *Government Regulation,* (Toronto: Ontario Economic Council, 1978), pp. 11–66, p. 16.

21. K.J. Arrow, *The Limits of Organization* (New York: Norton, 1974), p. 39ff.; Boulding, "Economics of Knowledge," op. cit. (nt. 18); A. Breton, *Bilingualism: An Economic Approach,* (Montreal: C.D. Howe Research Institute, 1978), pp. 1–3.

22. See for instance G.S. Becker, *Human Capital — A Theoretical and Empirical Analysis with Special Reference to Education* 2nd ed. (New York: Columbia U.P., 1975).

23. Arrow, *Limits,* op. cit. (nt. 21) p. 41.

24. Ibid.
25. Ibid., p. 42.
26. See, e.g., G.J. Stigler and G.S. Becker, "De Gustibus Non Est Disputandum," *Am. Econ. Rev.* 67 (1977):76–90.
27. Ross submits that consumers view the choice among alternatives as an investment. In empirical studies of consumer behavior, it was found that once his mind was made up, a consumer avoided information favouring the nonchosen alternative and had a heightened interest in information consistent with his choice. I. Ross, "Applications of Consumer Information to Public Policy Decisions," in *Marketing Analysis for Societal Problems*, J.N. Sheth and P.L. Wright, eds., (Urbana: U. Ill. P., 1974), p. 49.

Chapter 6

1. Becker, *Economic Approach*, op. cit. (ch. 1, nt. 12), p. 153.
2. Posner, *Economic Analysis of Law*, op. cit. (ch. 1, nt. 4), p. 4.
3. R.A. Posner, *Economic Analysis of Law*, 1st ed. (Boston: Little, Brown, 1972), p. 5. Not one reference is given to this "abundant evidence." But see, for instance, A. Alchian and W.R. Allen, *Exchange and Production: Competition, Coordination, and Control*, 2nd ed. (Belmont, Ca.: Wadsworth, 1976), p. 70ff. on evidence for the validity of the laws of demand. Mishan, on the contrary, believes that support has been exaggerated. Mishan, "Folklore of the Market," op. cit. (ch. 2, nt. 24). See also Blaug, *Methodology of Economics*, op. cit. (ch. 4, nt. 2), ch. 6.
4. Becker, *Economics Approach*, op. cit. (ch. 1, nt. 12), p. 153.
5. Ibid., p. 156; also R.M. Cyert, W.R. Dill, and J.G. March, "The Role of Expectations in Business Decision Making," in L.A. Welsch and R.M. Cyert, eds., *Management Decision Making* (New York: Penguin, 1970), pp. 86–109. On p. 109, they write:

> It would be a mistake to picture the biases introduced in either of these fashions as exceptionally great. In almost every case there are some reasonably severe reality constraints on bias. But where the decision involves choice between two reasonably equal alternatives, small biases will be critical.

6. Becker, *Economic Approach*, op. cit. (ch. 1, nt. 12), p. 157.
7. In general, see also for instance, R.R. Nelson, and S.G. Winter, "Factor Price Changes and Factor Substitution in an Evolutionary Model," *Bell J. Econ.* 6 (1975):446–486 and the literature cited there. Alchian and Allen, *Exchange and Production*, op. cit. (nt. 3), p. 305. For the law, P.H. Rubin, "Why Is the Common Law Efficient?" *J. Leg. Stud.* 6 (1977):51–63; G.L. Priest, "The Common Law Process and the Selection of Efficient Rules," *J. Leg. Stud.* 6 (1977):65–82; and other references at ch. 3, nt. 98.
8. W. Kirsch, *Entscheidungsprozesse*, 3 vols. (Wiesbaden: Betriebswirtschaftlicher Verlag Dr. Th. Gabler, 1970–71), vol. I, pp. 25–27; W. Kirsch, M. Michael, and W. Weber, *Entscheidungsprozesse in Frage und Antwort* (Wiesbaden: Betriebswirtschaftlicher Verlag Dr. Th. Gabler, 1973), p. 19.

9. Kirsch, *Entscheidungsprozesse*, vol. 1, op. cit. (nt. 8), pp. 25–27

10. General literature on the subject: W. Edwards and A. Tversky, eds., *Decision Making* (New York: Penguin, 1967), and Kirsch, *Entscheidungsprozesse*, op. cit. (nt. 8).

Psychological research: W. Edwards, "The Theory of Decision Making" (1954) and "Behavioral Decision Theory" (1961), in Edwards and Tversky, *Decision Making*, op. cit., pp. 13–95; G.M. Becker and C.G. McClintock, "Value: Behavioral Decision Theory," *Ann. Rev. Psych.* 18 (1967):239–286; P. Slovic, B. Fischhoff and S. Lichtenstein, "Behavioral Decision Theory," *Ann. Rev. Psych.* 28 (1977):1–39.

Normative decision theory: R.D. Luce and H. Raiffa, *Games and Decisions* (New York: Wiley, 1957); H. Raiffa, *Decision Analysis* (Reading, Mass.: Addison-Wesley, 1968); P.G. Moore, and H. Thomas, *The Anatomy of Decisions* (Harmondsworth, U.K.: Penguin, 1976); S.J. Thorson, "Axiomatic Theories of Preference-Based Choice Behavior," *American Behavioral Scientist* 20 (1976):65–92.

11. Edwards, "Theory," op. cit. (nt. 10), p. 16; R.D. Luce, "Psychological Studies of Risky Decision Making," in Edwards and Tversky, *Decision Making*, op. cit. (nt. 10), pp. 334–352.

12. N.H. Anderson, "Information Integration Theory: A Brief Survey," in D.H. Krantz et al., *Contemporary Developments in Mathematical Psychology* (San Francisco: Freeman, 1974), pp. 236–305.

13. R.N. Shepard, "On Subjectively Optimum Selections among Multi-Attribute Alternatives," in Edwards and Tversky, *Decision Making*, op. cit. (nt. 10), pp. 257–283.

14. Slovic et al., "Behavioral Decision Theory," op. cit. (nt. 10), p. 11.

15. For instance, B. Anderson, *Cognitive Psychology* (New York: Academic Press, 1975), p. 309, gives the following approximations:

$$u(x) \simeq \sqrt{x} \qquad \text{for } x > 0 \text{ (gain)}$$

$$u(x) \simeq -x^2 \qquad \text{for } x < 0 \text{ (loss)}$$

Similarly Kirsch, *Entscheidungsprozesse*, op. cit. (nt. 8), Vol. I, p. 111ff.; Raiffa, *Decision Analysis*, op. cit.; Moore and Thomas, *Anatomy*, op. cit. (nt. 10).

18. The idea of subjective probabilities goes back to L.J. Savage, *The Foundation of Statistics* (New York: Wiley, 1954). On methods for measuring subjective probabilities (uncertainty) and utility, see, for instance, the articles in Part I of G.M. Kaufman and H. Thomas, *Modern Decision Analysis* (Harmondsworth, U.K.: Penguin, 1977); the introduction gives references to review articles.

19. Well-known strategies of this kind are *minimax* (choose the option that entails the smallest loss, if one loses), *maximax* (choose the option promising the largest gain, if one wins), *minimum regret* (choose the option for which the difference between gain and loss is smallest).

20. The Bayesian rule is a statistical device that allows one to refine one's estimate of the probability of A on the basis of knowledge of the relation of A with some other factor B and of the probability of B's occurence. The formula is:

$$P(A_k/B) = P(B/A_k).P(B) \ / \ \sum_{j=1}^{n} P(B/A_j).P(B)$$

where A_1 to A_n are mutually exclusive and jointly exhaustive states of the world.

$P(X)$ means the probability that X and $P(X/Y)$ means the probability that X, given that Y.

Raiffa, *Decision Analysis*, op. cit. (nt. 10), p. 18ff.; Moore and Thomas, *Anatomy*, op. cit. (nt. 10), p. 78ff.

21. See, for instance, W. Edwards, H. Lindman, and L.D. Phillips, "Emerging Technologies for Making Decisions," in F. Barron and W. C. Dement, eds., *New Directions in Psychology* (New York: Holt, Rinehart and Winston, 1965), pp. 259–325; W. Edwards, "Optimal Strategies for Seeking Information: Models for Statistics, Choice Reaction Time, and Human Information Processing," *J. Math. Psych.* 2 (1965):312–29; W. Edwards, "Conservatism in Human Information Processing," in B. Kleinmuntz, *Formal Representation of Human Judgment* (New York: Wiley, 1968), pp. 17–52; L. Phillips and W. Edwards, "Conservatism in a Simple Probability Inference Task," in Edwards and Tversky, *Decision Making*, op. cit. (nt. 10), pp. 239–254; Slovic et al., "Behavioral Decision Theory," op. cit. (nt. 10), p. 3; H.A. Simon, "On How to Decide What to Do," *Bell J. Econ.* 9 (1978):494–507, pp. 502, 503.

22. See Edwards, "Theory," op. cit. (nt. 10), p. 36.

23. Slovic et al., "Behavioral Decision Theory," op. cit. (nt. 10), p. 8.

24. See, for example, Moore and Thomas, *Anatomy*, op. cit. (nt. 10); Kaufman and Thomas, *Modern Decision Analysis*, op. cit. (nt. 18). Even the normative use of the theory is now questioned. March writes in a recent article ["Bounded Rationality, Ambiguity, and the Engineering of Choice," *Bell J. Econ.* 9 (1978):587–608, p. 588] that models of rational choice appear to be more appropriate as predictions than as guides for intelligent action.

25. See Kirsch, *Entscheidungsprozesse*, op. cit. (nt. 8), vol. I, pp. 57–60; Raiffa, *Decision Analysis*, op. cit. (nt. 10), ch. 7.

26. Kirsch, *Entscheidungsprozesse*, op. cit. (nt. 8), vol. I, p. 101.

27. Decision theorists have elaborated models in which one succeeds in near optimal search by adopting such strategies as a fixed size sample or an optimal stopping rule based on the decrease in the new elements (or price variation) that each further visit to a supplier entails. On this subject, see A. Schwartz and L.L. Wilde, "Intervening in Markets on the Basis of Imperfect Information: A Legal and Economic Analysis," *U. Penn. L. Rev.* 127 (1979):630–682, p. 646ff. Classical articles on the subject are: G. J. Stigler, "The Economics of Information," *J. Pol. Econ.* 69 (1961):213–225; J.L. Gastwirth, "On Probabilistic Models of Consumer Search for Information," *Quart. J. Econ.* 90 (1976):36–50, and the earlier literature he cites; M. Rothschild, "Searching for the Lowest Price When the Distribution of Price is Unknown," *J. Pol. Econ.* 84 (1974): 689–712.

28. Slovic et al., "Behavioral Decision Theory," op. cit. (nt. 10), p. 1; Kirsch, *Entscheidungsprozesse*, op. cit. (nt. 8), p. 61ff.

29. See, for instance, H.A. Simon, *Administrative Behavior* 3rd ed. (New York: Free Press, 1976).

30. C.S. Colantoni, O.A. Davis, and M. Swaminuthan, "Imperfect Consumers and Welfare Comparisons of Policies Concerning Information and Regulation," *Bell J. Econ.* 7 (1976):602–615, p. 604 define unbounded rationality as a concept of human mind in which "there are neither rate nor storage limits on the powers of individuals to receive, store, retrieve and process information without error." See also Simon, *Administrative Behavior*, op. cit. (nt. 29), p. xxviiiff.; H.A. Simon,

"Theories of Bounded Rationality," in C.B. McGuire and R. Radner, *Decision and Organization: A Volume in Honor of Jacob Marschak* (Amsterdam: North-Holland, 1972), p. 162.

31. See D. W. Taylor, "Decision Making and Problem Solving," in Welsch and Cyert, *Management Decision*, op. cit. (nt. 5), p. 35.

32. Simon, "Theories," op. cit. (nt. 30), p. 170.

33. Taylor, "Decision Making," op. cit. (nt. 31), p. 37.

34. Simon, "Theories," op. cit. (nt. 30), p. 170; Kirsch, *Entscheidungsprozesse*, op. cit. (nt. 8), p. 88.

35. H.A. Simon, *The Shape of Automation for Men and Management* (New York: Harper Torch Books, 1965), p. 62; R. Wintrobe, "The Economics of Bureaucracy," unpublished thesis, University of Toronto, 1976, p. 4, for parallel distinctions made by other authors.

36. Simon, "Theories," op. cit. (nt. 30), p. 168; also Kirsch, *Entscheidungsprozesse*, op. cit. (nt. 8), p. 109. Kirsch notes that this way of assuming the level of aspiration fixed is increasingly abandoned in favor of the view that it should be treated as a learning process, sensitive to success and failure.

37. Simon, "Theories," op. cit. (nt. 30), p. 170. Similar problems are encountered in the determination of "optimal stopping rules." See nt. 27.

38. This tradeoff is reminiscent of the discussion in welfare economics about the prospects for collective welfare gains due to improvements in allocative efficiency and to innovation.

39. Boden defines a heuristic as "a method that directs thinking along the paths most likely to lead to the goal, less promising avenues being left unexplored" [*Artificial Intelligence and Natural Man* (Hassocks, U.K.: Harvester Press, 1977), p. 347]. Crombag, in reviewing the literature on heuristics, arrives at the conclusion that they are (my translation) "meta-rules, which govern not the problem at hand, but the rules to solve the problem. . . . What is one looking for in using (heuristic) rules of search? Rules or sequences of rules which, if applied correctly, may enable one to find a solution or a partial solution. Finding rules find solutions, search rules search finding rules" (*Vakspecifieke cognitieve psychologie III: Over het oplossen van meetkundige vraagstukken* (Subject specific cognitive psychology III: On the solution of geometry problems), Educational Research Center, Univ. of Leyden, 1977, p. 17).

40. H.A. Simon, *The Sciences of the Artificial* (Cambridge, Mass.: MIT Press, 1969), p. 33.

41. Ibid., ch. IV; also Simon, *Administrative Behavior*, op. cit. (nt. 29), pp. 20–21; Wintrobe, "Economics of Bureaucracy," op. cit. (nt. 35), p. 29ff.

42. March, in "Bounded Rationality" (nt. 24), on p. 589 refers to this problem and similar ones.

43. A.D. Hirschman and C.E. Lindblom, "Economic Development, Research and Development, Policy Making: Some Converging Views," in F.E. Emery, *Systems Thinking* (New York: Penguin, 1969), p. 358.

44. Ibid., pp. 368–369.

45. C.E. Lindblom, "Tinbergen on Policy Making," *J. Pol. Econ.* 66 (1958):531–538, p. 534.

46. Kirsch, *Entscheidungsprozesse*, op. cit. (nt. 8), p. 118; H.A. Simon, "Theories of Decision Making in Economics and Behavioral Science," in F.G. Castles et al., eds., *Decision, Organizations and Society* (New York: Penguin, 1971), p. 45.

47. L. Festinger, *A Theory of Cognitive Dissonance* (Palo Alto, Calif.: Stanford U.P., 1957); L. Festinger, *Conflict, Decision and Dissonance* (Palo Alto, Calif.: Stanford U.P., 1964); Kirsch, *Entscheidungsprozesse,* op. cit. (nt. 8), Vol. I, pp. 118–125.

48. Anderson, *Cognitive Psychology,* op. cit. (nt. 15), pp. 314–325, gives a variety of such techniques.

49. Simon, "Theories," op. cit. (nt. 46), p. 44; Kirsch, *Entscheidungsprozesse,* op. cit. (nt. 8), p. 112; March, "Bounded Rationality," op. cit. (nt. 24), pp. 602, 603.

50. Kirsch, *Entscheidungsprozesse,* op. cit. (nt. 8), p. 107ff.

51. Ibid., p. 115.

52. *Bell J. Econ.,* 9 (1978):491–608.

53. March, "Bounded Rationality," op. cit. (nt. 24); Simon, "On How to Decide" op. cit. (ch. 5, nt. 12). See also Simon's "From Substantive to Procedural Rationality," in F. Hahn and M. Hollis, eds, *Philosophy and Economic Theory* (New York: Oxford U.P., 1979), 64–85; Simon, "Rational Decision Making in Business Organizations," *Am. Econ. Rev.* 69 (1979):493–514.

54. March, "Bounded Rationality," op. cit. (nt. 24), p. 591. Some attempts at the formalization of the idea of bounded rationality have been made. Olander gives a partial formalization in his empirical study of satisficing versus maximizing. See his "Search Behavior in Non-Simultaneous Choice Situations: Satisficing or Maximizing," in D. Wendt and C. Vlek, eds., *Utility, Probability and Human Decision Making* (Dordrecht, Netherlands: Reidel, 1975), pp. 297–320; see also R. Radner and M. Rothschild, "On the Allocation of Effort," *J. Econ. Th.* 10 (1975):358–376.

55. March, "Bounded Rationality," op. cit. (nt. 24) (references omitted).

56. Ibid., p. 590.

57. Simon, "On How to Decide," op. cit. (nt. 21), p. 504.

58. Ibid.; also March, "Bounded Rationality," op. cit., pp. 591, 592.

59. March, "Bounded Rationality," op. cit. (nt. 24), p. 598.

60. Ibid., p. 601.

61. Slovic et al., "Behavioral Decision Theory," op. cit. (nt. 10), p. 4.

62. A. Tversky and D. Kahneman, "Judgment under Uncertainty: Heuristics and Biases," *Science* 185 (1974):1124–31; D. Kahneman and A. Tversky, "Prospect Theory: An Analysis of Decision under Risk," *Econometrica* 47 (1979):263–291; A. Tversky and D. Kahneman, "The Framing of Decisions and the Psychology of Choice," *Science* 211 (1981):453–458; earlier work by these authors, inter alia: Kahneman and Tversky, "Subjective Probability: A Judgement of Representativeness," *Cogn. Psych.* 3 (1972):430–454; Kahneman and Tversky, "On the Psychology of Prediction," *Psych. Rev.* 80 (1973):236–51; A. Tversky, "Intransitivity of Preferences," *Psych. Rev.* 76 (1969):31–48; Tversky and Kahneman, "The Belief in the Law of Small Numbers," *Psych. Bull.* 76 (1971):105–110; A. Tversky, "Elimination by Aspects: A Theory of Choice," *Psych. Rev.* 79 (1972):281–299; Tversky and Kahneman, "Availability: A Heuristic for Judging Frequency and Probability," *Cogn. Psych.* 5 (1973):207–232.

63. See A. Tversky, "Features of Similarity," *Psych. Rev.* 84 (1977):327–352.

64. Tversky and Kahneman, "Belief," op. cit. (nt. 62).

65. Tversky and Kahneman, "Judgment," op. cit. (nt. 62), in Johnson-Laird and Wason, eds. *Thinking,* (Cambridge: Cambridge U.P., 1977), p. 333.

66. S. Macaulay, "Non-contractual Relations in Business: A Preliminary Study," in V. Aubert, *Sociology of Law* (New York: Penguin, 1969), p. 198.

67. Slovic et al., "Behavioral Decision Theory," op. cit. (nt. 10), p. 6.

68. Tversky and Kahneman, "Judgment," op. cit. (nt. 62), p. 59.

69. Ibid., p. 60.

70. Tversky, "Elimination," op. cit. (nt. 62), p. 298.

71. Ibid., p. 298.

72. Slovic et al., "Behavioral Decision Theory," op. cit. (nt. 10), p. 8.

73. Tversky, "Elimination," op. cit. (nt. 62), p. 296; see Chapter 8.

74. This will be further discussed in Chapter 7 (misperception).

75. Van den Doel, following earlier literature, suggests the use of the terms *subjective* and *objective* rationality, which he defines in the following passage [*Democracy and Welfare Economics* (Cambridge: Cambridge U.P., 1979), p. 22].

A decision is subjectively rational if a decision-maker attempts to bring his objective function to the highest level. A decision is objectively rational if the maximum that could be achieved is actually achieved. The difference between objective and subjective rationality is due, on the one hand, to incomplete information about possible behavioural alternatives and implications, and, on the other hand, to the impossibility of digesting all information.

76. Schwartz and Wilde, "Intervening," op. cit. (nt. 27), pp. 630–639.

77. Trebilcock et al., "Markets," op. cit. (ch. 5, nt. 20), p. 44, submit that a clear example of this is the federal *Income Tax Act* in Canada.

78. G.S. Becker, "A Comment on Peltzman's 'Toward a More General Theory of Regulation,' " *J. Law Econ.* 19 (1976):245–248, p. 247.

79. Trebilcock et al., "Markets," op. cit. (ch. 5, nt. 20), pp. 43, 44.

80. S. Peltzman, "Toward a More General Theory of Regulation," *J. Law Econ.* 19 (1976):211–240; Trebilcock et al. "Markets," op. cit. (ch. 5, nt. 20) give a verbal exposé of this theory on pp. 35–36, 39, 46–48, 53.

81. See text around nt. 59.

82. Posner, *Economic Analysis* op cit. (ch. 1, nt. 4), p. 416.

83. This is at least my conclusion from reading texts such as the following: P. Weiler, *In the Last Resort — A Critical Study of Supreme Court of Canada* (Toronto: Carswell-Methuen, 1974); W. Twining and D. Miers, *How to Do Things with Rules* (London: Weidenfeld and Nicholson, 1976); E.H. Levi, *An Introduction to Legal Reasoning* (Chicago: U. Chic. P., 1948); R.A. Wasserstrom, *The Judicial Decision* (Palo Alto, Calif.: Stanford U.P., 1961); B.N. Cardozo, *The Nature of the Judicial Process* (New Haven, Conn.: Yale U.P., 1921); G. Gottlieb, *The Logic of Choice* (London: Allen and Unwin, 1968); J. Esser, *Vorverstaendnis und Methodenwahl in der Rechtsfindung* (Frankfurt am Main, Germany: Athenaeum Verlag, 1970); W. Van Gerven, *Het beleid van de rechter* (Zwolle, Netherlands: Tjeenk Willink, 1971); H.F.M. Crombag et al., *Een theorie over rechterlijke besslissingen* (Groningen, Netherlands: Tjeenk Willink, 1977); W. Kilian, *Juristische Entscheidung und elektronische Datenverarbeitung* (Frankfurt am Main, Germany: Athenaeum Verlag, 1974); C. Perelman, *Logique juridique — nouvelle réthorique* (Paris: Dalloz, 1976).

84. W.M. Landes and R.A. Posner, "Adjudication as a Private Good," *J. Leg. Stud.* 8 (1979):235–284, p. 235.

85. Ibid., pp. 239–240.

86. To see how this works, imagine a social cost-benefit analysis of the flexibility required in judicial decision making. If people are risk averse, the higher the rate of change in the law, the greater their uncertainty and hence the greater the "risk premium" they require to accept it (see further Chapter 8). On the benefit side change may be beneficial to some people because it makes possible more efficient solutions. Let us represent costs and benefits graphically. Normally costs and benefits are stated not as functions of the likelihood of change itself, but rather of its variance. If p is the probability that some rule will be changed — and hence an indicator of uncertainty in the law — the variance is equal to p (1-p). The cost and benefit graph will probably look like Diagram 6.1. In the upper-right-hand corner of the graph, where costs exceed benefits, there is room for political action aimed at obtaining greater certainty in the law. Near the origin one may expect pressure for legislative change in the law.

87. Elsewhere I wrote that courts implicitly minimize the sum of three types of cost: the cost of rule formation (lawyers, courts, delay), the cost of uncertainty, and the cost of inflexibility or inadequate fit (staying with outdated solutions, forgoing gains) ["Les notions floues en droit ou l'économie de l'imprécision," *Langeages* 12 (1979):33–50, p. 37ff.].

88. Perelman expresses it as follows [*Logique juridique,* op cit. (nt. 83), p. 123]:

En droit, par contre, il est essentiel que les litiges se terminent dans un laps de temps raisonnable, pour qu'on aboutisse à la paix judiciaire. . . . C'est la raison pour laquelle les problèmes de

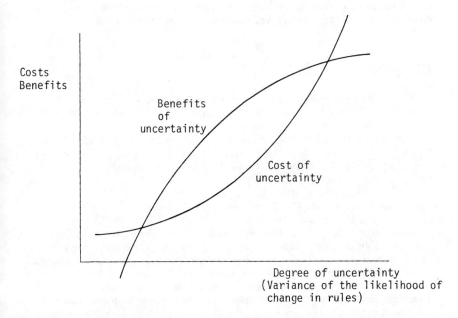

Diagram 6.1. Cost and Benefits of Uncertainty in the Law

compétence et, d'une façon plus générale, de procédure, feront l'objet d'une réglementation préalable, insérant le débat judiciaire dans un cadre approprié.

Such a passage would fit well into a discussion of procedural rationality as proposed by Simon. The nonbinding character of legal arguments is expressed as follows (p. 125):

> Les techniques d'argumentation fournissent tout un arsenal de raisons, plus ou moins fortes, plus ou moins pertinentes, mais qui peuvent, à partir d'un même point de départ, mener vers des conclusions différentes, et parfois même opposées. . . . L'argumentation n'est jamais contraignante, comme la démonstration, et c'est pourquoi on sera plus souvent d'accord sur le point de départ de l'argumentation que sur les conclusions vers lesquelles tend le discours de l'orateur.

Procedural rather than substantive rationality for judicial and other decisions is also the theme of N. Luhmann, *Legitimation durch Verfahren* (Darmstadt, Germany: Luchterhand, 1975).

89. See T. Viehweg, *Topik und Jurispurdenz* (Munich, Germany: C.H. Beck, 1954); G. Struck, *Topische Jurisprudenz* (Frankfurt am Main, Germany: Athenaeum, 1971), pp. 20–34 gives a catalogue of sixty-four *topoi*, including well known ones such as *audi et alteram partem, nec ultra petita, in dubio pro reo, de minimis non curat praetor, nemo plus juris transferre potest quam ipse habet*, equality, protection of trade and commerce, protection of good faith, and so on.

Chapter 7

1. P. Nelson, "Information and Consumer Behavior," *J. Pol. Econ.* 78 (1970):311–329, and "Advertising as Information," *J. Pol. Econ.* 82 (1974):729–754.

2. Nelson, "Information," op. cit. (nt. 1), p. 327.

3. M. Darby and E. Karni, "Free Competition and the Optimal Amount of Fraud," *J. Law Econ.* 16 (1973):67–88; see also G. Akerlof, "The Market for 'Lemons': Qualitative Uncertainty and the Market Mechanism," *Quart. J. Econ.* 89 (1970):488–500.

4. Darby and Karni, "Free Competition," op. cit. (nt. 3).

5. M.J. Trebilcock, C.J. Tuohy, and A.D. Wolfson, *Professional Regulation*, (Toronto: Ministry of the Attorney General, Ontario, 1979), pp. 51–52.

6. Trebilcock et al., in the study just mentioned, state that of the four professions of accounting, architecture, engineering and law, only the last might give rise to "demand generation" because "there is a sizeable household sector where consumers may need any one or more of a wide variety of services *but are generally uninformed about the types of services available. Nor are they usually able to assess the quality of legal services delivered*" (Ibid., p. 55) (emphasis added). In the other three professions clients have the ability — through in-house services, for instance — to evaluate the services and their need for it appropriately.

7. This term is taken from Darby and Karni, "Free Competition," op. cit. (nt. 3).

8. The analysis here is somewhat similar to that of the enforcement of laws in the face of possible violation. On this subject see G.J. Stigler, "The Optimum Enforcement of Laws," *J. Pol. Econ.* 78 (1970): 526–536.

9. Of course, the situation is rather hypothetical, since if one could immediately detect the information oneself, there would seem to be no reason to rely on what someone else provides.

10. More precisely:

expected value of the loss = p (discovery) ×

$\quad\quad\quad\quad\quad\quad\quad p$ (cease to buy/given discovery) ×

$\quad\quad\quad\quad\quad\quad\quad$ cost of lost business from those who cease to buy

where the "p" represent probabilities (see ch. 6, nt. 20).

11. A. Schwartz and L.L. Wilde, "Intervening in Markets on the Basis of Imperfect Information: A Legal and Economic Analysis," *Univ. Penn. L. Rev.* 127 (1979):630–682, pp. 636, 638, 660, 663.

12. The phenomenon is akin to what is known as adverse selection in the insurance literature. See the next chapter and text at Ch. 1, nt. 23.

13. B. Klein and K.B. Leffler, *The Role of Price in Guaranteeing Quality*, Discussion Paper No. 149, U. of Calif., Los Angeles, 1978; see also B. Klein, R.G. Crawford and A.A. Alchian, "Vertical Integration, Appropriable Rents, and the Competitive Contracting Process," *J. Law Econ.* 21 (1978):297–326, in particular p. 304, where the same idea of a "premium against cheating" is discussed in the context of the choice between a long-term contract and vertical integration.

See further, for instance, W.B. Cornell, "Price as a Quality Signal: Some Additional Experimental Results," *Econ. Inq.* 16 (1978):302–309.

14. Chapter 5, second section, Diagrams 5.1 and 5.2.

15. Chapter 5, fourth section.

16. Recall that methodologists require that theories be tested on "new" evidence, i.e., information not used for research leading to the initial formulation of the theory. The spy world is also painfully aware of this problem, at least if one is to believe an author like John Le Carré.

17. In a recent thesis it is argued that it is essentially this information problem that sets limits to the size of organizations. R. Wintrobe, "The Economics of Bureaucracy," Ph.D. thesis, Dept. of Political Economy, U. of Toronto, 1976.

18. McKenzie, "Methodological Boundaries," op. cit. (ch. 1, nt. 19).

19. A. Downs, *An Economic Theory of Democracy* (New York: Harper & Row, 1957), p. 210.

20. See Wintrobe, "Economics of Bureaucracy," op. cit. (nt. 17); H. Lepage, *Autogestion et capitalisme* (Paris: Masson, 1978).

21. Comanor and Wilson insist that "the provision of advertising messages and advertised products does not constitute *joint supply* in the standard economic sense of this term since the two do not arise from the same production process" [*Advertising and Market Power* (Cambridge, Mass.: Harvard U.P., 1974), p. 9]. Unfortunately they appear to have forgotten this remark already on p. 19 and following of the book.

22. Indeed, from the seller's point of view the combination may well be desirable *because of* the possibility of (slightly) misleading customers through the information he supplies them.

23. Darby and Karni, "Free Competition," op. cit. (nt. 3), pp. 84, 86.

24. Comanor and Wilson, *Advertising*, op. cit. (nt. 21), p. 12.

25. Ibid., pp. 12, 13.

26. Ibid.

27. Ibid., p. 245.

28. There may, of course, be other factors that explain how the salesman can exert "pressure" or influence on the customer. Here we are concerned only with those that have to do with the costliness of information.

29. This is in essence the thesis advanced by Kronman in his "Mistake, Disclosure, Information, and the Law of Contracts," *J. Leg. Stud.* 7 (1978):1–34.

30. If the seller is obliged to generate information even though he no longer sees an interest in doing so himself, the obligation is equivalent to an additional production cost or a tax on his product. The effects of such a tax are studied as part of standard microeconomics.

31. Schwartz and Wilde, "Intervening," op. cit. (nt. 11), p. 674, mention empirical studies that tend to show that if lists of unit prices for similar products are posted in supermarkets, customers will effectively choose less expensive commodities than they would have without them.

32. For instance, Quebec's *Consumer Protection Act*, (R.S.Q., Ch. P–40.1), sanctioned on 22 December 1978, states three levels of mandatory warranty on the sale of used cars:

1. 6 months or 10,000 kilometers for category A, defined as models less than two years old and where the car to be sold has run less than 40,000 kilometers.

2. 3 months or 5,000 kilometers for category B, defined as models, not in category A, that are less than three years old and where the car to be sold has run less than 60,000 kilometers.

3. 1 month or 1,700 kilometers for category C, covering cars not in A and B, where the model is less than five years old and the car has run less than 80,000 kilometers.

All remaining used cars (category D) carry no mandatory warranty (articles 159 and 160).

33. Dutch readers will recognise the statement on the label of boxes of Rademaker's Haagse hopjes that these are the *only authentic . . .* (emphasis added).

34. A.M. Spence, "Competitive and Optimal Responses to Signals: An Analysis of Efficiency and Distribution," *J. Econ. Th.* 7 (1974):296–332; A.M. Spence, *Market Signalling: Informational Transfer in Hiring and Related Screening Processes* (Cambridge, Mass.: Harvard U.P., 1974); A.M. Spence, "Informational Aspects of Market Structure: An Introduction," *Quart. J. Econ.* 40 (1976):591–97; A.M. Spence, "Signalling and Screening," unpub. Harvard Institute of Economic Research, Discussion Paper no. 467, 1976; K.J. Arrow, "Education as a Filter," *J. Pub. Econ.* 2 (1973):193–216; J.E. Stiglitz, "The Theory of Screening, Education and the Distribution of Income," *Am. Econ. Rev.* 65 (1975):283–300; Boudon, *Effets pervers et ordre social* (Paris: P.U.F., 1977), pp. 17–58. Also J.G. Riley, "Competitive Signalling," *J. Econ. Th.* 10 (1975):174–186; J.G. Riley, "Testing the Educational Screening Hypothesis," *J. Pol. Econ.* 87 (1979):S227–S252.

35. See, for instance, S. Salop, "Information and Monopolistic Competition," *Am. Econ. Rev.* 66 (1976):240–245; J.J. Laffont, "Information asymétrique et théorie de l'équilibre," *Rev. d'écon. pol.* (1975):806–810; S.J. Grossman and J.E. Stiglitz, "Information and Competitive Price System," *Am. Econ. Rev.* 66 (1976):246–253.

36. G.W. Nutter and J.H. Moore, "A Theory of Competition," *J. Law Econ.* 19 (1976): 39–66.

37. Among many others Rowley states this conclusion explicitly. C.K. Rowley, *Antitrust and Economic Efficiency* (London: Macmillan, 1973), p. 9.

38. Foremost among these views are those of Galbraith, in particular *American Capitalism* (New York: Penguin, 1963).

39. Nelson, "Information," op. cit. (nt. 1); L.G. Telser, "Advertising and Competition," *J. Pol. Econ.* 72 (1964):537–562; E.R. Jordan, and P.H. Rubin, "An Economic Analysis of the Law of False Advertising," *J. Leg. Stud.* 8 (1979):527–553. A good general survey of the problem is given by H.J. Wilton-Siegel, "Advertising, Competition and the Economy: A Survey," in *A Study on Consumer Misleading and Unfair Trade Practices*, Vol. 2, prepared for the Department of Consumer and Corporate Affairs, Ottawa, 1976, pp. 121–177, which contains a substantial bibliography.

40. For instance, P. Nelson, "Comments on Advertising and Free Speech," in A. Hyman and M.B. Johnson, eds., *Advertising and Free Speech* (Lexington, Mass.: Lexington Books, 1977), p. 54 ("The more the law protects against fraud, the more people think the law protects against fraud"). See also R.A. Posner, *The Regulation of Advertising by the FTC*, Am. Enterprise Inst. for Public Policy Research, 1973.

41. Comanor and Wilson, *Advertising*, op. cit. (nt. 21), p. 248. It should be noted that, as a recent study has found, "advertising need not always imply a barrier to entry in the usual sense" [A. Dixit and V. Norman, "Advertising and Welfare," *Bell J. Econ.* 9 (1978):1–17, p. 16]. But this study, too, is rather pessimistic with regard to the overall benefits of advertising. It concludes that "even when the case is loaded in favor of advertising, with welfare judged by postadvertising tastes and the monopoly profits contributed by advertising included in the measure of welfare, the market equilibrium level of advertising in a very wide range of circumstances is socially excessive" (p. 16). More favorable (to advertising): A. Glazer, "Advertising, Information, and Prices — A Case Study," *Econ. Inq.* 19 (1981):661–671. See also Y. Kotowitz, and F. Mathewson, "Advertising, Consumer Information and Product Quality," *Bell J. Econ.* 10 (1979):566–588.

42. Comanor and Wilson, *Advertising*, op. cit. (nt. 21), p. 253. See also G. Scherhorn and K. Wieken, "On the Effect of Counter-Information on Consumers," in B. Strumpel, J.N. Morgan and E. Zehn, eds., *Human Behavior in Economic Affairs* (New York: Elsevier, 1972), pp. 421–431; also Oi's reply to Goldberg, *Bell J. Econ. and Mgmt. Sc.* 5 (1974):689–696.

43. Akerlof, "Market for 'Lemons,' " op. cit. (nt. 3), p. 495.

44. One might also analyze this as a problem of adverse selection, a phenomenon to be discussed in Chapter 8.

45. Game theorists would analyze this situation as a prisoner's dilemma or a game of chicken. The particularity of these games is that if all are honest, they are better off than if they cheat. Yet if only one cheats, but the others don't, the cheater is far better off than under general honesty; the others, the "suckers," are

worse off than under general honesty and even worse than under general dishonesty (in the prisoner's dilemma, but not in the chicken game). On this subject see S.J. Brams, *Game Theory and Politics* (New York: Free Press, 1975), p. 31 (prisoner's dilemma) and p. 40 (chicken). That prisoner's dilemmas are a fecund source of legal rules has been argued convincingly in our view, by E. Ullmann-Margalit, *The Emergence of Norms* (Oxford: Clarendon Press, 1977).

46. Posner, *Economic Analysis of Law,* op. cit. (ch. 1, nt. 4), pp. 485–486; also his "The Behavior of Administrative Agencies," *J. Leg. Stud.* 1 (1972):395ff.

47. Recall, however, the scheme proposed by Klein et al., through which honesty in the supply of information by sellers can be guaranteed. Purchasers agree to pay a premium in the price of the commodity. This premium is set just high enough that its present value (taking into account future purchases) is higher than the net gain the seller can expect from cheating. See references at nt. 13.

48. Nelson, "Comments," op. cit. (nt. 40), p. 56. To some extent this effect is attained by making the content of advertising part of the seller's offer and, hence, of his contractual obligations. Quebec's *Consumer Protection Act,* op. cit. (nt. 32), stipulates this in art. 41 to 43.

49. Whybrow cites American statistics for the period 1960–1972, which show that private antitrust suits were always more than double the number of cases initiated by the government and in the last years well over ten times more (J. Whybrow, "The Case for Class Actions in Canadian Competition Policy: An Economist's Point of View," in *A Proposal for Class Actions under the Competition Policy Legislation,* prepared for the Department of Consumer and Corporate Affairs, Ottawa, 1976, p. 229). (The private prosecutor in such cases in the United States is entitled to treble damages if the action is well founded.)

50. Y. Barzel, "Some Fallacies in the Interpretation of Information Costs," *J. Law Econ.* 20 (1977):291–307, p. 299.

51. This looks like the arrangement made with young lawyers. Leibowitz and Tollison observe on the subject: "A typical pattern for a young lawyer is to become an associate in a large law firm at relatively low wages for six or eight years until partnership status is granted" ["Earning and Learning in Law Firms," *J. Leg. Stud.* 7 (1978):65–81]. They explain the initial low wage as containing an implicit reduction in salary in payment for practical education. It could equally well be explained in part by the idea of screening advanced by Barzel (nt. 50).

52. Hirsch and Scitovsky, for instance, argue that one needs general education as a productive skill necessary for deriving satisfaction from increasingly intricate forms of consumption [F. Hirsch, *The Social Limits to Growth* (Cambridge, Mass.: Harvard U.P., 1976); T. Scitovsky, *The Joyless Economy* (New York: Oxford U.P., 1976].

53. C.S. Colantoni, O.A. Davis, and M. Swaminuthan, "Imperfect Consumers and Welfare Comparisons of Policies Concerning Information and Regulation," *Bell J. Econ.* 7 (1976):602–615.

54. Ibid., p. 608.

55. Ibid., p. 611.

56. In the contract of sale in Quebec, for instance, the burden of unforeseen contingencies is on the purchaser (*periculum emptoris*) on the grounds that he is the owner of the object from the moment when the sale has been concluded. If the object perishes through force majeure — even before delivery — he still owes the purchase price. If, however, the object perishes as a result of a latent defect, he can

recover the purchase price already paid and, where the vendor is specialized in the type of product purchased or is its manufacturer, he can sue him for damages on the grounds that he is presumed to know the defect and has committed a *dol* (fraud) in not revealing it (art. 1527 C.C.).

57. Oi, "Reply to Goldberg," op. cit. (nt. 42).

58. This argument does not take into account the damage done to the manufacturer's reputation by the law suit. If Klein et al. are correct (see nt. 13), even a few law suits — resulting in damage awards well below the total social cost — may yet give the manufacturer the incentive to weight appropriately the option of making a less dangerous product.

59. V. Goldberg, "The Economics of Product Safety and Imperfect Information," *Bell J. Econ. and Mgmt. Sc.* 5 (1974):683–688, p. 683.

Chapter 8

1. Two remarks are in order. First, a gain foregone is also a loss. Second, not all uncertainty is unpleasant. Indeed, modest amounts of it are essential to a pleasurable life: people gamble, fashions change, the fun of many jokes lies in their unforeseen or surprising ending, and so on.

2. Raiffa illustrates risk aversion by a lottery with equal chances of winning or losing $500 and asks what a risk-averse person would pay — a form of insurance premium — in order not to have to assume such a lottery. The amount one would accept to pay would presumably go to zero as one's assets increase. (H. Raiffa, *Decision Analysis*, Reading, Mass.: Addison-Wesley, 1968, p. 92.)

3. J. Hirshleifer and J.G. Riley, "The New Economics of Information," unpublished paper, 21 pp., p. 6. Also their "The Analytics of Uncertainty and Information — An Expository Survey," *J. Econ. Lit.* 17 (1979):1375–1421.

4. Hirshleifer and Riley, "The New Economics," op. cit. (nt. 3), p. 7.

5. Raiffa, *Decision Analysis*, op. cit. (nt. 2), pp. 97–100.

6. M.J. Trebilcock, "The Doctrine of Inequality of Bargaining Power: Post-Benthamite Economics in the House of Lords," in Kronman and Posner, *Economics of Contract Law*, op. cit. (ch. 1, nt. 3), pp. 78–92, in particular p. 90.

7. Arrow writes on the subject: "Insurance against failure of businesses or of research projects has not arisen: the incentive to succeed may be too greatly reduced" [K.J. Arrow, "Insurance, Risk and Resource Allocation," in K.J. Arrow, *Essays in the Theory of Risk-Bearing* (Chicago: Markham Press, 1971), p. 143].

8. Recall the discussion of signaling in Chapter 7.

9. J. Umbeck, "A Theory of Contract Choice and the California Gold Rush," *J. Law Econ.* 20 (1977):421–437. On risk sharing in contracts see also W. Hallagen, "Self-selection by Contractual Choice and the Theory of Sharecropping," *Bell J. Econ.* 9 (1978):344–354; S. Shavell, "Risk Sharing and Incentives in the Principal and Agent Relationship," *Bell J. Econ.* 10 (1979):55–73.

10. Umbeck, "Theory," op. cit. (nt. 9), p. 422.

11. The discussion in the third section of Chapter 3 would suggest this.

12. Umbeck, "Theory," op. cit. (nt. 9), p. 433.

13. Art. 1871 of the Civil Code of Quebec (hereafter C.C.) (Formally called the Civil Code of Lower Canada and adopted in 1866).

14. Art. 1886 C.C.

15. If they can be replaced without ending the partnership, as the *Report on the Civil Code* (Quebec, Canada: Editeur Officel du Québec, 1978), suggests in art. 766 of Book V.

16. Art. 1892, 1895, 1896 C.C.

17. Art. 1887 C.C.

18. The decision is of the kind of an information tradeoff as discussed in Chapter 5.

19. The discussion of the decisions facing investors in the stock market also explains the basic mechanism driving various "futures markets" and other "speculative" institutions. Posner, *Economic Analysis of Law*, op. cit. (ch. 1, nt. 4), p. 34, has this to say on speculation: "Speculation is the purchase of a good not to use but to hold in the hope that it will appreciate in value. The speculator performs a valuable economic function in the adjustment of prices to changing values."

20. On this topic see, for instance, Posner, *Economic Analysis of Law*, op. cit. (ch. 1, nt. 4), p. 300ff.; a recent empirical analysis is G.L. Salamon and E.D. Smith, "Corporate Control and Managerial Misrepresentation of Firm Performance," *Bell J. Econ.* 10 (1979):319–328.

21. In civil law, creditors can invoke the nullity of such transactions, a power referred to as the *actio Pauliana*.

22. T.H. Jackson and A.T. Kronman, "Secured Financing and Priorities among Creditors," *Yale L.J.* 88 (1979):1143–1182, p. 1148, propose this argument.

For different views see: A. Schwartz, "Security Interests and Bankruptcy Priorities: A Review of Current Theories," *J. Leg. Stud.* 10 (1981):1–37; M. Write, "Public Policy Toward Bankruptcy: Me-First and Other Priority Rules," *Bell J. Econ.* 11 (1980):550–564.

23. See nt. 45 of ch. 7. Kronman and Posner, *Economics of Contract Law*, op. cit. (ch. 1, nt. 3) present an interesting excerpt on the subject on pp. 16–21. It is taken from R.L. Birmingham, "Legal and Moral Duty in Game Theory: Common Law Contract and Chinese Analogies," *Buffalo L. Rev.* 18 (1969):99ff.

24. Ullmann-Margalit, *Emergence of Norms*, op. cit. (ch. 7, nt. 45), argues that this is one of the general functions of law.

25. Jackson and Kronman, "Secured Financing," op. cit. (nt. 22).

26. R.A. Posner and A.M. Rosenfield, "Impossibility and Related Doctrines in Contract Law: An Economic Analysis," *J. Leg. Stud.* 6 (1977):83–118, p. 92. See also R.E. Speidel, "Excusable Non-Performance in Sales Contracts: Some Thoughts

on Risk Management," *South. Calif. L. Rev.* 32 (1980):241–280; R.E. Speidel, "Court-Imposed Price Adjustments under Long-Term Supply Contracts," *Northw. U.L. Rev.* 76 (1981):369–422.

27. G. Calabresi, *Costs of Accidents,* op. cit. (ch. 1, nt. 4), pp. 28 and 39ff.

28. S. Shavell, "Accidents, Liability, and Insurance," Harvard Inst. of Economic Research, Discussion Paper no. 685, pp. 23, 24. See also his "Risk Sharing and Incentives in the Principal and Agent Relationship," *Bell J. Econ.* 10 (1979):55–73, p. 65.

29. K.J. Arrow, "Uncertainty and the Welfare Economics of Medical Care," in K.J. Arrow, *Essays in the Theory of Risk-Bearing* (Chicago: Markham Press, 1971), p. 185; see also J.M. Buchanan and G. Tullock, *The Calculus of Consent* (Ann Arbor: U. Mich. P., 1962), pp. 192–199. T.M. Carroll, et al., "The Market as a Commons: An Unconventional View of Property Rights," *J. Econ. Iss.* 13 (1979):605–627, suggest that protection of value (insurance) is one stage in the development of property rights as an institution (p. 616ff.). They write: "A guarantee of value restricts the arbitrary and capricious market movement of property values or incomes stemming from the ownership of property." They argue that this desire can explain the striving for (monopolistic) market power and that the courts accepted this tendency inasmuch as it did not "abuse in the market the property rights of exclusion and free exchange" (p. 617).

Chapter 9

1. B. Masse and M. Marois, *La règle du jeu — Enquête auprès des organismes de consommation et des consommateurs plaignants,* Groupe de recherche en jurimétrie, Montréal, 1976, p. 1 (my translation).

2. D.A. Dagenais et al, "La consommation," in *Guide d'information en droit,* (Montreal: Société québécoise d'information juridique, 1978), p. 3 (my translation).

3. Ibid., p. 4.

4. C. Masse, "L'information et l'exploitation des consommateurs," *La Revue de droit de l'Université d'Ottawa* 10 (1979):90–131, p. 99 (my translation). See also his study with M. Marois, "La règle du jeu," op. cit. (nt. 1).

5. Ibid. At the time of the survey the *Consumer Protection Act* of 1971 was in force.

6. Dagenais et al., "La consommation," op. cit. (nt. 2), p. 2.

7. Ibid., p. 1.

8. Masse, "L'information," op. cit. (nt. 4), p. 98.

9. Ibid., p. 5.

10. Dagenais et al., "La consommation," op. cit. (nt. 2), p. 3.

11. Masse, "L'information," op. cit. (nt. 4), p. 96.

12. Ibid., pp. 101–104.

13. Masse and Marois, "La règle du jeu," op. cit. (nt. 1).

14. Whether the incentives are optimal is a disputed question. See J. Hirshleifer, "The Private and Social Value of Information and the Reward to Inventive Activity," *Am. Econ. Rev.* 61 (1971):561–574; K.J. Arrow, "Economic Welfare and the Allocation of Resources for Invention," in K.J. Arrow, *Essays in the Theory of*

Risk-Bearing (Chicago: Markham Press, 1971), pp. 144–163; H. Demsetz, "Information and Efficiency: Another Viewpoint," *J. Law Econ.* 12 (1969):1022ff.; C.K. Rowley, *Antitrust and Economic Efficiency* (London: Macmillan, 1973), pp. 33–43 and 55–57. An extensive review of the literature can be found in A. Heertje, *Economics and Technical Change* (New York: Wiley, 1977), Chapters 11 and 12.

15. See art. 1509 C.C.

16. J.L. Baudouin, "La protection du consommateur et la formation des contrats civils et commerciaux," in Travaux de l'Association Henri-Capitant des amis de la culture française, Vol. 24 (1973): *La protection des consommateurs* (Paris: Dalloz, 1975) pp. 3–15, p. 5 (my translation).

17. Ibid., p. 6.

18. Ibid., p. 4.

19. Posner, who generally sees not much of a problem for the consumer, writes on this subject [*Economic Analysis of Law*, op. cit. (ch. 1, nt. 4), p. 81]:

> A more plausible basis for a belief that fraud is apt to be a graver problem in consumer than in commercial transactions is the difficulty of devising effective legal remedies where the stakes are small.

Note that the models of the development of the common law, which show a trend toward efficiency among litigants whose stakes are large, would predict in conflicts opposing large stakes to small stakes (which consumers are) a gradual shift of the law in favor of the former. See P.H. Rubin, "Why Is the Common Law Efficient?" *J. Leg. Stud.* 6 (1977):51–63, p. 55ff. See also Hollander and Mackaay, "Judges," op. cit. (ch. 3, nt. 98).

20. On this subject see E.J. Mishan, *Cost-Benefit Analysis*, 2nd ed. (New York: Praeger, 1976), pp. 298–320 (Loss of Life and Limb). Consider that in the seventeenth and eighteenth centuries, Dutch sailors would enroll on ships to the East Indies with the prospect that a substantial proportion — perhaps even half — of the crew would not survive the voyage.

21. See the discussion on bounded rationality in Chapter 6 and on misperception in Chapter 7.

22. Schwartz and Wilde, "Intervening," op. cit. (ch. 7, nt. 11) discuss this question on p. 660ff.

23. Standard economic reasoning with respect to information would lead one to expect that the amount of information produced will be just so much that the benefits consumers derive from it and for which they are willing to pay are just equal to the cost of producing it. Unfortunately, in many markets this equality will not hold, because the information supplier incurs not only production costs but also what might be termed image costs. Trebilcock expresses it very well ["The Doctrine of Inequality of Bargaining Power — Post-Benthamite Economics in the House of Lords," U. of T. L.J. 29 (1976):359–385, pp. 371, 372]:

> While the marginal *social* costs to the non-competitive firm of disclosing information to consumers that makes clear the inferiority of its terms may be trivial, the marginal *private* costs to the firm of disclosure (in terms of lost sales) will induce suppression of the information *even though consumers may be willing to pay the marginal social costs of its production.* (Emphasis added).

Trebilcock fears that the problem will be particularly severe with regard to expensive, complex or infrequently purchased goods and services, on which consumers have little experience information.

24. D. Stager, *Economic Analysis and Canadian Policy* 2nd ed. (Toronto: Butterworths, 1976), pp. 28–30.

25. The company may, of course, bring this onto itself by deliberately flouting certain groups of customers. But it may then simply destroy its own reputation, rather than focus public attention on a particular aspect of the product for the industry as a whole.

26. M.J. Trebilcock, "Winners and Losers in the Modern Regulatory State: Must the Consumer Always Lose?" *Osgoode Hall L.J.* 13 (1975):619–647, p. 624ff.

27. M. Olson, *The Logic of Collective Action* (Cambridge, Mass.: Harvard U.P., 1974), p. 132ff.

28. M.J. Trebilcock, et al., "Markets for Regulation: Implications for Performance Standards and Institutional Design," in *Government Regulation* (Toronto: Ontario Economic Council, 1978), pp. 57, 58.

29. Government intervention entails other kinds of failure. An interesting article on the subject is C. Wolf, "A Theory of Nonmarket Failure: Framework for Implementation Analysis," *J. Law Econ.* 22 (1979):107–139. See also Dales, "Beyond the Marketplace," op. cit. (ch. 2, nt. 11).

30. M.J. Trebilcock, "Doctrine," op. cit. (nt. 23) makes a similar argument with respect to alleged abuse of market power.

31. See M.J. Trebilcock et al., "Markets," op. cit. (nt. 28).

32. See Stigler's article mentioned in nt. 8 of ch. 7.

33. Quebec's *Consumer Protection Act* (R.S.Q., Ch. P–40.1) mentions permits for itinerant vendors, money lenders, and health studio operators (art. 321). Regulations made under the act can stipulate that requests for permits must be accompanied by security or surety (art. 323). This obligation already exists for car dealers under art. 22 of the (Quebec) *Highway Code* (R.S.Q., ch. C–24). Any merchant who receives advance payment from a consumer must place it in a trust account (art. 254 of the *Consumer Protection Act)* (my translation of act titles). (Consumer Protection Act will be abbreviated C.P.A. hereafter).

34. J.L. Baudouin, *Les Obligations*, (Montreal: P.U.M., 1970), p. 78 (No. 127). See, however, P. Legrand, "Pour une théorie de l'obligation de renseignement en droit civil canadien," *McGill L.J.* 26 (1981):206–288; and in French law, J. Ghestin, *Traité de droit civil, Tome II: Les obligations — Le contrat*, (Paris: Librairie générale de droit et de jurisprudence, 1980), Nos. 457–508 (pp. 373–412), on the "obligation précontractuelle de renseignements."

35. Kronman, "Mistake, Disclosure," op. cit. (ch. 7, nt. 29).

36. *Consumer Protection Act*, op. cit. (nt. 33), art. 45.

37. Ibid., art. 47.

38. Ibid., art. 155. For a relevant empirical study see K. McNeil et al., "Market Discrimination Against the Poor and the Impact of Consumer Disclosure Law: The Used Car Industry," *Law & Soc. Rev.* 13 (1979):695–720.

39. It might be asked why, if case law so far is compatible with Kronman's economic theory, development of further disclosure rules should not be left to the courts. The answer is perhaps that, because of the consumer's small stakes, he has little interest in going to court and the case law would not develop in his favor, as we argued in nt. 19. It is also argued that courts are unlikely to pinpoint the specific

information requirements that the act defines. This is probably true. Whether such specificity is more than a short-term advantage to the consumer is a debatable question; the more precise the formula, the more likely it is that loopholes will be found.

40. Newspaper report in the Montreal *Gazette* of 6 August 1979.

41. See articles by Posner cited in ch. 7, nts. 40 and 46.

42. *Combines Investigation Act* (R.S.C. 1970, ch. C–23), art. 36, 36.1, 36.2, 37, 37.1.

43. *Consumer Protection Act*, op. cit. (nt. 33) in Title II (Business Practices), art 215ff. (my translation of titles).

44. Ibid., art. 40 to 43.

45. Baudouin, op. cit. (nt. 16), p. 10.

46. Trebilcock, "Doctrine," op. cit. (nt. 23), p. 364; see also my "The Costliness of Information and its Effect on the Analysis of Law," in J.S. Ziegel, ed., *Proceedings of the Seventh Annual Workshop on Commercial and Consumer Law (1977)*, (Toronto: Canada Law Book, 1979), p. 133.

47. Trebilcock, Ibid. See also W.M. McGovern, "Forfeiture, Inequality of Bargaining Power and the Availability of Credit: An Historical Perspective," *Northw. U.L. Rev.* 74 (1979):141–165; and some empirical studies on the effect of protecting consumers from harsh repossession clauses: W.C. Whitford and H. Laufer, "The Impact of Denying Self-Help Repossession of Automobiles: A Case Study of the Wisconsin Consumer Act," *Wisconsin L. Rev.* (1975):607–657; C.W. Grau and W.C. Whitford, "The Impact of Judicializing Repossession: The Wisconsin Consumer Act Revisited," *Wisconsin L. Rev.* (1978):983–996.

48. Trebilcock, "Doctrine," op. cit. (nt. 23), p. 375.

49. Ibid., p. 372.

50. See Schwartz and Wilde, "Intervening," op. cit. (ch. 7, nt. 11), pp. 660, 661.

51. Quebec's *Consumer Protection Act*, op. cit. (nt. 33) contains in art. 136 a prohibition of clauses authorizing a merchant to repossess a good sold under a conditional sales contract without the explicit consent of the consumer or the court.

52. Warranties and a guarantee of the availability of parts are prescribed, for instance, in arts. 37 to 39 and 53, 54 of the act.

53. Until 1980 the Quebec Civil Code prescribed a standard lease for residential premises.

54. V.P. Goldberg, "Institutional Change and the Quasi-Invisible Hand," *J. Law Econ.* 17 (1974):461–496.

55. Trebilcock, "Doctrine," op. cit. (nt. 23), p. 375.

56. Art. 44 of the *Consumer Protection Act*, op. cit. (nt. 33) stipulates that in a conventional warranty, exclusions are valid only if made in separate and successive clauses. Recall also efforts starting in the state of New York to formulate standard contracts (insurance policies, for instance) that are directly intelligible to the laymen (the plain-English movement).

57. The discussion has crystallized in a memorandum of the Consumer Protection Office (May 1979), in which the problem at issue here is discussed on p. 76ff.

58. For conditional sales the restrictions are given in art. 139 and following of the *Consumer Protection Act*. Official notice must be given and the consumer is granted a reprieve of thirty days. If more than half of the total amount has been

paid, repossession is permitted only by authorization of the court. Art. 1040aff. of the Civil Code contain a similiar obligation to give notice, followed by a term of grace for the debtor, with respect to immovable property.

59. General Motors and other car manufacturers have, however, started to experiment with "extended protection plans" in which, for a modest price at the time of purchase of a new car, the owner is protected against all repair costs for a substantial period (two or three years). One should not despair of the market.

60. Trebilcock, "The Doctrine," op. cit. (nt. 23), p. 376.

61. Masse, "L'information," op. cit. (nt. 4), p. 102.

62. See text surrounding nt. 3.

63. The *Food and Drug Act* (R.S.C. 1970, ch. F–27) and the *Hazardous Products Act* (R.S.C. 1970, ch. H–3).

64. According to Dagenais et al., "La consommation," op. cit. (nt. 2), pp. 67, 68.

65. Ibid., p. 69.

66. Ibid., p. 73ff.

67. W. Oi, "The Economics of Product Safety," *Bell J. Econ. and Mgmt. Sc.* 4 (1973):3–28 and his "Reply to Professor Goldberg," *Bell J. Econ. and Mgmt. Sc.* 5 (1974):689–696; R.A. Posner, "The Behavior of Administrative Agencies," in G.S. Becker and W.M. Landes, eds., *Essays in the Economics of Crime and Punishment,* (New York: Columbia U.P., 1974), pp. 215–261; R.S. Higgins, "Producer's Liability and Product-Related Accidents," *J. Leg. Stud.* 7 (1978):299–321. See also references at ch. 3, nt. 79 and ff.

68. N.W. Cornell, R.G. Noll, and B. Weingast, "Safety Regulation," in H. Owen and C.L. Schultze, eds., *Setting National Priorities — The Next Ten Years* (Washington, D.C.: Brookings, 1976), p. 470.

69. *Report on the Quebec Civil Code — Vol. I: Draft Civil Code,* (Quebec, Canada: Editeur Officiel du Québec, 1978). Art. 102, Book V reads:

A manufacturer of all or part of a moveable thing, and any other person who distributes that thing under his name or as his own, is responsible for the damage caused by a defect in the design, manufacture, preservation or presentation of the thing, unless the defect was apparent. The same applies when the user is given no indication necessary to his protection concerning risks and dangers that he could not himself detect.

70. Cornell et al., "Safety Regulation," op. cit. (nt. 68), p. 477.

71. Ibid.

72. Ibid.

73. Enumerated in art. 23 C.P.A., op. cit. (nt. 33). It applies to contracts with itinerant vendors, loans, conditional sales, sales of used cars, repair services and so on.

74. For instance, in art. 168 (for car repairs) and 183 (for repairs of domestic appliances) C.P.A., op. cit. (nt. 33).

75. Art. 263 C.P.A., op. cit. (nt. 33).

76. See, for instance, Posner, *Economic Analysis of Law,* op. cit. (ch. 1, nt. 4), pp. 448, 449. The agreement provides that if the case is lost the lawyer receives no payment, whereas if he wins he takes a percentage of the award. As the lawyer

assumes a risk, his payment in the latter case is of course higher than would be expected in jurisdictions where fees must be set independent of the outcome.

77. It is feared that lawyers will be more tempted to "cut corners" and to settle cases out of court. On these questions see M.J. Trebilcock, C.J. Tuohy, and A.D. Wolfson, *Professional Regulation* (Toronto: Ministry of the Attorney General of Ontario, 1979), p. 320 and the literature cited there. On lawyers for consumers generally, see S. Macaulay, "Lawyers and Consumer Protection Laws," *Law & Soc. Rev.* 14 (1979):114–171 and G. Calabresi, "Access," op. cit. (ch. 4, nt. 15).

78. Baudouin, "La protection," op. cit. (nt. 16), pp. 13 and 14.

79. 1001ff. C.C. But note that the proposed Code (op. cit., nt. 69) introduces such a concept in art. 37 of Book V. *Révision* is proposed in art. 75 and 76 of the same book.

80. Art. 8 C.P.A., op. cit. (nt. 33). See also art. 272 C.P.A., which provides for the reduction of the consumer's obligations as a general sanction to the merchant's or manufacturer's failing to meet any of the obligations imposed on him by the act.

81. Trebilcock, "Doctrine," op. cit. (nt. 23). See also A. Leff, "Thomist Unconscionability," *Can. Bus. L.J.* 4 (1979–80):424–428.

82. Trebilcock, "Doctrine," op. cit. (nt. 23), p. 376–377.

83. Art. 272 C.P.A., op. cit. (nt. 33).

Name Index

Subject Index